INTERNATIONAL THEMES AND ISSUES

VOLUME

1

A WORLD BEYOND BORDERS

INTERNATIONAL THEMES AND ISSUES

A joint series of the Canadian Historical Association
and the University of Toronto Press

SERIES EDITOR | Beverly Lemire

Canadian
Historical Association

Société historique
du Canada

UTP

INTERNATIONAL THEMES AND ISSUES
A joint series of the Canadian Historical Association
and the University of Toronto Press

SERIES EDITOR | Beverly Lemire

A WORLD BEYOND BORDERS

An Introduction to the History of
International Organizations

DAVID MACKENZIE

University of Toronto Press

Library and Archives Canada Cataloguing in Publication

MacKenzie, David (David Clark), 1953–
    A world beyond borders : an introduction to the history of international organizations / David MacKenzie.

(International themes and issues ; 1)
Includes bibliographical references and index.
Also issued in electronic formats.
ISBN 978-1-4426-0182-6

    1. International agencies—History. I. Title. II. Series: International themes and issues (Toronto, Ont.) ; 1

JZ4839.M33 2010   341.209   C2010-903928-9

We welcome comments and suggestions regarding any aspect of our publications—please feel free to contact us at news@utphighereducation.com or visit our Internet site at www.utphighereducation.com.

North America
5201 Dufferin Street
North York, Ontario,
Canada, M3H 5T8

2250 Military Road
Tonawanda, New York,
USA, 14150

orders phone: 1-800-565-9523
orders fax: 1-800-221-9985
orders e-mail: utpbooks@utpress.utoronto.ca

UK, Ireland, and continental Europe
NBN International
Estover Road, Plymouth, PL6 7PY, UK
orders phone: 44 (0) 1752 202301
orders fax: 44 (0) 1752 202333
orders e-mail: enquiries@nbninternational.com

The University of Toronto Press acknowledges the financial support for its publishing activities of the Government of Canada through the Canada Book Fund.

Printed in Canada

RECYCLED
Paper made from
recycled material
FSC® C021757

Contents

Acknowledgements

There are always people to thank in writing a book and this one is no exception. First I must thank Beverly Lemire and the other members of the Canadian Historical Association committee for their support and advice from the very beginning of the project. At various stages, the anonymous readers offered sound criticism and advice that I found useful; hopefully, their suggestions have helped me write a better book. Special thanks go to Natalie Fingerhut of the University of Toronto Press, who has believed in this project and guided it through to completion. Also, I would like to thank Betsy Struthers for copy editing the manuscript, Beate Schwirtlich for coordinating the book's production at the University of Toronto Press, and François Trahan for preparing the index. My wife, Teresa Lemieux, and daughters, Claire and Elizabeth, have provided constant support, and to the three of you I say, again, thank you.

List of Abbreviations

ACCT	l'Agence de Cooperation Culturelle et Technique
ACP	African, Caribbean, and Pacific Group of States
AFTA	ASEAN Free Trade Area
AMIS	African Union Mission in Sudan
APEC	Asia Pacific Economic Cooperation
ARF	ASEAN Regional Forum
ASEAN	Association of South East Asian Nations
AU	African Union
BINGO	business and industry NGO
BRAC	Bangladesh Rural Advancement Committee
CARE	Cooperative for Assistance and Relief Everywhere
CARICOM	Caribbean Community
CENTO	Central Treaty Organization
CHR	Commission on Human Rights
CIDI	Inter-American Council for Integral Development
CIDSE	Coopération internationale pour le développement et la solidarité
CITEJA	Comité International Technique d'Experts Juridiques Aériens
CPLP	Community of Portuguese Language Countries
DONGO	donor-organized NGO
EAU	UN Electoral Assistance Unit
EC	European Community

ECOSOC	Economic and Social Council
ECSC	European Coal and Steel Community
EEC	European Economic Community
EFTA	European Free Trade Association
EU	European Union
FAO	Food and Agriculture Organization
G77	Group of 77
G8	Group of 8
GATT	General Agreement on Tariffs and Trade
GCC	Gulf Cooperation Council
GNP	Gross National Product
GONGO	government-organized NGO
IACHR	Inter-American Commission on Human Rights
IATA	International Air Transport Association
ICAN	International Commission for Air Navigation
ICAO	International Civil Aviation Organization
ICC	International Criminal Court
ICJ	International Court of Justice
ICTFY	International Criminal Tribunal for the former Yugoslavia
ICTR	International Criminal Tribunal for Rwanda
IDB	Inter-American Development Bank
I-FOR	NATO Peace Implementation Force
IGO	intergovernmental organization
ILO	International Labour Organization
IMF	International Monetary Fund
INGO	international non-governmental organization
IRO	International Refugee Organization
MSF	Medécins Sans Frontières
NATO	North Atlantic Treaty Organization
NIEO	New International Economic Order
NGO	non-governmental organization
NPT	Treaty on the Non-Proliferation of Nuclear Weapons
NWICO	New World Information and Communication Order
OAS	Organization of American States
OAU	Organization of African Unity
OECD	Organization for Economic Co-operation and Development
OEI	Organization of Iberian-American States for Education, Science and Culture
ONUC	Opération des Nations Unies au Congo

OPEC	Organization of Petroleum Exporting Countries
OSCE	Organization for Security and Cooperation in Europe
Oxfam	Oxford Committee for Famine Relief
PCIJ	Permanent Court of International Justice
PINGO	public-interest NGO
PLO	Palestinian Liberation Organization
QUANGO	quasi-autonomous NGO
R2P	responsibility to protect
SALT I	(SALT II) Strategic Arms Limitation Treaties
SCO	Shanghai Cooperation Organization
SEATO	South East Asia Treaty Organization
SHAPE	Supreme Headquarters, Allied Powers, Europe (NATO)
START	Strategic Arms Reduction Talks
UDHR	Universal Declaration of Human Rights
UN	United Nations
UNAMID	UN-AU Mission in Darfur
UNAMIR	UN Assistance Mission to Rwanda
UNCTAD	UN Conference on Trade and Development
UNDP	UN Development Program
UNEF	UN Emergency Force
UNEP	UN Environment Program
UNESCO	UN Educational, Scientific, and Cultural Organization
UNFICYP	UN Force in Cyprus
UNHCR	United Nations High Commissioner for Refugees
UNICEF	UN International Children's Emergency Fund
UNIFIL	UN Interim Force in Lebanon
UNITAF	Unified Task Force (Somalia)
UNMIH	UN Mission in Haiti
UNOMIL	UN Observer Mission in Liberia
UNMOGIP	UN Military Observer Group in India and Pakistan
UNOSOM	UN Operation in Somalia
UNPROFOR	UN Protection Force (Yugoslavia)
UNRRA	United Nations Relief and Rehabilitation Administration
UNTAG	UN Transition Assistance Group in South-West Africa
UNTSO	UN Truce Supervision Organization
UPU	Universal Postal Union
USSR	Union of Soviet and Socialist Republics
WHO	World Health Organization
WTO	World Trade Organization
WWF	World Wildlife Fund

List of Figures

1 | An Introduction to International Organizations

States created international organizations to do things that they could not do on their own or to prevent from happening things that were not in the state's interests. International intergovernmental organizations did not create themselves or exist on their own; they were designed, supported, and operated by the countries that created them. At the same time, individuals and groups of individuals created international non-governmental organizations to reflect common concerns, accomplish shared goals, and solve problems that often transcended the ability or purview of government. Both kinds of organizations appeared because they served a purpose.

Along with the rise of the nation-state came conflict between states and the need for international cooperation, especially among the major powers. Major states could use their power to force or coerce weaker ones, but between major powers an alternative to war was sometimes necessary. Establishing international organizations was not the only way to relieve these tensions or solve these kinds of problems, but it did offer a vehicle to manage conflict between states and to set normal international standards of behaviour.

It is a little harder to be certain about the nature of international organizations. They are cooperative ventures between, among others, governments, peoples, businesses, scientists, organized labour, and professionals; they are involved in virtually all aspects of human life from politics, culture, and business to the environment, human rights, and disarmament; and they are found almost everywhere: in the developed and the developing worlds, among the rich and the poor, and across the political and ideological spectrum. They act, advocate, observe, study and report, aid, and teach; and, in rare cases, they coerce states, people, institutions, and so on to act or refrain from acting in a variety of different ways.

Many existing organizations have grown in terms of membership and responsibilities over the years, and many new ones have been created. At the start of the twentieth century, there were relatively few international organizations; today, there are tens of thousands of them. They all play an expanding role in the international system and exhibit a degree of freedom unimagined a century ago. "Investigate almost any violent conflict, environmental concern, financial meltdown, or humanitarian crisis," two scholars wrote, and "you will find international organizations involved, probably in a leading role. These organizations do much more than simply execute international agreements between states. They make authoritative decisions that reach every corner of the globe and affect areas as public as governmental spending and as private as reproductive rights.... A whole variety of [international organizations] are busily defining human rights, refugee rights, children's rights, and women's rights, shaping how these rights are understood at the international and the domestic level."[1]

But do international organizations transcend the nation-state in any way? On this question there is considerable debate between those who see the nation-state as the prime actor in international affairs, using and controlling international organizations to achieve their own ends, and those who argue that international organizations play a much more autonomous role and can achieve goals beyond the reach of individual states. To the former, international organizations are the tools of the state, especially the great powers like the United States of America, and have little independent existence on their own; to the latter, international organizations are a more positive force in the world whose activities in a broad range of social, cultural, and economic fields have gradually expanded into a vast network of interrelated functions that, while not replacing them, have increasingly curbed, restricted, and, in some cases, transcended the powers of the state.[2]

There are other questions to bear in mind, especially concerning the ability and effectiveness of international organizations. Are they capable of doing what they are created to do? There are more international organizations than ever before actively involved in human rights, economic development, and the environment; at the same time, the past two decades have seen some of the most horrific human rights abuses in history, the destruction of the ecosystem continues, and the gap between rich and poor continues to grow. The use of torture, rape, and murder is as common now as it was 50 years ago, despite the best efforts of hundreds of international organizations.[3] For some observers, international organizations are key players in many important global efforts to create a better world, and the need for them is greater than ever; for others, international organizations, at best, reflect the interests of the powerful states and, at worst, have a negative impact on others. An argument has been made, for example, that the development loans of the International Monetary Fund (IMF) do not enhance but actually impair economic growth in developing countries.[4] It is important to bear these points in mind when examining the history of international organizations. It is also safe to say that the effectiveness of international organizations does not correspond to their size or number.

Each international organization is unique in its own way. They come in various shapes and sizes, and like all institutions they develop their own style, culture, "spirit," and bureaucracy. Nevertheless, they share some common characteristics and functions. First, they all do things, in that they are established for a purpose, operate with their own rules, and try to achieve their stated goals (that is, help refugees, stop a war, clean up the environment, prevent the spread of disease, protect the interests of their members, and so on). These goals can change over time and are often never achieved or result in unintended consequences. Second, international organizations serve as an arena for things to happen; in other words, they provide the machinery to foster negotiations, establish norms of behaviour, fashion international law, act as a forum for debate for the weak as well as the strong, and so on. Third, international organizations serve as clearing houses for information. They collect and publish information and statistics; report on and study issues of importance to the institution; and inform, educate, influence, persuade, and disseminate the organization's values and beliefs.[5]

International organizations arose from the shared concerns and interests of governments and people—interests that transcended national borders and the concerns of a single state. This is not to suggest that they worked at odds with the nation-state, only that they appeared as the best possible way to serve mutual international interests and to solve mutual international problems. As one historian wrote, "nations and peoples had to be strongly aware that they shared certain interests and objectives across national boundaries and that they could best solve their many problems by pooling their resources and effecting transnational cooperation, rather than through individual countries' unilateral efforts."[6] International organizations connect governments and people all over the world; they are cooperative by necessity and international by design.

There is debate over when the first international organization appeared. Some scholars point to medieval Europe; others go back as far as ancient Greece and Rome, crediting anyone who called for some kind of international cooperation as being a supporter of international organizations. International relations, the rise of the nation-state, and the various organizations to which states belonged have been the focus of study for centuries. Dante, Machiavelli, Sun Tzu, Immanuel Kant, Hugo Grotius, Henri de Saint-Simon, and many others wrote of international cooperation, world government, and associations of states. The rise of the Catholic Church can be seen as a kind of early international organization, centralized in the Vatican, with a permanent secretariat, and drawing support and allegiance from all over the Western world.

We can trace the origins of modern international intergovernmental organizations (the focus of this book) to the rise of the European nation-state. The Treaty of Westphalia (1648), which ended the Thirty Years War, is usually acknowledged as the moment when the sovereign state was recognized as the "basic unit of social organization," first in Europe and then for the rest of the world.[7] From this point, nation-states made the rules and created a variety of international intergovernmental organizations, which they directed and controlled.

More often than not, early efforts at international organization came following the end of major conflicts when the victors gathered to decide what to do with the vanquished and to settle problems left over from the war. The most important of these conferences, at least for the rise of international organizations, was the Congress of Vienna in 1815. The major European powers used it to re-establish borders, dynasties, and territories in the aftermath of the Napoleonic Wars and to start the process of reintegrating France into the European system. It was followed by the creation of the Quadruple Alliance (Austria, Britain, Prussia, and Russia), which called for the staging of international conferences to help maintain peace in Europe. The Alliance evolved into the Congress System, or the Concert of Europe, an informal series of conferences among the major European powers based on the recognition of complete national sovereignty. Decisions required unanimity; any agreements reached applied only to those who accepted them; and there were no sanctions against those who failed to live up to their agreements. The Concert of Europe created a kind of balance of power among the great powers and offered a level of protection to the smaller powers. Here we see the rough structure of future international organizations, with the great powers meeting in council to ensure peace and maintain stability through international collaboration, arbitration, and the discussion of mutual problems.[8]

The Concert of Europe was not an international organization in the true sense, as it had no formal structure or secretariat and its conferences were staged irregularly and only when there was something of import to discuss.[9] Nevertheless, several dozen conferences were held over the course of the nineteenth century. In 1884 a large conference was held in Berlin to discuss African colonial possessions; in the last half of the century six conferences dealt with health issues; other conferences covered such topics as security, borders, trade, immigration, and communications. The Concert of Europe broke down and failed to prevent the outbreak of war in 1914, but it helped establish a process of international cooperation that was imitated by later international organizations.

The Industrial Age spawned other international organizations concerned with technological change. The appearance of new inventions from the telegraph to the airplane had international implications, and easier travel and improved communications accelerated the spread of ideas and information. More specialized and technical organizations dealt with specific issues, and although they were never totally free from outside influences, they tended to be less political and usually benefited all participant states. The first of these were the international commissions established to regulate the use of European rivers that crossed international borders: the Elbe (1821), Rhine (1831), and Danube (1856). Other specialized organizations followed, such as the International Telegraph Union Bureau (1865) and the Universal Postal Union (1874); these organizations had permanent secretariats and, ultimately, a continuous existence.[10]

Similarly, a few international non-governmental organizations appeared. The rise of a small but widespread peace movement led to the creation of peace societies, mainly in Europe and the United States, and they too began to pressure governments for action and organized international conferences. The International Red Cross, formally established in 1864, was a mixture of governmental and non-governmental efforts. It emerged from an international conference in Geneva that agreed to an international convention on the treatment of the sick and wounded and the neutrality of hospitals and ambulances during a time of war. The Geneva Convention was ratified by governments, and the International Committee of the Red Cross was born, but it operated via local Red Cross societies in each member state. The Red Cross continued to provide services in peacetime as well as war in response to natural disasters, epidemics, and other moments of crisis.

The growing peace movement was partly responsible for the holding of two conferences, which also included representatives of the smaller powers, at The Hague in the Netherlands in 1899 and 1907. The first was attended primarily by European states, but the 1907 conference included more than 40 countries, many from Latin America and Asia. They expanded the earlier Geneva Convention to include warfare at sea and produced some agreement to increase international arbitration as a way of settling disputes. The conferences helped to establish some basic rules for international behaviour, although they failed to keep the peace; indeed, plans for a third conference in 1915 were interrupted by the outbreak of the First World War.

These early efforts at international organization were in no way the exclusive preserve of the European states. In the Western Hemisphere the "Pan American movement" evolved in the nineteenth century, culminating in the First International Conference of American States in Washington, DC, in 1889–90. It established a regional body to enhance hemispheric trade relations and to aid the settlement of inter-American disputes. The International Bureau of American Republics was formed by 21 American republics in 1890; in 1910 it became known as the Pan American Union, and its mandate was broadened to include the carrying out of conference resolutions and to collect and disseminate information dealing with economic, social, and cultural affairs.

The Pan American Union, with its headquarters in Washington, had a permanent secretariat and staff of librarians, translators, secretaries, and so on, as well as a director-general and governing board. It held fairly regular conferences on matters of regional importance and established several regional specialized agencies, such as the Pan American Sanitary Bureau (1902), the Pan American Child Institute (1927), the Inter-American Commission of Women (1928), and the Pan American Institute of Geography and History (1929). The Pan American Union was open to all American republics (and therefore excluded countries like Canada and the British colonies in the Caribbean), and its goal was to promote economic development as well as peace and friendship in the Western Hemisphere.

Moreover, in the years after its civil war, the United States increasingly turned to international arbitration to settle its disputes with other states. Both the United States and Britain were eager to resolve amicably problems regarding fishing rights, boundary disputes, and trade relations with

Canada; to do so, they established a series of Anglo-American Joint High Commissions—from the Treaty of Washington in 1870 to the 1903 Alaska Boundary Dispute—in which several issues were discussed simultaneously and either settled or given over to international arbitration. This kind of arrangement was institutionalized in 1909 with the Anglo-American Boundary Waters Treaty, which created the International Joint Commission (Canada–United States) to examine boundary water issues and anything else the two governments wanted to direct its way. The IJC continues to function today.

Consequently, at the start of the twentieth century, a number of international organizations—both governmental and non-governmental—were operating not only in Europe but in the Americas, parts of Asia, and indirectly in the European colonial empires. Moreover, the use of international arbitration to settle disputes was widely embraced (provided the two sides involved in the dispute agreed), and there was a growing body of international law that was acknowledged if not always followed by an increasing number of states. International cooperation in technical matters was a reality reflected in several specialized international organizations. Furthermore, a system of international conferences sponsored by the great powers took responsibility for maintaining international stability, discussing major mutual problems, and producing a process for international cooperation. When the First World War broke out in 1914, therefore, international organizations were an established fact, and many of the ideas and processes that would be embodied in the League of Nations were already commonly accepted, especially in the West.

Notes

1. Barnett and Finnemore, *Rules for the World*, 1.
2. See Karns and Mingst, *International Organization*, 34–55.
3. See Cmiel, "The Recent History of Human Rights," 117–35.
4. Vreeland, *The International Monetary Fund*, 132–33.
5. Adapted from Archer, *International Organizations*, 135–47.
6. Iriye, *Global Community*, 9.
7. Weiss et al., *The United Nations and Changing World Politics*, 4–5.
8. Morgenthau, *Politics Among Nations*, 438–47.
9. Yoder, *The Evolution of the United Nations System*, 4.
10. Murphy, *International Organization and Industrial Change*, 46–48.

2 | The League of Nations

The League of Nations, a fascinating experiment in international organization, has attracted enormous attention in the almost 100 years since its creation at the end of the First World War. Not only is its own history appealing, it has had the added attraction since 1945 of serving as a foil for the United Nations (UN). Compared to the UN, where for many years mass bloc voting, stalemate, and impotency have seemed to dominate, the League has been romantically viewed as a place where great ideas could be debated and diplomats could make a difference. The League's noble beginning and tragic end have always given it an additional allure as well as providing a prime source for speculation: although it ultimately failed to stop the next world war, could it have worked under different circumstances? Or was it doomed by its own internal flaws and contradictions?

The idea of setting up an association of nations to maintain peace can be traced back to the earlier efforts at international organization discussed in Chapter One. Pacifists, internationalists, dreamers, members of technical organizations, and even some politicians began calling for some kind of international organization to deal with political questions. These feelings intensified and became much more vocalized during the First World War. In Britain, a League of Nations Society appeared months after the war began when Foreign Secretary Lord Grey and Conservative politician Lord Robert Cecil, among others, began calling for an organization to prevent the outbreak of future wars. In 1917 the British Imperial War Cabinet, which included representatives from the Dominions, debated the idea of a

9

postwar international organization. In addition, by 1916 members of the European Peace societies—and millions of other Europeans who longed for peace—supported the idea of an organization to guarantee peace and perhaps even save European civilization. Europe was in upheaval, millions were dead and wounded, millions more were displaced from their homes. Everyone wanted peace, and there was significant support for a League in government, in the press, and on the street.[1]

Added to the growing public support for an international peace organization was the need to implement and enforce the peace treaties that would come at the end of the war—regardless of the outcome. There were concerns about how to deal with Germany and the other enemy states, their empires, and the myriad problems that would linger once hostilities stopped. New borders would be drawn; new governments established; and refugees, reparations, and reconstruction would present more difficulties. On top of everything else, there were security concerns, particularly in France but also in other states that felt threatened by German economic and military power. An international organization could help to re-establish European society and create a more secure Europe. If nothing else, it could also be used to enforce the peace by ensuring that Germany paid for its crimes and was prevented from ever rising again. The Allied powers would make the decisions about the peace settlement, but an international organization could serve as one tool to help implement them.

The League of Nations was an integral part of the settlement of the First World War. It was created with the memory of the war still fresh, and the desire not to repeat the mistakes that led to its outbreak was a major consideration. In a sense, its supporters started by looking backwards in an effort to prevent something that had already happened from happening again. It was widely believed that the European states fell into war through a series of accidents that might have been prevented had there been time to cool off or negotiate. A series of secret treaties and alliances had created a domino effect as one state after another mobilized for war; there was no existing machinery to prevent the catastrophe from unfolding. Open diplomacy and collective security, it was argued, were the keys to preventing the outbreak of future wars and would offer a degree of safety that did not exist in 1914.

The League, therefore, was a product of its time, emerging from competing and even contradictory impulses. It was meant to enhance stability in the world and guarantee its members' national frontiers by establishing a system of collective security; it was supposed to prevent the outbreak of future wars by providing the machinery for arbitration and settlement of international disputes; it was designed to serve as the vehicle for the great powers to implement aspects of the peace agreement and to deal with various problems that remained after the war, ranging from the supervision of colonies and the staging of plebiscites to the repatriation of refugees; and it was also intended to promote and provide the forum for a number of worthwhile endeavours from disarmament to economic and social reconstruction. One thing the League would not do, however, was replace the existing system of international affairs or supersede the power of the state. The League would be used by its creators to do what they wanted, and it would reflect the varying interests of the states that created it.[2]

It is interesting that even with the strong support in Western Europe for the creation of a League—and given the European problems that were waiting for the League to address—the real leadership for its creation came from the United States, a state that until 1917 was neutral in the war. Like the Europeans, millions of Americans were already looking towards the creation of an international body to maintain peace. As early as 1910 President Theodore Roosevelt, while accepting his Nobel Peace Prize, called for the formation of a "league of peace" to prevent war. In 1915 a group of prominent Americans launched the League to Enforce Peace, which included in its program a call for a new international organization to establish international law to maintain peace, with the United States playing a key role. The group opened branches across the country and attracted widespread support from both political parties. A National Congress was created in 1916, and speakers at its first meeting included President Woodrow Wilson.

Wilson, the son of a Presbyterian minister, had both a law degree and a PhD in political science, and he had served as president of Princeton University and governor of the state of New Jersey. He was an intense and passionate man, with rather conservative views on moral and racial issues, although his political platform, dubbed the "New Freedom," supported many of the progressive causes of the day. He also embodied a strong sense of mission and idealism concerning the place of the United States in the world that influenced everything he did. Wilson may not have been the first person to come up with the idea of a League but, as one journalist later wrote, the "force, the passion, and the rhetoric [behind the League] were uniquely American and Wilsonian."[3]

By the time the United States entered the war in April 1917, Wilson was speaking publicly about "peace without victory" and the right of self-determination for all people. Many of his ideas were embodied in his January 1918 statement of American war aims in which he proclaimed his famous "Fourteen Points." He called for an end to secret diplomacy, which he believed had caused the war, and for arms reduction, the lowering of tariffs, the freedom of the seas, and self-determination. He also made several specific points concerning a number of disputed European territorial boundaries. The fourteenth point—the key one for Wilson—called for the creation of an international organization to oversee the peace and to guarantee the new revised borders. The Fourteen Points were widely welcomed in Europe and around the world, but many were vague, and not everyone agreed with them, even among those states friendly with the United States. Those nations, including France, Italy, and Britain, which had paid a very heavy price for victory, were less enthusiastic about the meaning of "peace without victory," so a clash with Wilson was almost inevitable.[4]

Wilson took the unprecedented step of attending the Paris Peace Conference, which opened 12 January 1919. He arrived in France to a hero's welcome, and he came prepared to oversee the creation of a League of Nations—and there was no question in his mind that the United States would play the leading role in it. He asked that the League be the first order of business at the Conference, and a Commission to draft its Covenant was created immediately. The Commission included representatives from the five great powers (the United States, Britain, France, Italy, and Japan) and ultimately from nine smaller states. There were no representatives from the Soviet Union, Germany, or any of the defeated states, and they were not asked for their opinions about the League; the draft Covenant and the League itself were produced by and reflected the views of the victors of the war.

The leaders of the great powers could not agree on many issues. Each pursued his own nation's interests at the negotiating table and brought a different view about the nature and powers of the proposed League. Wilson concentrated on the breakdown of the old system and balance of power in Europe and the rise of bolshevism and revolutionary socialism; for him, the League could help preserve the peace and stabilize the postwar world. Premier Georges Clemenceau of France was concerned above all else with his country's security and wanted to ensure that Germany would never again threaten France; the League was a secondary issue and valuable only if it could help solidify France's position by tying other countries to its defence. British Prime Minister David Lloyd George had just won re-election on a platform of making Germany pay for British reconstruction; he was less sure about the freedom of the seas or the idea of self-determination and was unwilling to give the League any significant powers. Italian Prime Minister

Vittorio Orlando invested considerable effort in the shaping of the League, even though his country's demand for territory, promised in a secret treaty of 1915, seemed to counter several of its founding principles. The Japanese delegation, led by Baron Nobuaki Makino, had its own proposals, including a failed attempt to achieve international acknowledgement of racial equality, but creating a powerful League with a broad mandate was not first among them, so the Japanese didn't play a significant role in drafting the Covenant. Many of the smaller states were enthusiastic supporters of the League idea, but its creation rested in the hands of the "Big Four."

The Treaty of Versailles, signed on 28 June 1919, was a dictated peace that reflected the animosity and bitterness felt towards Germany and left a legacy of resentment in that country; as a result, its fate and that of the League of Nations were inseparable. The Treaty, in redrawing the boundaries of Germany and much of Eastern Europe, left millions of Germans living in other countries; territory was ceded to Czechoslovakia and to a reconstituted Poland, which now included a corridor to the Baltic Sea and the new free city of Danzig, which was under the direction of the League and whose population of 350,000 consisted roughly of 42.5 per cent Germans. The colonial empires of the defeated states were confiscated; Germany was required to pay huge reparations and was largely disarmed; the Rhineland was demilitarized; and the industrial output of the Saar Valley, approximately 800 square miles near the border with France, was put in the hands of the French government for 15 years. The victors would use the new League of Nations to supervise and oversee the implementation of various aspects of the Treaty and to handle any remaining unresolved issues that they chose to hand over to it.

In many ways the League was a testament to Wilson's vision and determination, but it turned out to be the biggest defeat of his life. The Democrat Wilson erred in not bringing any Republicans with him to Paris to help in the Treaty negotiations, and on his return he steadfastly refused to accept any revisions to it. The opposition was led by Republican Senator Henry Cabot Lodge, chair of the important Senate Foreign Relations Committee, who liked neither Wilson nor his League, believing that it would undermine American sovereignty and commit the United States to sending military forces around the world under the direction of the European-dominated organization. Lodge produced a list of 14 "reservations" to the Treaty (to match Wilson's Fourteen Points), which must be met before he would support it. The whole issue became embroiled in partisan politics, and the two sides hardened in their positions. Wilson faced a Republican-dominated

Congress and was unable to sway many votes; by early 1920 both Lodge's reservations and the original Treaty suffered Congressional defeat, and subsequent efforts to resurrect it failed. In the election of 1920, the Republican Warren Harding won a landslide victory, and all talk of the ratification of the Treaty of Versailles and American involvement in the League of Nations evaporated. The League was born, but without American involvement it was wounded at the very start.[5]

The Covenant of the League of Nations (see Appendix 1), the organization's constitution, was included as part of the Treaty of Versailles; indeed, it was included in all of the five peace treaties signed. Its final wording and intent appeared far different from what had been originally planned. No one saw the League as a replacement for great power cooperation; if it functioned well as an organization, it might help, at best, to facilitate that cooperation. It was not a democracy, and although it included the basic premise of "one member one vote," it was not founded on the concept of equality of nations. The great powers had a larger voice and more influence than the others in the decision-making process. Moreover, Wilson's Fourteen Points were not incorporated into the Covenant—self-determination was neither granted nor accepted as a right, and colonial peoples were still seen as being in need of care to help them along the road to self-government. The other objectives of arms reduction, open covenants, freedom of the seas, and tariff reductions remained unrealized and only as distant goals to be achieved sometime in the future. Thus, the League of Nations was to wear many hats: keeper of the Treaty, handmaiden of the great powers, provider of collective security, colonial overseer, social activist, and the voice of peace for humankind.

The League's basic structure included an assembly of all members, a smaller permanent council of the larger powers, and a permanent secretariat. It was open to all self-governing states, including the British Dominions, and although it initially consisted primarily of the victors of the First World War, new members were gradually brought in with the approval of two-thirds of existing members. There were 42 original members, primarily from Europe and Latin America but with global representation from China, India, and Australia. Within two years another 10 states were welcomed, including Luxemburg, Lithuania, Albania, and former enemy states Austria, Bulgaria, and Hungary. South Africa and Liberia were the lone African members until the arrival of Ethiopia in 1923 and, much later, Egypt in 1937.

The Assembly, in which each member had one vote, was in charge of the League's expenses and set its budget. The Council consisted of nine states

FIGURE 2.1 Members of the League of Nations

Member	Entrance	Exit	Member	Entrance	Exit
Afghanistan	1934		Ireland	1923	
Albania	1920	1939	Italy ♦		1937
Argentina ♦			Japan ♦		1933
Australia ♦			Latvia	1921	
Austria	1920	1938	Liberia ♦		
Belgium ♦			Lithuania	1921	
Bolivia ♦			Luxembourg	1920	
Brazil ♦		1926	Mexico	1931	
Bulgaria	1920		Netherlands ♦		
Canada ♦			New Zealand ♦		
Chile ♦		1938	Nicaragua ♦		1936
China ♦			Norway ♦		
Colombia ♦			Panama ♦		
Costa Rica	1920	1925	Paraguay ♦		1935
Cuba ♦			Persia ♦		
Czechoslovakia ♦			Peru ♦		1939
Denmark ♦			Poland ♦		
Dominican Republic	1924		Portugal ♦		
Ecuador	1934		Rumania ♦		1940
Egypt	1937		Salvador ♦		1937
Estonia	1921		Siam ♦		
Ethiopia	1923		South Africa ♦		
Finland	1920		Spain ♦		1939
France ♦			Sweden ♦		
Germany	1926	1933	Switzerland ♦		
Greece ♦			Turkey	1932	
Guatemala ♦		1936	United Kingdom ♦		
Haiti ♦		1942	USSR	1934	1939
Honduras ♦		1936	Uruguay ♦		
Hungary	1922	1939	Venezuela ♦		1938
India ♦			Yugoslavia ♦		
Iraq	1932				

♦ Original member

at first, with representatives of the five great powers—Britain, France, Italy, Japan, and the United States (the Americans, of course, never occupied their seat)—plus four representatives from smaller powers on a rotating basis. Any member could be invited to sit in on council meetings when matters specifically dealing with that state were under discussion. The Council was to meet once a year and at any other time considered necessary. The Council and Assembly worked by unanimity on all but procedural matters, so, technically, everyone had a veto. Procedural matters (Article 5) included the appointment of committees to investigate particular issues; thus, it was possible to circumvent the need for unanimity by making the approval of reports with recommendations a procedural matter, so that the views of the League could not be vetoed by one member.

The Secretariat provided a continuous existence for the League, organizing the meetings and conferences, creating services to facilitate the organization, providing the interpreters and secretaries, and publishing the proceedings. The Secretariat included a variety of "Sections" established to oversee key areas of League work, including the mandates, disarmament, minorities, and political, social, economic and financial, and administrative issues. The secretary-general, appointed by the Council but approved by the Assembly, had relatively little power and was essentially a caretaker of the organization, but he had the right to call a meeting of Council at the request of any League member. All positions in the League were specifically open to both men and women, but the League, like most international organizations of that time, was dominated by men. There were many important exceptions, of course. Briton Rachel Crowdy, for example, was appointed head of the Section on Social Problems and was probably the highest ranking woman in the League Secretariat.

The heart of the Covenant was found in Articles 10 through 19. Article 10 called for League members to "respect and preserve as against external aggression the territorial integrity and the existing political independence of all members of the League" and left it up to the Council to decide "the means by which this obligation shall be fulfilled." Here was the concept of collective security, and this article was one of the most hotly contested. For the French and many smaller states it expressed the very essence of the League by announcing to all potential aggressors that an attack on one member would be considered an attack on all; the Americans, British, Canadians, and several other British Dominions were concerned that by guaranteeing all existing borders Article 10 would drag their nations into endless conflicts in which they were not concerned. Article 10 applied only to "external" aggression and left national sovereignty intact; it was gently qualified by Article 19, which permitted the Assembly to reconsider "treaties which may have become inapplicable" and "international conditions whose continuance might endanger the peace of the world."

Articles 11 through 18 established the procedure for the settlement of international disputes. All members were called upon to submit their disputes to the League, or to arbitration, or to the Permanent Court of International

Justice, and not to go to war for at least three months after a judicial decision or the Council had made its report. This cooling-off period would give the two sides the opportunity to negotiate an agreement regardless of the League's subsequent actions. The outbreak of hostilities, or any threat of war, could be brought to the attention of the League by any member, whether or not they were a party to the dispute, and the secretary-general could summon a meeting of the Council. If arbitration failed, the Council would study the situation, issue a report, and hopefully effect a settlement by unanimous decision (parties to the dispute could attend the meetings but could not vote). If the Council could not make unanimous recommendations, each member could consider its own response and actions, and the Council could hand the problem over to the Assembly, where the same rules and procedures applied. In such cases it was technically still possible for the parties to go to war if they had not negotiated a settlement. But if the Council reached a unanimous agreement, then all members agreed not to go to war with any of the parties that complied with its recommendations; if one of the parties disregarded the League decision and went to war in contravention of the Covenant, it was deemed to have committed an act of war against all members and was to be immediately subject to sanctions and the severance of diplomatic, trade, and financial relations. The Council would also recommend whatever military action was necessary. No country could be forced to go to war to defend another, but all members would be morally obligated to uphold League decisions.

In addition, the Covenant established the procedure for dealing with those colonies and territories that had been taken away from the defeated Central Powers "as a consequence of the late war." In patronizing tones the drafters of the Covenant agreed that those territories "which are inhabited by peoples not yet able to stand by themselves under the strenuous conditions of the modern world" should be divided among the more developed nations. The territories were placed into three categories—A, B, or C—based on their ability to govern themselves, and a mandate system was established to oversee their development.

A Permanent Mandates Commission was created to advise the Council on the mandate system, but the actual responsibility for the territories was granted to various League members. The mandates over the former German colonies of New Guinea, Western Samoa, and South West Africa were granted, respectively, to Australia, New Zealand, and South Africa. In Africa, Tanganyika was made a British mandate, Ruanda-Urandi was given to the Belgians, and the Cameroons and Togoland were divided between

France and Britain. In the Middle East, mandates over Iraq, Transjordan, and Palestine were granted to Britain while Syria and Lebanon went to France.

The Mandates Commission received annual reports from the administering states and could offer comments and recommendations, but the administration of the mandate territories remained firmly in the control of the states. It created a new kind of arrangement, with the mandated territories in a kind of limbo, neither official colonies of the administering state nor under the complete supervision of the League. However, theoretical sovereignty was about all that the territories maintained, and they were treated largely as colonies by the mandatory powers. Despite the lofty rhetoric of self-determination and the ostensible goal of independence, at least for the more advanced mandates, little progress was made before the Second World War. Indeed, strategic interests and disputes over trading rights in the mandate territories between the major powers, including the United States, likely hindered the movement towards independence.[6] Of all the mandates, only Iraq was granted independence (1932) before the outbreak of the Second World War. The others—from Palestine to South West Africa—remained in limbo, and the problems they faced were left for others to resolve.

The League was also entrusted with responsibility for a range of social issues such as public health and the control of diseases, working conditions, communications, the suppression of slavery, and the control of illegal drugs and prostitution. Existing international bodies dealing with non-political issues—such as the Universal Postal Union—were to be brought under the direction of the League (but only with their consent) and the Covenant (in Article 24) created a kind of "League System," which would be repeated in the UN. Several new organizations were created and brought under the auspices of the League as well. Examples include the League's Communications and Transit Organization (1921), set up (under Article 23) to collect and disseminate information on the technical aspects of all forms of transportation, and the International Committee on Intellectual Cooperation (1922), established to promote cooperation in cultural and intellectual activities. In some cases, the new organizations largely embraced or supplanted existing prewar associations; for example, the Office International d'Hygiène Publique, established in Paris in 1907, essentially evolved into the League's Health Organization (1923). This organization won universal acclaim for its efforts in combating typhus and cholera epidemics in Russia and Eastern Europe, and it helped spark technical advances in sanitation. It was eventually transformed into the World Health Organization (WHO).[7]

Perhaps the most important League-associated organization was the International Labour Organization (ILO), based in Geneva and created in 1919 by terms laid out in the Treaty of Versailles. The ILO had its own constitution and autonomy, a permanent secretariat, and a director-general, and all League members were automatically members. Consisting of representatives of workers and employers, as well as government, the ILO studied working conditions and fashioned international conventions to establish labour standards on working hours, wages, unemployment benefits, the protection of women and children, and other matters. It survived the League to become a specialized agency of the UN, and it continues to operate today.

Because the war had demonstrated the great destructive capacity of aviation, discussions during the Paris Peace Conference led to the signing of the International Air Navigation Convention (known as the Paris Convention), followed by the creation of the International Commission for Air Navigation (ICAN) in 1922. ICAN, with its headquarters and secretariat in Paris, was a permanent body established to oversee, implement, and modify the Paris Convention; to collect aviation statistics; and to settle aviation disputes between its members. Although not specifically tied to the League, its fortunes rose and fell with the League, and it suffered from some similar problems. All League members were members of ICAN, but Germany, the Soviet Union, and others at first were excluded. Likewise, the United States and most of Latin America remained outside the organization (they formed their own group with the Pan American Convention on Commercial Aviation signed in Havana in 1928).

Note should also be made of the creation of the Permanent Court of International Justice (PCIJ) in The Hague in 1921. A judicial tribunal of 11 (later 15) judges, the PCIJ was established by the Covenant (Article 14) to "hear and determine any dispute of an international character which the parties thereto submit to it." The Court was envisioned to play a role in the arbitration and settlement of disputes, and, although it had fairly limited powers, it made more than 50 judgements that were accepted by the international community. Most of these decisions, however, related to largely non-critical issues and were focused primarily on small-scale European disputes; for example, the Court ruled in Denmark's favour against Norway over the possession of Eastern Greenland.

The League of Nations began in January 1920 and ended in April 1946. Its history is often portrayed in two halves—its "rise" in the 1920s when the air was filled with optimism, it enjoyed great public support and even enthusiasm, and there were relatively few serious security threats facing the great powers; and its "fall" in the 1930s when things came apart. The world slipped into depression and war while the League stood by, impotent and unable to prevent the catastrophe. There is a degree of truth in this view. In the 1920s the League was very popular; large League of Nations Societies in several countries enhanced its moral authority; and it was not uncommon for heads of government and foreign ministers to lead their delegations to the League Assemblies in Geneva. Compared to the 1930s, the first postwar decade was one of optimism and idealism about the potential of the League, an idealism that came to be regarded in later years as simple naiveté. It was equally true that the 1920s was a decade of relative stability when the League was not forced to confront major disputes between any of the great powers. The public had faith in the League, which rode this popular support to achieve some modest goals, if only in non-political areas.

It is important to recall that the League was created to do different things, some of which it did achieve: helping to settle minor border disputes, containing the spread of diseases, assisting in the repatriation and resettlement of refugees and prisoners of war, encouraging international cooperation in the inspection and distribution of drugs, and generally aiding in postwar reconstruction. Its Refugee Committee oversaw the repatriation of tens of thousands of former prisoners of war and displaced Russians, Poles, and Armenians. Dr. Fridtjof Nansen, the Norwegian explorer, was put in charge, and over a two-year period he was able to help more than 400,000 men, women, and children return to their homes. Nansen was named the League's first "High Commissioner for Refugees" and became a powerful moral force, winning the Nobel Peace Prize in 1923. In the Saar Valley the League kept the peace and administered the territory for 15 years before supervising a 1935 plebiscite in which the population voted to return to Germany.

On the major issues of the day, concerning revolution and war in Eastern Europe, Turkey, and elsewhere, the League was uninvolved, but it did experience some minor successes in other areas.[8] In 1920 a dispute between Finland and Sweden over the possession of the Aaland Islands off the southern coast of Finland was decided in Finland's favour by a League commission. Sweden accepted the decision, even though most of the islands' 26,000 residents spoke Swedish and Finland was not yet a member of the League. In a somewhat similar situation, the League established a commission to decide the boundary dispute between Germany and Poland in Upper

Silesia; the commission divided the territory in two, largely along ethnic lines, and an agreement was signed in 1921.

In 1923 Italy bombed and occupied the Greek Island of Corfu, following the killing of an Italian diplomat who was working on League business along the border between Greece and Albania. Outraged Italian dictator Benito Mussolini issued an ultimatum to the Greek government, and the Greeks appealed to the League. Following an investigation the League called on Greece to compensate Italy for its losses and for Italy to pull out of Corfu—both sides agreed. League supporters saw this as an example of both the League's effectiveness when its leading powers worked together and its potential to do even better things; detractors (and most historians) called it a humiliation for Greece and a victory for Mussolini, who had acted like a bully and got away with it. Two years later, in 1925, even more serious fighting broke out along the border between Greece and Bulgaria; there was a real threat of war, with Greek forces crossing the Bulgarian frontier. The League Council acted swiftly, issuing an ultimatum for both sides to withdraw and to establish a cease-fire. The two sides complied, Greece agreed to compensate Bulgaria for the damage caused by its troops, the League dispatched observers to monitor the border, and war was averted.[9]

These examples of success were real but minor. Disputes involving Finland, Sweden, Greece, Bulgaria, and even Italy did not pose a serious security threat to the great powers, and that made them that much more open to solution. However, serious matters of national security remained in the hands of national governments, colonial questions were left to the colonial powers, and the concerns of non-members like the Soviet Union and United States were totally outside the League's jurisdiction. In the Western Hemisphere, the League was usually turned to, if at all, only as a last resort. In 1933 the League was asked for help to stop the Chaco War between Bolivia and Paraguay only after the failure of arbitration involving several neighbouring states and the Pan American Union. The League helped end the war, and a treaty was signed in 1938, but only after thousands had died.

In addition, internal affairs were just that—internal to the state in question. The League could do little to affect them. The repression and murder of Armenians, for example, produced no response from the League, and when Armenia was occupied and turned into a Soviet Republic the League remained silent. More positively, the idea of protecting minority rights (as opposed to individual human rights) was included in several peace treaties and was part of the League's mandate. The League received hundreds of petitions and complaints from minority groups about their treatment in their home country, but it acted on only a few of them and then only in the role of mediator. The League could not impose its will on any state, its interference in the domestic affairs of any member would have been greatly resisted and resented, and no state—especially none of the great powers—was eager to fight to protect the rights of minorities in other states. The League was less than completely successful in its efforts, but at least it put the issues of the protection of minority rights and self-determination on the table.[10]

The biggest challenge throughout the League's history was to provide a system of collective security for its members in order to prevent the outbreak of another major war. In the middle of this larger question were France and Germany, the Treaty provisions, borders, war guilt, and reparations. Relations between France and Germany rose and fell during the 1920s, and guaranteeing France's security while reintegrating Germany into Europe was an intractable problem. Not only was the League weak without the backing of the United States, but its Covenant established such a slow process for arbitration that it was possible for states still to go to war. Article 10 came under attack from countries that had, like the United States, serious concerns about being dragged into wars that were not of their concern. The Canadians, for example, made repeated attempts to remove or dilute Article 10, and, although they did not distinguish themselves by their efforts, they were not alone, and it was gradually acknowledged that no member would be forced to take any action without its consent.

At first, several attempts were made within the League to guarantee French security, but they all failed. In 1923–24 a draft Treaty of Mutual Assistance failed. In 1924, the British Labour government of Ramsay MacDonald issued the Geneva Protocol, an anti-aggression pact that would have established a process of compulsory arbitration and binding decisions. Opposition to it rose immediately (particularly in Britain and the Commonwealth), and a newly elected Conservative British government withdrew its support. It collapsed early in 1925. A solution of sorts was found outside the League, with the signing of the Locarno Treaty in 1925 by France, Germany, and Belgium, with guarantees by Britain and Italy. Its aim was to maintain the status quo in Western Europe by guaranteeing the borders of Germany, France, and Belgium (it also maintained a demilitarized Rhineland).[11]

Locarno was largely negotiated by the foreign ministers of the three great European powers: Aristide Briand of France, Gustav Stresemann of Germany, and Austen Chamberlain of Britain. In addition to representing their respective governments, these three men symbolized the success of the League in the 1920s. Neither Stresemann nor Chamberlain was an enthusiastic supporter of the League; however, the presence of this trio of foreign ministers—with larger-than-life personas—and their apparent willingness to collaborate seemed to auger well for its future. Hopes were raised even higher thanks to the Locarno arrangements, which called for the entrance of Germany into the League (Germany was already a member of a few technical organizations and the ILO).

Germany entered the League in February 1926. There were mixed feelings about this move, from the British, who thought that it would help rehabilitate Germany and give a boost to European stability, to the French, who were less enthusiastic over the prospect of a stronger Germany, and to the Germans, who saw League membership as a way to overturn aspects of the Treaty of Versailles and to re-establish Germany as a great power. German entrance sparked a minor crisis, however. The Germans insisted on and were granted permanent membership on the League Council.[12] The governments of Brazil, Spain, and Poland immediately demanded equal treatment. The League sought a compromise and offered to expand the non-permanent Council membership (three of whom could be re-elected). The Brazilians refused to accept and resigned from the League and in so doing reinforced the sense of the League as a European organization. Conversely, the presence of Germany seemed to usher in a new era for the League—no longer merely an association of the victors of the First World War, it appeared stronger and more stable than ever before.

Military disarmament was another goal aimed at ensuring European peace, but it was an objective never attained by the League. Several of the peace treaties called for disarmament and the general reduction in arms, and the Covenant (Article 8) gave the League a role to play in making plans for arms reduction (and to limit arms manufacturing), which the various members would implement. It was also given the task of collecting information on the industrial output and military stockpiles in each member state and in supervising the international trade in arms. It was a thankless task, even though all members agreed to accept the armaments regulations established by Article 1. The League could not impose its will on any of its own members, let alone those states that remained outside. Even within the League there were great divisions over both the process of disarmament and its ultimate goal.

The League worked very hard for disarmament and the regulation of the trade in arms.[13] The Assembly had its own disarmament committee, and a

Disarmament Section was established in the Secretariat. The latter launched a series of publications of statistics on armaments and the arms trade: the *Armaments Year-Book* and the *Statistical Year-Book of the Trade in Arms and Ammunition* were both published between 1926 and 1938. The Permanent Armaments Commission called for in Article 9 was established by the Council in 1920 and consisted of military representatives speaking on behalf of their nation's self-interest; the Temporary Mixed Commission on Armaments of both military and non-military personnel studied disarmament questions. Finally, the Preparatory Commission for the Disarmament Conference was established in 1926 to make preparations for a general disarmament conference that was to negotiate an international disarmament treaty.[14]

The World Disarmament Conference opened in Geneva in February 1932 with representatives from 59 countries (including representatives from the United States and the Soviet Union), each with their own idea about disarmament. The Versailles Treaty called for the disarmament of Germany, and the thinking was that general disarmament would follow from there. Beyond that there was disagreement. The Germans did not like being disarmed when others were not. The French spoke in favour of disarmament but were never convinced that the reduction of the French military would make France any safer—for them it was more important first to establish French security before moving to general disarmament. The British were also concerned but were already in the process of disarming. Finding an acceptable formula that everyone could live with was impossible. Everything was connected: the different services and the different kinds of weapons and hardware within each service; one side would agree to cuts only if the other side would agree to cuts somewhere else.[15] The conference dragged on for months with little progress. In the meantime Japan invaded Manchuria and Hitler came to power in Germany. In October 1933, Germany walked out of both the Conference and the League, and the Disarmament Conference collapsed a few months later, in June 1934. The League may have helped establish some standards for arms regulation that were gradually embraced by the international community,[16] but it failed to achieve any kind of general disarmament or to limit or regulate the manufacture and trade in arms. Soon it was hard to find anyone willing even to discuss disarmament.

The collapse of the Disarmament Conference, along with the failure of the World Monetary and Economic Conference (held in London in the summer of 1933 to discuss trade and tariff issues), was a symbolic turning point in League history. Before, there was the hope, dream, and chance—however slight—of international cooperation; after, there was depression, pessimism, and the slow descent into war. In the face of the threat posed by Nazism, fascism, and militarism, the weaknesses of the League began to show, and the whole structure began to crumble. The contempt for the League demonstrated by the Axis powers of Germany, Italy, and Japan became unrestrained, and the other great powers regularly bypassed the League, relying on old-style diplomacy to solve their international problems.

Two international events of the 1930s were significant tests for the League, and both revealed its inherent weakness: the Japanese invasion of Manchuria and the Italian-Ethiopian Crisis of 1935. In the first, the Japanese military seized power at home and launched a very aggressive policy in Asia, including the invasion of the Chinese province of Manchuria in September 1931. The Japanese claimed they were there to "restore order" and blamed the Chinese, but it was a vicious and cruel attack that killed thousands and led to the creation of the Japanese-dominated state of Manchukuo. For many outside Japan it was also a clear violation of the League Covenant and blatant aggression against a League member. As a result, the Chinese appealed to the League.[17]

It is hard to imagine an international crisis that the League was less likely to be willing or able to deal with effectively. First, the aggression was committed by a great power and a League member; to force Japan out of Manchuria would have been a next-to-impossible task. Second, League members could not automatically count on American support in their efforts to constrain the Japanese. The American government was outraged by the Japanese actions but was divided over the best course of action to take and made no promises to support any subsequent League action. Third, the aggression occurred in China far away from the Euro-dominated and Euro-focused League. There was little information and much confusion about exactly what had occurred in Manchuria, and there was little enthusiasm in London or Paris for taking on a major power on the other side of the world when the deteriorating security conditions in Europe were far more troubling.

In the event, in December 1931 the League Council appointed a Commission of Inquiry under the Earl of Lytton to travel to Japan and Manchuria and then to report on its findings. The Lytton Commission reported in September 1932, blaming Japan for its aggression and vindicating China. In the Assembly there was considerable support for action against Japan, especially among the smaller states, but the leading states— the ones that would be called upon to enforce any League action—were hesitant to get involved, even in the implementation of sanctions against Japan. In February 1933 the Assembly agreed to not recognize the new state of Manchukuo; even that was too much for the Japanese. The Japanese delegation walked out of the Assembly; a few weeks later, in March 1933, Japan withdrew from the League.

An armistice was signed between China and Japan—with the support of the League—to put an end to the fighting, but it left Japan in control of Manchuria. What little the League did probably only strengthened the evolving alliance between Japan, Germany, and Italy. Japan soon denounced earlier arms agreements and, in 1937, launched a murderous campaign in northern China. The League did nothing to stop it; by then there was little that it could have done. The territorial integrity of China was not preserved and no sanctions were applied under Articles 15 and 16. It was a total failure for the concept of collective security.

The Italian-Ethiopian Crisis was a more immediate predicament for the League and the biggest failure in the League's history.[18] The Italians had been in Eritrea since the late nineteenth century, and there were skirmishes along the border with Ethiopia in the 1920s and early 1930s. Mussolini was looking for a reason to move against Ethiopia and used the excuse of a border incident in December 1934 to allow fighting to break out. By early 1935 an Italian invasion of Ethiopia appeared imminent and a wider war threatened. Ethiopia, a League member, appealed its case in Geneva, and public opinion in most states tended to support it against Italy. Discussions in both the Council and Assembly raised the possibility of sanctions against the Italians, but there was little more than talk. The French and British were more worried about the rise of Hitler in Germany and had hopes that Mussolini could be turned into an ally. They sympathized with the plight of the Ethiopians, and may have been willing to help, but not if it meant a wider war with Italy. Furthermore, it was unknown how the United States would react if sanctions were applied against Italy—would the Americans go along or would they continue to trade with the Italians? If the latter, would the League attempt to enforce its sanctions against the United States? American opinion was divided, but to most outsiders it looked like the United States was moving into an isolationist shell with the passage in 1935 of the first of several Neutrality Acts.

In October 1935 Italy invaded Ethiopia, sparking public outrage across Europe and North America and producing a serious crisis for the League. Sanctions were discussed, including trade embargoes and the banning of imports from Italy, the freezing of loans, and a proposal to close the Suez Canal to Italian ships. Fifty of 54 members of the Assembly voted that Italy had resorted to war and was in violation of the Covenant. As a result, the implementation of sanctions by these states was automatic, but the real debate focused on what sanctions—if any—the League should apply. Most members accepted an arms embargo and restrictions on loans to Italy, and many introduced trade bans on specific products. The debate on the inclusion of oil on the list of sanctions was particularly difficult, and a decision was postponed several times. It was agreed that cutting off Italy's oil supply would make it very difficult for the Italians to continue fighting, but would this mean the blockading of all oil shipments, including those from the United States? Without American cooperation the sanctions would probably fail and serve little purpose other than driving Mussolini into a closer relationship with Hitler. Tough sanctions might also spark a broader European war—a war nobody wanted. In the end it was left to each state to decide for itself what sanctions to apply.

The crisis exposed the limitations of the League. An argument can be made that the League successfully operated as it was supposed to—it met, studied, debated, and called for sanctions against an aggressor state—and that the weakness or failure was not in the League but in the states themselves for not standing up to Italy. But this way of thinking was lost on most observers at the time. For millions of people around the world this was a clear example of aggression and the violation of a League member's territory. Many of the League delegates who were filled with the "spirit of Geneva" felt that it was imperative that the League act. For many smaller states that might have occasion in the future to turn to the League to protect their security, it was also important to take a stand. In government circles of the great powers, however, there were other considerations. The only "great powers" in the League were France and Britain, so the heaviest burden would fall to them (especially Britain, in this case); in their efforts to find a way out of the crisis, the League was more of a hindrance than a help. Efforts to negotiate a settlement outside the League—the Hoare-Laval Pact of December 1935—sparked public outrage and were denounced by Ethiopian Emperor Haile Selassie when they were revealed, largely because the deal offered most of Ethiopia to Italy. The collapse of the deal led to the resignation of British Foreign Secretary Sir Sam Hoare but did not prompt a new direction in British or French policy, and their reluctance to impose more serious sanctions on Italy remained.

Things did not improve in 1936, as Germany, Italy, and Japan formed the Axis alliance and Hitler militarily reoccupied the Rhineland, denouncing both Locarno and the League in the process. The Italians moved across Ethiopia using tanks, airplanes, and mustard gas against practically defenceless Ethiopian troops. Emperor Selassie appeared before the League and demanded action but was met by indifference mixed with hostility. For British Prime Minister Chamberlain, Hitler was the bigger worry and continuing any kind of sanctions against Italy just didn't make sense. Those few sanctions that had been applied were lifted in the summer, just as civil war broke out in Spain, shifting the world's attention away from Ethiopia. Selassie fled into exile, Ethiopia was annexed as an Italian colony, and Italy left the League in 1937.

The League never had "real" power—at least with respect to maintaining collective security—but the crisis over the Italian invasion of Ethiopia left it in shambles, stripping it of its remaining "moral" authority. The dictators condemned the League as an agent of international communism (and fascist Spain withdrew its membership) and the British, French, and others began openly questioning its value and called for its reform. The events that led to war in 1939, therefore, unfolded outside the League, without reference to it, and often without even discussion within it. In November 1939, following the Soviet invasion of Finland, the League performed its last task—expelling the Soviet Union, which had joined only in 1934. Then it adjourned to await its anticipated revival once the war was over. The revival never came, and in April 1946 the League met one last time, paid its debts, wrapped up its remaining business, and voted itself out of existence.

Few people mourned the passing of the League at the end of the Second World War, but many have speculated since then about its shortcomings and why, in the end, it failed. The shortest answer is that the League was, in fact, successful in many of its roles, such as in helping repatriate refugees, overseeing the implementation of the peace treaties, solving lesser disputes, and giving a voice to smaller countries and peoples. In addition, its various conferences, commissions, committees, and associated agencies—several of which survived the League's demise—did important work. Even in areas considered to be failures, such as disarmament, economic affairs, and the protection of minority rights, the League helped to establish international norms, procedures, and knowledge that were embraced by the international community and integrated into the UN, its specialized agencies, and other international organizations. But on the larger issues of war and peace it is clear that the League never had the capacity to prevent a war between great powers.

The great powers used the League when it could serve their national interests and tended to ignore it when it could not, and the old international rivalries never really disappeared. It is doubtful that any government seriously believed that the League would be able to achieve its ultimate goal of collective security because it relied on moral force alone. It had neither military nor economic power and could not force or coerce a state to act in any particular way if it chose not to; it could provide a forum for debate, and it could investigate and provide for the arbitration of disputes. And when both sides in the dispute agreed to cooperate it could be—and was— effective. Critics charged that it was naive to believe that nations would be deterred by moral argument alone or by the force of international public opinion, and the Covenant was criticized as an idealistic and overly optimistic document—a League "without teeth" was doomed to failure. The Covenant and League were founded on the conditions and premises of 1914; its calls for open diplomacy, cooling-off periods, and arbitration were out of step with the kind of interwar aggression in which declarations of war were rare, and cooling-off periods and lengthy investigations only made it easier for aggressive states to secure their goals. It was even argued that the League aggravated international crises by involving itself in situations where it could have no real impact. It was unable to stop aggression in Manchuria or Ethiopia, but the public debate and condemnation of Japan and Italy only served to drive them further into alliance with Germany.

It is hard not to point to the decision of United States to remain outside as a partial explanation for the weakness of the League. From the very start the League was hampered by the absence of American leadership and power. Without the United States the share of the burden on those who remained was that much greater; having a great power sitting outside the League was an example that made it easier for other countries to do the same; and the American withdrawal was seen by many as a failure in American moral responsibility. American support or compliance with League actions was never a given and in some cases was not forthcoming. This made it harder for the League to act. Without American leadership in the Pacific region, for example, there was little that the League could do to restrain Japanese expansion. The League never fully recovered from this initial blow. This weakness was a constant thought in the minds of many of those who came together in the Second World War to ensure the presence of the United States in the new UN.

In addition, the absence of other important states was a constant hindrance to the League's ability to act effectively. It was never a truly global organization; for most of its existence it resembled a Eurocentric collection of the victors of the First World War. The United States never joined;

Germany came in 1926 and left in 1933; Japan withdrew in 1933; Italy and Spain followed; the Soviet Union joined only in 1934 and was expelled in 1939; and others dropped out along the way, including Brazil, Chile, Venezuela, and several other Latin American states. With each resignation the stature, authority, and effectiveness of the League diminished. This is not to suggest that the presence of all these states would have averted war in 1939 or turned the League into a powerful force for peace in the world. The Soviet Union, had it been a member in the 1920s, would have been just as hostile as it was sitting on the outside, and it is unrealistic to think that League membership alone would have had any measurable impact on the governments of Germany, Japan, and Italy in the 1930s.

The demise of the League of Nations was not an indication of the end of international organizations generally or of the idea and goal of international collaboration. The experience probably helped reinforce the idea of international organization and cooperation; even in failure, it helped foster and promote support for internationalism. Likewise, the failure of collective security did not lessen the need for it in the future. The legacy of the League of Nations spoke to the promise of collective security and international cooperation; its history provided a blueprint for future experiment; its failure to prevent war underlined the need for a stronger, more assertive international organization.

Notes

1 Walters, *A History of the League of Nations*, 17–21.
2 Steiner, *The Lights That Failed*, 349.
3 Bendiner, *A Time for Angels*, 4.
4 Egerton, *Great Britain and the Creation of the League of Nations*, 73–74.
5 For the American defeat of the treaty, see Bendiner, 139–59.
6 See Crozier, "The Establishment of the Mandates System," 483–513, and Gorman, "Liberal Internationalism," 449–77.
7 For a review of the various institutions, see Walters, 176–93.
8 For a list of League accomplishments, see Yoder, *The Evolution of the UN System*, 14–16.
9 Steiner, 357–59.
10 See Fink, "Minority Rights as an International Question," 389–91.
11 Dexter, *The Years of Opportunity*, 193–203.
12 Kimmich, *Germany and the League of Nations*, 58–59.
13 See Stone, "Imperialism and Sovereignty," 213–30.
14 Webster, "The Transnational Dream," 501–05.
15 Steiner, 373–74.
16 See Webster, "Making Disarmament Work," 551–69.

17 On the Manchurian crisis, see Scott, *The Rise and Fall of the League of Nations*, 207–41.

18 For an examination of the crisis, see Scott, 317–68.

3 | Wartime Internationalism and International Organizations

The Second World War provided both the motive and opportunity for the expansion of international organizations, and by the time it was over their number, scope, and variety had grown significantly. The inability of the League of Nations to prevent the war was not widely interpreted as a reason not to have any other international organizations; if anything, the experience of the 1930s only emphasized how important it was to have in place some kind of system or structure to pursue international peace and security. In addition, there was a growing understanding that the difficult economic and social conditions of the Depression in the 1930s were factors in the outbreak of the war, and the link between social and economic issues and general international security was never clearer. The logical conclusion for many people was that a stronger, broader, and more encompassing organization was necessary.

The war produced a strong movement towards internationalism, especially among the Western Allies who had come together in a common cause and had achieved an impressive record of cooperation. They showed what could be accomplished by working together in war—why could that spirit of cooperation not be harnessed in peacetime and used to prevent future wars or solve transnational social problems? Technology was also continuing to bring the whole world together—for both good and evil. In the fields of communications and transportation, the need for international regulation, setting of standards, and the sharing of information in broadcasting, telecommunications, aviation, scientific research, and so on was accelerated by wartime technological advancements. Technological change had also made the world a more dangerous place, and disarmament and the control of atomic energy were issues that, for many people, transcended national boundaries and required international collaboration.

The war also created new conditions and enormous problems that would need to be confronted once victory was achieved. Tens of millions were dead; millions more were homeless—and stateless. There would be major challenges in rehabilitating both the defeated Axis states and those nations that had been overrun and occupied. Not only would they have to be rebuilt from the ground up, not only in terms of immediate relief but also in long-term reconstruction, but questions remained about their collapsing empires—what was to become of all the colonies, territories, and peoples liberated by the end of the war? For many, thinking about these questions could not wait for the war to end. It was a heady time for many internationalists because the war had produced a unique opportunity—the chance to rebuild the world in the image of the victors before the old national rivalries and tensions reappeared. Thus, although the war led to the creation of many international organizations, few of them were focused exclusively on war-related issues; indeed, almost all of them were created for what would come after—a chance to build and shape the postwar world.

Most nations, however, were left out of the process. There was no question of involving the Axis powers, and many neutral states such as Spain, Argentina, Portugal, and Switzerland were unwelcome and often not invited. The participation in discussions of those states defeated or occupied was difficult if not impossible. Those in the colonial world often had more pressing issues to deal with, and they were largely ignored. Realistically, only a handful of states had the time, the financial and human resources, and the inclination to devote much effort and consideration to discuss the development of future postwar international organizations.

Interest and support was found in many countries, although serious work was undertaken in relatively fewer states. Included in this group were Australia, New Zealand, Canada, several Latin American states, and a few European countries. It was, however, Britain and the United States that made the greatest contribution to the development of international organizations during the war. In Britain, the government and dozens of non-governmental groups immersed themselves in postwar planning from almost the moment the war began. Before it was over, numerous government departments and committees, religious groups, charities, university associations, and individuals had produced an array of reports, studies, books, and articles, as well as organizations and movements, focused in varying degrees on postwar reconstruction, education, human rights, disarmament, and peace. A similar situation developed in the United States in that, from early in the war and in a thousand different ways, both government departments and civilian groups began the process of study and debate over postwar organizations and internationalism generally. The difference was that the United States had far greater human and financial resources to dedicate to these questions than anyone else and the economic and military power to do something about them. The American government could not work in isolation, and great efforts were made to attract and maintain outside support for American goals. But, invested as it was with the spirit of internationalism (what some critics called a desire to remake the world in the American image) and endowed with great resources, the United States became the prime mover behind the incredibly busy few years that led to the creation of many important international organizations, in particular the United Nations (UN).

International organizations had not disappeared in the 1930s, but their emphasis and focus tended more towards the social and cultural spheres than political ones. Most of these interwar international organizations and non-governmental organizations (NGOs) began in the West and spread to other parts of the globe. These included the International Confederation of Students, the International Federation of University Women, the World Association for Adult Education, the International Research Council, the Save the Children International Union, and the Institute of Pacific Relations, and their success or failure should not be measured only by their inability to prevent the outbreak of war. From the International Olympic Committee to the World Jewish Congress, these NGOs strove to enhance international cooperation and understanding in a variety of ways and, in many cases, against great odds. By 1932 the League's *Handbook of International Organizations* contained more than 500 international organizations, the great majority of which were NGOs.[1]

The experience of the war intensified these efforts, especially in the field of humanitarian assistance and, as the war progressed, in reconstruction, peace and disarmament issues, and international cooperation. Many religious service and aid groups and other charities organized to provide relief, and some looked for international contacts. Early in the war a group of independent British aid organizations met to establish the Oxford Committee for Famine Relief (Oxfam) to provide food relief in Nazi-occupied Europe. After the war Oxfam opened a series of charity stores in Britain and expanded to dozens of countries around the world, establishing Oxfam International in the 1970s. In the United States similar humanitarian organizing began during the war. The largest NGO was CARE, the Cooperative for American Remittances to Europe (1945) which was set up by a group of voluntary agencies to provide relief for devastated Europe. CARE worked closely with other agencies, in particular the UN, and after the war its mandate was broadened to include humanitarian assistance throughout the developing world. In the postwar era and renamed the Cooperative for Assistance and Relief Everywhere, branches of CARE were established in more than 60 countries.

Similar patterns of cooperation appeared on the governmental level, first for military collaboration and then for more humanitarian reasons. The destruction and dislocation caused by the war produced an enormous demand for emergency relief, which the Allied governments acknowledged almost from the beginning. A variety of ad hoc committees were created, and, starting in 1940, Allied representatives gathered in London to discuss European relief needs. Once in the war, the United States assumed a leading role and oversaw the creation of the UN Relief and Rehabilitation Administration (UNRRA) in November 1943. UNRRA was set up to provide relief—food, shelter, clothing, medical services, and other supplies—to those in need both during and after the war. UNRRA accepted aid donations from those states that had not been invaded and divided it among those that had; by 1946 some 20 countries, including Greece, Poland, the Ukraine, and China, had received approximately $4 billion in aid ($2.7 billion from the United States). UNRRA also played a significant role in helping refugees and displaced persons to return to their homes after the war (a different group, the International Committee on Refugees [1939] attempted to find homes in other countries for refugees). By 1947 UNRRA had sheltered, clothed, and fed hundreds of thousands of people; had built hospitals and helped check the spread of diseases; and had given millions of dollars for economic reconstruction. All of UNRRA's functions were ultimately assumed by other organizations, and it was officially terminated in March 1949.

The most important organization created during the war was the UN. The idea of setting up a new world organization was much discussed throughout the war; because the end of the second war was anticipated much earlier than the first, internationalists had years to plan for the future. Supporters of a new organization also had the benefit of hindsight and could learn from the League of Nations example.

The new organization found a champion in American President Franklin D. Roosevelt, and it is tempting to compare Roosevelt and the UN to Wilson and the League. Roosevelt had supported Wilson and his League idea and had run as a Democratic vice-presidential candidate in the 1920 election on a platform of support for entrance into the League. His indifferent attitude to the League in the 1930s reflected more his feelings about its ineffectiveness than it did a loss of faith in international cooperation, and in the Second World War he became a staunch supporter of a new organization.[2] Roosevelt's idea was to have an organization with a basic structure similar to the League, but to make it more effective he wanted much stronger enforcement powers entrenched in the hands of the great powers—they would be expected to carry the security/military burden and therefore deserved to have this power. Centralizing the power in the hands of the "policemen" would make the new organization more effective and more likely ensure the participation of the great powers, in particular the United States and the Soviet Union. Roosevelt was also determined not to repeat the mistakes Wilson had made: he insisted that any new organization safeguard American sovereignty; he courted public opinion through speeches and regular radio broadcasts; he was determined to act immediately and not to wait for the war to end; and he worked to remove partisanship from the debate over membership in the new organization by bringing in members of the Republican Party right from the start and having them working from the inside. It was a successful strategy in that membership in the UN did not become a major political issue in the 1944 election (as the League had for Wilson in 1918), and by 1945 the American people were fairly well informed and generally supportive of the idea, while political leaders were, for the most part, onside when it came to securing Congressional approval.

In August 1941, several months before the official American entrance into the war, Roosevelt met with British Prime Minister Churchill off the coast of Newfoundland. Together they issued the Atlantic Charter, which, among other things, committed their countries to the creation of a "wider and permanent system of general security." The principles of the Atlantic Charter were endorsed by 26 allied states on the first day of January 1942, less than a month after the American entrance into the war, in the Declaration of the United Nations. Thus, from the moment the United States entered the war, its government was committed to the creation of a postwar international organization. By 1943 the State Department had produced a tentative draft charter for the new organization, and by the end of the year resolutions in its support passed both the Senate and the House of Representatives. Roosevelt was ready to initiate discussions on postwar organization with the major allies; in particular, the concurrence of Churchill and Stalin was central to any proposal for a general security organization. Neither the British nor Soviet leader was enthusiastic about Roosevelt's plans, but both agreed to discuss the issue.[3]

Several conferences were held in 1943–44 at which the UN's structure was established: in Moscow (October 1943), Tehran (November 1943), Washington (August–October 1944), and Yalta (February 1945). The first produced the Moscow Declaration, which announced to the world that the four great powers (Britain, the United States, the Soviet Union, and China, which did not attend but agreed to it subsequently) intended to establish a general security organization at the end of the war. At Tehran the "big three"—Roosevelt, Churchill, and Stalin—held preliminary discussions on some basic questions, but no consensus was reached. At the 1944 conference at Dumbarton Oaks, a mansion in Washington, the basic structure began to take shape and a full document of proposals was produced. The great powers agreed that there would be an organization to maintain peace and security in the world, with an assembly and secretariat, a social and economic function, an international court, and what would become the Security Council dominated by themselves.[4] It was subsequently agreed that the name for the new organization would be the United Nations and that, with the inclusion of France, there would be five permanent members of the Council.

The Yalta Conference was one of the biggest and most important of the wartime summits. It dealt with several war-related issues, such as the division of Germany and the future of Poland, but several questions regarding the UN were also discussed. First was the great power veto, which was absolutely necessary for the Soviets as well as the Americans. Roosevelt believed that without it the Soviets might walk away from the UN altogether; in his own case, a veto would help reduce political opposition at home by ensuring that the United States could never be forced to act against its own interests. Second, at Dumbarton Oaks it was agreed that all "peace loving nations" could be members of the UN, but did this include the enemy states? Or the neutral states? Or all states? At Yalta "peace loving" was agreed to include any state that had declared war on the Axis powers as of 1 March 1945 (and therefore did not include Argentina). Plus, after considerable wrangling between the three leaders, it was agreed that India (although not completely independent) and the two Soviet republics of Ukraine and Belarus would become original members (the Soviets originally asked for 15 seats for its republics). Third, it was agreed that the UN would be more than a security organization (as the Soviets wished) and that it would include a social and economic dimension, but the discussion did not go much further than that basic agreement. Fourth, the three leaders discussed the issue of colonies and possessions and agreed that the UN would play a role as trustee for such territories, but on British insistence it was agreed that this trusteeship would apply only to certain colonies—the former League mandates, colonies of the Axis states, and any other territories that a member wanted to have included. No Allied state, including the British, would be forced to place its colonies in trusteeship.[5]

As a result of these meetings and conferences (and in stark contrast to Wilson's experience in Paris in 1919), by the time the international conference at San Francisco was called to write the constitution of the new organization, there was already much agreement between the great powers on some very basic issues, and they had a draft agreement in the Dumbarton Oaks proposals (with a few amendments from Yalta thrown in). If the weakness of the League was the lack of great power support, the experience leading up to San Francisco was quite the reverse. If anything, it was the smaller powers that felt left out, complaining that decisions were being made without public consultation and that they were being overlooked in the process. The Australians, Canadians, and other middle powers had established their own groups to study the Dumbarton Oaks proposals, and they began to offer suggestions limiting the powers of the Security Council and enhancing the role of the Assembly. In the developing world, especially in those territories recently freed from colonial rule, there was anxiety over what had been agreed to regarding trusteeship. Across Latin America, there were concerns about the lack of place for themselves in the new organization and whether the UN would displace the role of the Pan American Union in the settlement of hemispheric disputes. At a conference at Chapultepec Castle in Mexico City, in February–March 1945, the members of the Pan American Union essentially created a common front on several key issues (especially on the role of regional organizations and smaller powers), which would be maintained through the creation of the UN.[6]

The United Nations Conference on International Organization was convened in San Francisco to draw up the UN Charter. It took place during the final days of the European war (25 April–26 June 1945), which gave the whole affair a certain extra significance. Fifty states attended the conference, but it was really an American affair. The United States hosted, set the agenda, paid for most of it, ran it from its delegation's hotel room, and reportedly tapped the telephones and intercepted secret messages of the other delegations.[7] Ultimately, it housed the UN Charter in its archives and served as headquarters of the organization.

Beyond the plenary sessions, multiple committees, and delegation meetings that are common in large international conferences, there were two parallel conferences at work in San Francisco. The first comprised negotiations among the great powers, especially between the Soviets and Americans, and the second between the great powers and the smaller states. The veto and when it could be used, for example, was discussed in both camps, and the Americans found themselves somewhat in the middle between the Soviets, who wanted a largely unrestricted veto, and a group of smaller states—headed by Australia—that wished to limit it to a few key areas. Ultimately it was agreed that the veto could be used only for substantive issues and not for procedural ones, but the catch was that it would apply to any disagreements over what was to be considered "substantive." The great powers also agreed to the creation of the permanent Military Staff Committee, consisting of their Chiefs of Staff, to oversee the use of force by the UN. The committee never proved effective, but its creation—and the thought that it might send UN troops into battle—does help explain the American and Soviet demand for a veto.

Several other changes to the draft agreement were made, although none, individually, fundamentally altered the basic structure of the new UN. The Latin American bloc had a few successes: it fought for the inclusion of Argentina as an original member and pushed for (with American support) the inclusion of an article permitting the creation of regional alliances (Articles 52–53). The Canadians, reflecting concerns similar to those they had had over Article 10 of the League Covenant, convinced the great powers to include an article stating that before any member would be compelled to use force, its government would be able to participate in the meeting of the Security Council dealing with the use of its military forces (Article 44). This proposal, it has been pointed out, was already acceptable to both the British and the Americans.[8] The smaller countries also achieved a degree of success with the broadening of the powers of the General Assembly to include the right to discuss security issues (providing the Security Council was not), and it was given control over the UN budget. Perhaps most important, the Latin American states, a few other smaller states, and the large group of some 42 (mainly American) NGOs that had been invited to the Conference pressured the great powers to include the issue of human rights in the Charter. They were successful; the Charter makes seven references to human rights. However, as two scholars point out, the American delegation already supported the idea, and these references to human rights were rather vague and statements of principle only.[9]

With these changes the Charter was signed on 26 June 1945 by 50 states (Poland made it 51 when it later signed as an original member). The Charter easily passed through the American Senate (the vote was 89 to 2). It was a testament to the work of President Roosevelt, even though he died on 12 April so did not live to see it happen. It was left to the new president, Harry Truman, to ratify the Charter on 8 August 1945. The Charter came into force on 24 October 1945, when enough member governments had ratified it (50 per cent plus all five great powers), and this date has been recognized as its birth date. All signatories ratified the Charter by the end of the year. A Preparatory Committee was set up and, on 10 January 1946, the General Assembly held its first session in London, England.

The first thing that strikes a reader of the Charter is the Preamble, which hints at some of the fundamental contradictions in the Charter and history of the UN (see Appendix 2). The Preamble speaks of the "peoples" of the UN—not the states—and announces their resolve to maintain peace and security, to practise tolerance, and to promote the "economic and social advancement of all peoples." In addition to stopping wars, the people reaffirm their "faith in fundamental human rights, in the dignity and worth of the human person, in the equal rights of men and women and of nations large and small." It was the strongest international endorsement of the concept of human rights yet agreed to and a remarkable achievement. But beyond these statements of principles, there are no measures included for the implementation of these lofty goals and no sanctions or penalties against those states that fail to live up to them. Furthermore, this is the only part of the Charter that mentions "people"; the articles that follow focus almost exclusively on states, and, indeed, many essentially permit the states to ignore basic human rights, especially in their own territories. For example, Article 2 states that the UN was not to intervene in matters "within the domestic jurisdiction" of each member, and this provision—demanded by the great powers especially—effectively ruled out intervention in the affairs of a state to curb human rights abuses. Human rights were now a fundamental goal, but the states would be the vehicle to achieve that goal. And this tension between the concept of absolute national sovereignty and the concept of universal human rights—between the rights of states and the rights of individuals—remains in the UN to this day.

FIGURE 3.1 Structure of the General Assembly

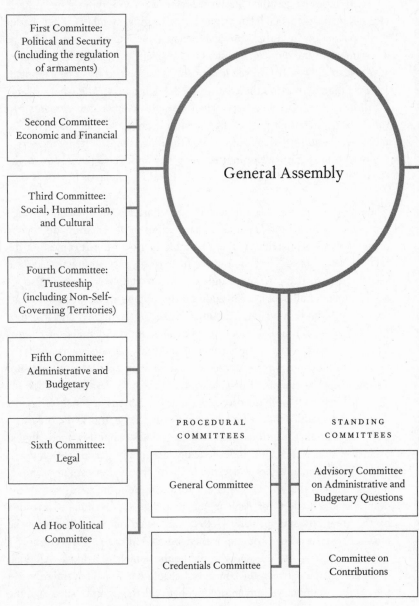

MAIN COMMITTEES

First Committee: Political and Security (including the regulation of armaments)

Second Committee: Economic and Financial

Third Committee: Social, Humanitarian, and Cultural

Fourth Committee: Trusteeship (including Non-Self-Governing Territories)

Fifth Committee: Administrative and Budgetary

Sixth Committee: Legal

Ad Hoc Political Committee

General Assembly

PROCEDURAL COMMITTEES

General Committee

Credentials Committee

STANDING COMMITTEES

Advisory Committee on Administrative and Budgetary Questions

Committee on Contributions

OTHER EXISTING BODIES ESTABLISHED BY THE GENERAL ASSEMBLY

Interim Committee of the General Assembly
Disarmament Commission
  Sub-Committee on Disarmament
Panel for Inquiry and Conciliation
Peace Observation Commission
  Balkan Sub-Commission
Advisory Committee on the International Conference on the Peaceful Use of Atomic
    Energy
Scientific Committee on the Effects of Atomic Radiation
Collective Measures Committee
  Panel of Military Experts
Committee of Good Offices on the Admission of New Members
United Nations Commission to Investigate Conditions for Free Elections in Germany
United Nations Commission for the Unification and Rehabilitation of Korea
United Nations Korean Reconstruction Agency
United Nations Relief and Works Agency for Palestine Refugees in the Near East
Italian-Libyan Mixed Arbitration Commission
United Nation Children's Fund (UNICEF)
Ad Hoc Committee on a Special United Nations Fund for Economic Development
Office of the United Nations High Commissioner for Refugees
Ad Hoc Commission of Prisoners of War
United Nations Advisory Commission for Somaliland
United Nations Plebiscite Commissioner (for the Trust Territory of Togoland under
    British Administration)
Committee on South West Africa
Committee on Information from Non-Self-Governing Territories
Sub-Committee on the Revision of the Questionnaire (relating to Trust Territories)
Advisory Commitee for the United Nations Memorial Cemetery in Korea
Negotiating Committee for Extra Budgetary Funds
Board of Auditors
United Nations Administrative Tribunal
United Nations Staff Pension Committee
Investments Committee
Committee to Review the Salary, Allowances, and Benefits System of the United Nations
Committee on Application for Review of Administrative Tribunal Judgments
International Law Commission
Committee on Calling of a Charter Review Conference
Special Committee on Defining Aggression

Source: *Yearbook of the United Nations, 1955* (p. xii) © United Nations, 1956.
Reproduced with permission.

The UN was established as a collective security organization of states, and its role and functions are set out in the Charter's 19 chapters. Its purpose is to "maintain international peace and security" and to "take effective collective measures for the prevention and removal of threats to the peace." The member governments agree to settle disputes peacefully, based on the "respect for the principle of equal rights and self-determination of peoples" and to seek international cooperation "in solving international problems of an economic, social, cultural, or humanitarian character, and in promoting and encouraging respect for human rights and for fundamental freedoms for all without distinction as to race, sex, language, or religion" (Article 1).

The remaining chapters detail the functions of the six main UN bodies: the General Assembly, the Security Council, the Economic and Social Council, the Trusteeship Council, the International Court of Justice, and the Secretariat. The General Assembly (Chapter 4) consists of all members, each with one vote (provided the member hasn't fallen two years behind in paying its dues), and important decisions are made on the basis of a two-thirds majority vote. Meetings are held annually, and it may discuss, initiate studies, set up sub-committees, pass resolutions, and make recommendations on any questions—social, economic, cultural, peace and security, and so on—that it wishes, bringing to the attention of the Security Council any situation that may disturb the peace. The only exception is when the Security Council is itself discussing a dispute; then, the Assembly must refrain from making recommendations on that topic (Article 12). It has no executive decision-making or enforcement powers, and its resolutions are not legally binding; the General Assembly is primarily a place for discussion of important world issues, a place, as Roosevelt said, "to allow all the small nations to blow off steam."[10] But it was given the power to approve the annual budget, to elect the non-permanent members of the Security Council and other bodies, to appoint the secretary-general (on the recommendation of the Security Council), and to supervise the work of other UN bodies. In subsequent years its influence grew, along with the membership, and it became more involved, for example, in the creation and supervision of peacekeeping missions.

The Security Council (Chapters 5–7) consists of the five permanent members (Britain, United States, Soviet Union, China, and France), also known as the P-5; in contrast to the General Assembly, it meets on an almost continuous basis. Each member of the P-5 has a veto on all Council decisions except on "procedural matters" (although the word "veto" does not appear—Article 27 calls for decisions with the "concurring votes of the permanent members"). Amendments to the Charter need an Assembly vote with a two-thirds majority plus the concurrence of the P-5. In addition, the Security Council at first included six non-permanent members (with no veto) elected on two-year terms (the number was raised to 10 non-permanent members in 1965). These members were to be chosen based not only on merit but also to reflect "geographical distribution" (Article 23). The Security Council can also create various kinds of select committees and special commissions to investigate specific issues.

The Security Council is the real focus of power in the UN. It is charged with the "primary responsibility for the maintenance of international peace and security" (Article 24), although states are urged to seek settlement at first through negotiation, arbitration, regional organizations, and the International Court of Justice. Nevertheless, the Security Council decides when there has been aggression (Article 39), what to do about it, and who should do it (Article 48). If diplomatic efforts and economic sanctions fail, then the Security Council "may take such action by air, sea, or land forces as may be necessary to maintain or restore international peace and security" (Article 42). Plans for these actions would be drawn up by the Military Staff Committee, consisting of P-5 military commanders, who also advise and assist the Security Council. The General Assembly, in turn, carries out the decisions of the Security Council (Article 25).

ECOSOC, the Economic and Social Council (Chapter 10), was established as a permanent body to study, report, and make recommendations on "international economic, social, cultural, educational, health, and related matters" and to promote human rights. All the specialized agencies brought into relationship with the UN fall under the purview of ECOSOC and submit annual reports to it, but it does not control or direct their activities. It can focus attention on issues, create commissions (such as regional commissions) to study various problems of an economic or social nature, coordinate the activities of the specialized agencies, and establish relations with a host of NGOs, but it relies on moral authority more than anything else. ECOSOC meets annually; it began with 18 elected members (votes are based on a simple majority, with no veto) but has grown since 1945 to 27 (1965) and 54 (1973).

The Secretariat (Chapter 15) consists of the secretary-general and his or her staff. It is divided into various departments, each headed by an assistant secretary-general. Staff members are non-political and do not represent their nations; although they are to be selected on the basis of merit, they must reflect "as wide a geographical basis as possible" (Article 101). The secretary-general is the UN's chief administrative officer and is elected for a five-year, once renewable term by the General Assembly on the recommendation of the P-5 (and therefore cannot be elected without P-5 support). Since the appointment of Trygve Lie as the first secretary-general, a debate has continued over the nature of the position—is it to be *secretary* (administrative and passive) or *general* (political and active)? In many ways it is both, in that the secretary-general oversees the functioning of the staff and office and reports to the General Assembly, but he or she also has the right to bring peace and security issues before the Security Council (Article 99) and to attend Security Council meetings (and the meetings of most of the other UN bodies). This right enables the secretary-general to assume a more political role and has led to some antagonism with members of the P-5; it has also permitted some in the position to become important international figures in their own right.

Mention should also be made of the International Court of Justice (Chapter 14) and the Trusteeship Council (Chapters 12 and 13). The statute establishing the ICJ is annexed to the UN Charter; it became the UN's "principal judicial organ," essentially taking over from the earlier Permanent Court of International Justice. All members—but only states—are parties to the Statute, and all members agree to abide by its decisions. The Trusteeship Council was established under the authority of the General Assembly to supervise the UN trust territories—the small collection of territories placed in the hands of the organization. The goal of the trustee system was to promote the advancement of the people in the territories and their "progressive development towards self-government or independence." There were 11 Trust Territories in 1945, about half in Africa, three groups of Pacific islands, New Guinea, and Nauru. Most achieved independence within 20 years.

Included in the Charter are also those articles mentioned above that permit regional organizations to act in maintaining peace and security so long as they are "consistent with the Purposes and Principles of the United Nations" (Article 52). This article reflected the desire of the United States and the Pan American Union to keep the Western Hemisphere on its own, while Article 44 gives the right of consultation and consent for any state before its troops are committed to action. In addition, Article 71 enables ECOSOC to consult with NGOs in its area of interest, an arrangement that increased in importance in later years as the relationship between NGOs and the UN grew. Finally, Article 51 guarantees the "inherent right" of self-defence for any member if attacked, a right demanded by the United States for both security and political reasons.

The Charter that was signed in 1945 remains virtually unchanged today—
it has been amended only to enlarge the Security Council and ECOSOC.
The interpretation of many of its articles has evolved over the years, and
some parts of it have fallen into disuse, but the basic principles remain.

One of the most significant outcomes of the burst of wartime internationalism was the creation of the multiple international organizations that comprise the UN system. The specialized agencies, several of which predate
the UN itself, are largely social and cultural or technical in nature. Most
are focused on what are called the "soft" fields (as opposed to the "hard"
fields of peace and security) and deal with humanitarian concerns, women
and children's issues, poverty, social and economic development, and the
environment, as well as an array of technical fields. In general they try to
promote the creation and implementation of international standards and
regulations in their areas of expertise, and they serve other roles as debating
societies, research engines, and clearing houses for information. Most work
well out of the international media spotlight, but their work is essential to
the success of the UN system.

One of the UN's first tasks was to bring into relationship the specialized agencies that comprise its system. Being "brought into relationship"
means that they report to the UN, generally try to cooperate and prevent
overlap with each other, and cannot have members that are unacceptable
to the UN, although they can have members that are not in the UN and
vice versa; the Soviet bloc, for example, had a mixed membership in the
different agencies. The specialized agencies have their own budgets, which
gives them some independence and makes them less reliant on voluntary
contributions like the UN's commissions and offices dealing with similar
issues. Loosely under the oversight of ECOSOC, the specialized agencies
work on their own, and most consist of an assembly (or board, or conference) of all members that meets annually or biannually; a smaller council
(or executive board, or board of directors) that is much smaller in size but
meets more frequently and makes the important decisions; and a permanent
secretariat that performs the bureaucratic functions of the organization.
Most also have a director general or president. The names of the bodies
and positions vary, as do the voting procedures, membership requirements,
financial assessments, enforcement measures (if any), and so on, but in most
cases the organizations are controlled by the larger, more powerful states,
in particular, the United States. Moreover, being relatively independent of
the Security Council and General Assembly has not meant that they have

FIGURE 3.2 Organs of the UN

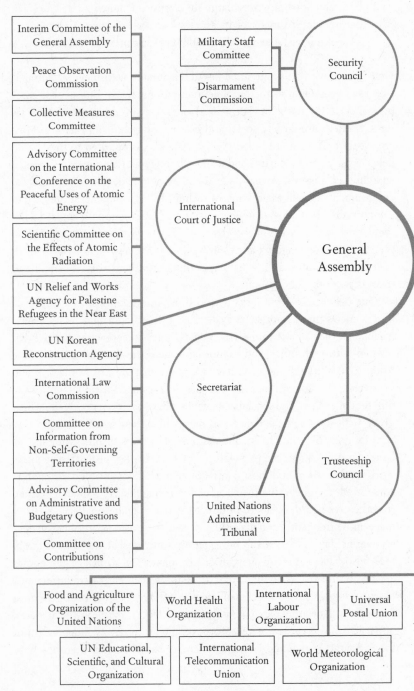

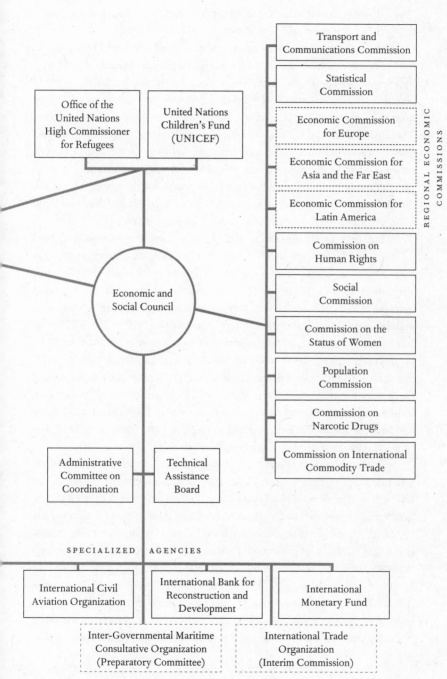

Source: *Yearbook of the United Nations, 1955* (p. ci) © United Nations, 1956. Reproduced with permission.

been immune to the kinds of problems facing those bodies. In the postwar era all the specialized agencies were impacted in varying degrees by Cold War tensions, decolonization, membership disputes, development issues, the fight against apartheid, and so on.

Most of the specialized agencies can trace their origins to two sources: those maintained from the era of the League and those created to deal with the devastation of the Second World War. For example, the ILO, which began in 1919, became a UN specialized agency in 1946, maintaining its unique structure of representatives from states, employers, and workers. The Universal Postal Union (UPU) dates back to 1874. UNRRA, discussed above, was replaced by the International Refugee Organization (IRO), established in 1946–48 to oversee the protection and repatriation of refugees. After helping the resettlement of hundreds of thousands of people, the IRO was replaced, in 1951, by the Office of the United Nations High Commissioner for Refugees (UNHCR), based in Geneva.

Rebuilding and maintaining the world's food supply was a central problem for the postwar world. With this in mind, the American government invited 44 allied states to an international conference in Hot Springs, Virginia, in May 1943. The result was the creation of an Interim Commission to look at the establishment of a permanent food organization, leading ultimately to the Food and Agriculture Organization (FAO). The FAO is an informational body that collects and maintains statistics on food supplies, production, and nutrition, and provides technical assistance to help developing nations increase their agricultural output. It provides the permanent machinery for international discussions and agreements on food policy and, in general, promotes international cooperation in the field of agriculture and food. FAO held its first meeting in Quebec City, Canada, in 1945, and its permanent headquarters was established in Rome, Italy, in 1951.

In November 1944, 52 nations met in Chicago to create the International Civil Aviation Organization (ICAO) to establish technical standards for international civil aviation (airport regulations, meteorological services, licensing of crew, facilitation of air travel, and so on). In a fashion similar to several other new organizations, ICAO absorbed the remains of ICAN (including some of its personnel), and in 1947 its Legal Committee, which was established to produce conventions dealing with international air law, absorbed the remains of CITEJA, the Comité International Technique d'Experts Juridiques Aériens, an earlier organization of aviation legal experts created in Paris in 1925. ICAO has produced standards for noise pollution and the transport of dangerous materials; since the 1960s, it has focused much serious attention on international conventions to combat air piracy, sabotage, and attacks against international airports. At almost the same time that ICAO was created, an NGO of airlines was established—the International Air Transport Association or IATA (built on an interwar organization of the same name)—and the two organizations continue to operate from their separate headquarters in Montreal, Canada.

One of the most important agencies established in the early postwar years was the World Health Organization (WHO). It grew out of the remains of the League's Health Organization and a 1946 ECOSOC conference in New York City, which established its constitution and an interim organization to operate until it received sufficient ratifications. The WHO officially came into existence on 7 April 1948 (headquartered in Geneva), and its mandate is to study and report on health issues, to establish standards in medical/health fields, and to distribute information and give advice on health issues. In particular, the WHO fights against the spread of diseases and, ultimately, strives to help eliminate them. In 1947, for example, the interim organization responded to a serious outbreak of cholera in Egypt and called for support from the international community.[11] Many states responded with vaccines and equipment, the WHO coordinated their distribution, and the epidemic was under control within a matter of weeks.

Likewise, the UN Educational, Scientific, and Cultural Organization (UNESCO) traces its roots to the earlier International Institute of Intellectual Cooperation, but it was officially created at an international conference in 1945 and began operations in Paris in 1946. UNESCO's mandate is to encourage the spread of science, education, and culture; to promote intellectual collaboration; to organize exchange groups and to initiate projects such as ending illiteracy; to conduct research; and to educate, train, proffer advice, and provide technical assistance in these fields. It began with the optimistic sense that collaboration in these fields could help prevent the outbreak of future wars, but over the following decades the organization became greatly divided along East-West and North-South lines until it became a focal point for critics of the UN.

Financial reconstruction was of equal importance. In July 1944, 44 states met in Bretton Woods, New Hampshire, at the UN Monetary and Financial Conference to discuss the reconstruction of Europe and the re-establishment of international trade and the world's financial system at the end of the war. Bretton Woods led to the creation of two separate but related international organizations: the International Monetary Fund (IMF) and the International Bank for Reconstruction and Development, which became known as the

World Bank. The IMF was created to monitor and promote the stability of international trade, currencies, and exchange rates, and to make loans to states experiencing balance of payment and currency problems. In addition to financial assistance for states suffering financial crises, the IMF collects information on monetary and fiscal issues, offers advice and technical assistance, and provides a forum for debate on economic and financial matters. The IMF created a fund from the contributions (or quotas) of the participating nations. The World Bank was not exactly a central bank for the world (as some had hoped); it established a capital fund for longer term assistance to states in need. As its official name suggests, the World Bank was created for both reconstruction—mainly in Europe, at first—and development. After the war, its focus shifted to assisting developing countries and offering reconstruction assistance following humanitarian disasters. The Articles of Agreement for these two organizations were ratified by a sufficient number of countries and came into force in December 1945, and both were operating by 1947. That year the World Bank made its first reconstruction loan of US$250 million to France, and within two years almost a dozen states had made drawings on the IMF's reserves.

The Bretton Woods organizations were largely dominated by the United States and, to a lesser degree, Western Europe. Headquarters for the IMF and World Bank were established in Washington, DC, and the president of the World Bank has always been an American; IMF managing directors have all been Europeans. Capital for the Bank and the IMF come from member contributions or quotas, which are based on each member's gross domestic product and other calculations, and the main decision-making power rests in the hands of the executive directors and largest contributors. In both cases the United States is the largest contributor and thus controls the greatest share of voting power (more than $3 billion of the original total commitment of $9 billion came from the United States).

Both organizations also became prime vehicles for economic development, but with mixed success. The IMF's role of stabilizing and monitoring exchange rates disappeared with the collapse of fixed exchange rates in the early 1970s, and increasingly both organizations focused on loans and economic projects in the developing world. Dozens of countries have turned to the IMF and World Bank for aid and advice, but over time much criticism has appeared over the conditions demanded by the organizations, especially the IMF, to qualify for aid. These conditions increased in number over the years and often involved demands for deregulation, tariff adjustments, changes to tax policies, and even privatization.[12] For many states these conditions were seen as an infringement on state sovereignty.

Efforts to establish an International Trade Organization failed, but in 1947 the General Agreement on Tariffs and Trade (GATT) was signed, and it performed many of the functions of a trade organization through a series of negotiation "rounds." Until it was replaced by the World Trade Organization (WTO) in 1995, the GATT worked to reduce tariffs and quotas and to minimize trade discrimination among its members. The WTO is a more powerful organization with broader enforcement powers and a dispute settlement mechanism. Although related to the IMF and World Bank, neither the GATT nor the WTO were or are UN specialized agencies.

There are now 15 specialized agencies within the UN (including the International Atomic Energy Agency); in addition, since 1945 a host of other programs, commissions, and committees reporting directly to ECOSOC have been created, including the UN Environment Program (UNEP) and the Commission of the Status of Women. One of the most important, although not an international organization in the usual sense, is the UN International Children's Emergency Fund (UNICEF) created by the General Assembly on 11 December 1946. UNICEF was originally set up to raise money from private and government sources to help children in war-devastated countries, and its efforts were straightforward even if its goals were unreachable—the provision of milk and food, health care, clothing, and so on to those in need. In 1953 UNICEF became a permanent entity within the UN family.

The end result of all this activity has been a complex patchwork quilt of committees, commissions, and organizations, sometimes overlapping and duplicating each other's work, at other times working at cross-purposes, while, in the meantime, undertaking countless projects, functions, and roles in the international community. As one historian has recently written, there is no point in mincing words, "the UN is a structural monstrosity, a conglomeration of organizations, divisions, bodies, and secretariats all with their distinctive acronyms that few can ever imagine being able to master."[13]

The UN followed and replaced the League of Nations, picking the remains of its moribund predecessor and attaching some of them (such as the ILO and UPU) directly, remaking others into new entities (WHO, UNESCO, ICAO, etc.), and incorporating them all into the UN system. The UN was wholly new, but in many ways it was based on the example of the League. Both were a response to world war, and both were established to deal with the legacy of the war and to prevent similar wars from breaking out in the future. They also shared some basic principles—the sovereignty of the nation-state, the equality of member states, and the idea of collective security—and they were both international institutions set up to deal with issues of peace and security. In addition, they had similar structures, including the assembly, a smaller council of great powers, a secretariat, international court, and a mandates/trusteeship arrangement for colonial territories.

There were also great differences. The most significant dealt with the power of the two organizations and was symbolized by the P-5 veto. The League was based on a fairly idealistic view that states shared common interests and that war could be prevented through common action; thus, it was founded on the principle of unanimity, especially in the application of economic and military sanctions. All members effectively had a veto, except under Article 15 of the Covenant in which the state involved in a dispute under consideration by the Council lost its vote. This meant, in theory at least, that even a great power—if it were a party in the dispute—could not block League action against it. The UN is quite different in that it is based on a more realistic view that war is unlikely to disappear and that an international organization needs much stronger powers to enforce collective security. To achieve this, the Security Council was given greater authority, the P-5 were given the veto, and the other members were bound to follow out the Security Council's decisions. Consequently, in the League it was harder to take action because of the need for unanimity but possible to take action contrary to the wishes of a Council member, even permanent ones. In the UN it is easier to take action because only the P-5 have a veto but also almost impossible to take action against one of the P-5 because they can veto any Security Council decision they do not like. The result is a more powerful Security Council in which the power and interests of the great powers are rarely if ever jeopardized. In this way, one of the key weaknesses of the League—its inability to attract and keep the great powers as members—is avoided in the UN, where no great power can be threatened by UN action. To date no great power has left the UN, and rarely do they threaten to leave because the cost and dangers of staying are minimal.[14] Not only has this prevented the UN from shrinking and fracturing, it has permitted it to grow into a truly global organization with a greater emphasis on social and economic issues and a much more diverse membership than ever found in the League.

Another major—if somewhat obvious—difference was the presence of the United States in the UN. The United States emerged from the Second

World War as the most powerful nation in the world—economically, militarily, culturally—and it was present at the creation of a new world order largely of its own design. To many states, the experience of the League without American membership only reinforced their desire to ensure that the United States joined the new organization. To be successful, any kind of global collective security organization would need the force of American power to ensure the peace, and few American allies wished for its retreat into isolationism. One way to solidify the connection, of course, was to situate the UN headquarters in American territory, and there was little opposition to this decision. Thanks to a generous donation from the Rockefeller family and a loan from the American government, the Manhattan site was purchased and the permanent UN building opened in October 1952. It was the beginning of a new era in the history of international organizations.

Notes

1 Iriye, *Global Community*, 28–35.
2 Hoopes, *FDR and the Creation of the UN*, 9–11.
3 Ryan, *The United Nations and International Politics*, 9–11.
4 Hilderbrand, *Dumbarton Oaks*.
5 Krasno, "Founding the United Nations," 27–30.
6 Krasno, 30–31.
7 Schlesinger, *Act of Creation*, 93–97.
8 Chapnick, *The Middle Power Project*, 132.
9 Normand and Zaidi, *Human Rights at the UN*, 129–31; see also Mazower, "The Strange Triumph of Human Rights," 379–98; Sherwood, "'There Is No New Deal for the Blackman in San Francisco,'" 71–94.
10 Quoted in Normand and Zaidi, 110.
11 Lee, *The World Health Organization*, 14–15.
12 Vreeland, *The International Monetary Fund*, 24.
13 Hanhimäki, *The United Nations*, 26.
14 Grigorescu, "Mapping the UN–League of Nations Analogy," 25–42.

4 | The UN in the Cold War Years

The UN was born at the end of the Second World War, but it came of age in the Cold War and its history is linked to it. The roots of the conflict can be traced back to the war, and the effects of divisions between East and West can be seen in the wording of the UN Charter and the organization itself (from disputes over membership, human rights, use of the veto, and so on). The UN was not responsible for the Cold War, but the Cold War descended on the UN and all of its specialized agencies, and for more than four decades it served as a backdrop to the UN's activities.

The Cold War may have set the context, but the UN played only a bit part in its history. From the disputes over the future of Germany and Eastern Europe and the descent of the Iron Curtain in the 1940s to the War in Vietnam, the Soviet invasion of Afghanistan, and the Chinese invasion of Vietnam in the 1970s and 1980s, the UN found itself either completely ignored, shut out from any but a minor support role, or frozen into impotency in an East-West stalemate. Most of the world fractured into two heavily armed, ideologically opposed, and mutually hostile and suspicious camps. The UN could do nothing to restrain the superpowers, and the promise of the UN as a collective security organization evaporated fairly quickly.

Nevertheless, the divisions unleashed by the Cold War reverberated within the Security Council and the whole UN system. Discussions on the makeup of the Military Staff Committee exposed deep divisions and ultimately ground to a halt, ending any thought of a standing UN military force, although the Committee lives on. Early plans to share information and responsibility for the development of nuclear energy and to control the spread of nuclear weapons through the UN Atomic Energy Commission were equally unsuccessful. On a few occasions the Security Council served as the stage on which Cold War events played out; for example, during the 1962 Cuban Missile Crisis the tension-filled debates in the Security Council made for good television, but it was still a bit of a sideshow to the main event. Similarly, in 1983, following the Soviet destruction of a South Korean airliner, with the death of all aboard, the Security Council provided the venue for Cold War antagonisms to be expressed, but it did not influence events in a significant way. When it came to disputes involving the United States and the Soviet Union, either alone or together, the superpowers were able to keep the UN from interfering in their actions. The United States, for example, rejected any UN involvement in the War in Vietnam—even help in getting out; for their part, the Soviets vetoed any UN role in their dealings with Eastern Europe, especially following the invasions in Hungary (1956) and Czechoslovakia (1968).

The veto, which was necessary to ensure great power participation in a collective security organization, seemed in the Cold War to be the major stumbling block to collective security action. If a P-5 member—especially one of the two superpowers—was involved in an armed dispute, it was almost always possible to prevent the Security Council from taking action against it. In the first decade, the Soviets cast the overwhelming number of vetoes (77 of the first 80) and by the end of the Cold War had used it 114 times. The United States could usually count on the support of the three other P-5 members and a majority of states in the General Assembly to get its way without recourse to the veto; as a result, it did not use its first veto until 1970. Since the 1960s, with the entrance of dozens of new members from the developing world who were more sympathetic to the Soviet Union, the United States began to use the veto more frequently. Between 1970 and 1992 it used the veto 69 times to the Soviet Union's 13.[1]

The deadlock in the Security Council likely had the unintended consequence of enhancing the prestige of the secretary-general, enabling him to take a more active and public role as the world's top international civil servant. With the P-5 unable to provide leadership, the secretary-general was often consulted for action, although each secretary-general brought his own personality and style to the position. The Norwegian Trygve Lie, the first secretary-general, alienated the Soviets with his actions in the Korean War and was prevented from serving two full terms. Dag Hammarskjöld (1953–61) set the standard for the active secretary-general through his tireless work in the development of UN peacekeeping, although he too antagonized the Soviets. On Hammarskjöld's death in 1961, U Thant from Myanmar (Burma) took over and, although an able man, had only modest success in enhancing the role of the UN in the Cold War. The Austrian Kurt Waldheim (1972–1981) was an ambitious and active secretary-general who worked in cooperation with the P-5 rather than in opposition to them. However in 1981 his try for a third term was opposed, especially by the Chinese, and the Security Council settled on a compromise candidate, Javier Perez de Cuellar, a Peruvian diplomat with long experience at the UN. Perez de Cuellar served until the end of the Cold War, retiring in 1991.[2]

The Cold War also affected UN membership. With the rehabilitation of many states, including former enemies, and the emergence of dozens of new states from the former colonial empires, many potential members wanted to get in. Joining the UN is relatively simple in that a country needs the approval of the Security Council and a two-thirds majority in the General Assembly. A few new members were admitted (Iceland and Sweden, for example), but Cold War animosities led the two rivals to block each other's candidates. The Americans blocked the entrance of Soviet allies and satellites (Albania, Hungary, Bulgaria, etc.), while the Soviets vetoed membership of friends of the Americans (Portugal, Italy, Ireland, and others). By the mid-1950s it had become a significant problem, with almost one of every two Soviet vetoes being used to block the entrance of new members. In 1955 this embarrassing situation was resolved with a "package deal" agreement, under which a group of 16 states from both sides was welcomed into UN membership.[3] Once this logjam was broken, membership rose rapidly, surpassing 100 members early in the 1960s and reaching 184 in 1993. Similar kinds of membership squabbles erupted in other organizations and specialized agencies.

Moreover, the establishment of a communist government in China in 1949 reverberated in the Security Council as the United States refused to recognize it. While many members established relations with the People's Republic, the United States, and many others, insisted that the Chinese seat in the Security Council (and in most specialized agencies) be maintained by the nationalist government in Formosa/Taiwan. Whatever the merits of the issue, it led to endless problems in the UN and other organizations as sessions became more acrimonious and divided. Other membership issues arose in similar ways in the UN and the specialized agencies over the presence of the divided Korea, Vietnam, and Germany, and later, over the continued or potential membership of South Africa, Israel, Palestine, and

FIGURE 4.1 UN Member States

Member	Date of Admission	Member	Date of Admission
Afghanistan	19 November 1946	Dominican Republic	24 October 1945
Albania	14 December 1955	Ecuador	21 December 1945
Algeria	8 October 1962	Egypt[6]	24 October 1945
Andorra	28 July 1993	El Salvador	24 October 1945
Angola	1 December 1976	Equatorial Guinea	12 November 1968
Antigua and Barbuda	11 November 1981	Eritrea	28 May 1993
Argentina	24 October 1945	Estonia	17 September 1991
Armenia	2 March 1992	Ethiopia	13 November 1945
Australia	1 November 1945	Fiji	13 October 1970
Austria	14 December 1955	Finland	14 December 1955
Azerbaijan	2 March 1992	France	24 October 1945
Bahamas	18 September 1973	Gabon	20 September 1960
Bahrain	21 September 1971	Gambia	21 September 1965
Bangladesh	17 September 1974	Georgia	31 July 1992
Barbados	9 December 1966	Germany[7]	18 September 1973
Belarus[1]	24 October 1945	Ghana	8 March 1957
Belgium	27 December 1945	Greece	25 October 1945
Belize	25 September 1981	Grenada	17 September 1974
Benin	20 September 1960	Guatemala	21 November 1945
Bhutan	21 September 1971	Guinea	12 December 1958
Bolivia	14 November 1945	Guinea-Bissau	17 September 1974
Bosnia and Herzegovina[2]	22 May 1992	Guyana	20 September 1966
Botswana	17 October 1966	Haiti	24 October 1945
Brazil	24 October 1945	Honduras	17 December 1945
Brunei Darussalam	21 September 1984	Hungary	14 December 1955
Bulgaria	14 December 1955	Iceland	19 November 1946
Burkina Faso	20 September 1960	India	30 October 1945
Burundi	18 September 1962	Indonesia[8]	28 September 1950
Cambodia	14 December 1955	Iran	24 October 1945
Cameroon	20 September 1960	Iraq	21 December 1945
Canada	9 November 1945	Ireland	14 December 1955
Cape Verde	16 September 1975	Israel	11 May 1949
Central African Republic	20 September 1960	Italy	14 December 1955
Chad	20 September 1960	Jamaica	18 September 1962
Chile	24 October 1945	Japan	18 December 1956
China	24 October 1945	Jordan	14 December 1955
Colombia	5 November 1945	Kazakhstan	2 March 1992
Comoros	12 November 1975	Kenya	16 December 1963
Congo (Republic of the)	20 September 1960	Kiribati	14 September 1999
Costa Rica	2 November 1945	Kuwait	14 May 1963
Côte d'Ivoire	20 September 1960	Kyrgyzstan	2 March 1992
Croatia[3]	22 May 1992	Lao People's Democratic Republic	14 December 1955
Cuba	24 October 1945	Latvia	17 September 1991
Cyprus	20 September 1960	Lebanon	24 October 1945
Czech Republic[4]	19 January 1993	Lesotho	17 October 1966
Democratic People's Republic of Korea	17 September 1991	Liberia	2 November 1945
		Libya	14 December 1955
Democratic Republic of the Congo[5]	20 September 1960	Liechtenstein	18 September 1990
		Lithuania	17 September 1991
Denmark	24 October 1945	Luxembourg	24 October 1945
Djibouti	20 September 1977	Madagascar	20 September 1960
Dominica	18 December 1978		

Member	Date of Admission	Member	Date of Admission
Malawi	1 December 1964	Sao Tome and Principe	16 September 1975
Malaysia[9]	17 September 1957	Saudi Arabia	24 October 1945
Maldives	21 September 1965	Senegal	28 September 1960
Mali	28 September 1960	Serbia[12]	1 November 2000
Malta	1 December 1964	Seychelles	21 September 1976
Marshall Islands	17 September 1991	Sierra Leone	27 September 1961
Mauritania	27 October 1961	Singapore	21 September 1965
Mauritius	24 April 1968	Slovakia[13]	19 January 1993
Mexico	7 November 1945	Slovenia[14]	22 May 1992
Micronesia (Federated States of)	17 September 1991	Solomon Islands	19 September 1978
		Somalia	20 September 1960
Monaco	28 May 1993	South Africa	7 November 1945
Mongolia	27 October 1961	Spain	14 December 1955
Montenegro[10]	28 June 2006	Sri Lanka	14 December 1955
Morocco	12 November 1956	Sudan	12 November 1956
Mozambique	16 September 1975	Suriname	4 December 1975
Myanmar	19 April 1948	Swaziland	24 September 1968
Namibia	23 April 1990	Switzerland	10 September 2002
Nauru	14 September 1999	Sweden	19 November 1946
Nepal	14 December 1955	Syria[15]	24 October 1945
Netherlands	10 December 1945	Tajikistan	2 March 1992
New Zealand	24 October 1945	Thailand	16 December 1946
Nicaragua	24 October 1945	The former Yugoslav Republic of Macedonia[16]	8 April 1993
Niger	20 September 1960		
Nigeria	7 October 1960	Timor Leste	27 September 2002
Norway	27 November 1945	Togo	20 September 1960
Oman	7 October 1971	Tonga	14 September 1999
Pakistan	30 September 1947	Trinidad and Tobago	18 September 1962
Palau	15 December 1994	Tunisia	12 November 1956
Panama	13 November 1945	Turkey	24 October 1945
Papua New Guinea	10 October 1975	Turkmenistan	2 March 1992
Paraguay	24 October 1945	Tuvalu	5 September 2000
Peru	31 October 1945	Uganda	25 October 1962
Philippines	24 October 1945	Ukraine	24 October 1945
Poland	24 October 1945	United Arab Emirates	9 December 1971
Portugal	14 December 1955	United Kingdom	24 October 1945
Qatar	21 September 1971	United of Republic of Tanzania[17]	14 December 1961
Republic of Korea	17 September 1991		
Republic of Moldova	2 March 1992	United States	24 October 1945
Romania	14 December 1955	Uruguay	18 December 1945
Russian Federation[11]	24 October 1945	Uzbekistan	2 March 1992
Rwanda	18 September 1962	Vanuatu	15 September 1981
Saint Kitts and Nevis	23 September 1983	Venezuela	15 November 1945
Saint Lucia	18 September 1979	Viet Nam	20 September 1977
Saint Vincent and the Grenadines	16 September 1980	Yemen[18]	30 September 1947
		Zambia	1 December 1964
Samoa	15 December 1976	Zimbabwe	25 August 1980
San Marino	2 March 1992		

Source: "United Nations Member States," UN Press Release, L/37/06, 3 July 2006. ©
United Nations, 2006. Reproduced with permission.

FIGURE 4.1 UN Member States (continued)

1 On 19 September 1991, Byelorussia informed the UN that it had changed its name to Belarus.

2 The Socialist Federal Republic of Yugoslavia was an original member of the United Nations, the Charter having been signed on its behalf on 26 June 1945 and ratified 19 October 1945, until its dissolution in 1992. The Republic of Bosnia and Herzegovina was admitted as a member of the UN by General Assembly resolution A/RES/46/237 of 22 May 1992.

3 See note 2 above. The Republic of Croatia was admitted as a member of the United Nations by General Assembly resolution A/RES/46/238 of 22 May 1992.

4 Czechoslovakia was an original member of the United Nations from 24 October 1945. In a letter dated 10 December 1992, its permanent representative informed the secretary-general that the Czech and Slovak Federal Republic would cease to exist on 31 December 1992 and that the Czech Republic and the Slovak Republic, as successor states, would apply for membership in the UN. Following the receipt of its application, the Security Council, on 8 January 1993, recommended to the General Assembly that the Czech Republic be admitted to UN membership. The Czech Republic was thus admitted on 19 January 1993 as a member state.

5 Zaire joined the UN on 20 September 1960. On 17 May 1997, its name was changed to the Democratic Republic of the Congo.

6 Egypt and Syria were original members of the UN from 24 October 1945. Following a plebiscite on 21 February 1958, the United Arab Republic was established by a union of Egypt and Syria and continued as a single member. On 13 October 1961, Syria, having resumed its status as an independent state, resumed its separate membership in the UN. On 2 September 1971, the United Arab Republic changed its name to the Arab Republic of Egypt.

7 The Federal Republic of Germany and the German Democratic Republic were admitted to membership in the UN on 18 September 1973. Through the accession of the German Democratic Republic to the Federal Republic of Germany, effective from 3 October 1990, the two German states have united to form one sovereign state.

8 By letter of 20 January 1965, Indonesia announced its decision to withdraw from the UN "at this stage and under the present circumstances." By telegram of 19 September 1966, it announced its decision "to resume full cooperation with the UN and to resume participation in its activities." On 28 September 1966, the General Assembly took note of this decision, and the president invited representatives of Indonesia to take seats in the Assembly.

9 The Federation of Malaya joined the UN on 17 September 1957. On 16 September 1963, its name was changed to Malaysia, following the admission to the new federation of Singapore, Sabah (North Borneo), and Sarawak. Singapore became an independent state on 9 August 1965 and a member of the UN on 21 September 1965.

10 Montenegro held a 21 May 2006 referendum and declared itself independent from Serbia on 3 June. On 28 June 2006 it was accepted as a UN member state by General Assembly resolution A/RES/60/264.

11 The Union of Soviet Socialist Republics was an original member of the UN from 24 October 1945. In a letter dated 24 December 1991, Boris Yeltsin, the President of the Russian Federation, informed the secretary-general that the membership of the Soviet Union in the Security Council and all other UN organs was being continued by the Russian Federation with the support of the 11 member countries of the Commonwealth of Independent States.

12 In a letter dated 3 June 2006, the President of the Republic of Serbia informed the secretary-general that the membership of Serbia and Montenegro was being continued by the Republic of Serbia, following Montenegro's declaration of independence. On 4 February 2003, following the adoption and promulgation of the Constitutional Charter of Serbia and Montenegro by the Assembly of the Federal Republic of Yugoslavia, the official name of "Federal Republic of Yugoslavia" was changed to Serbia and Montenegro. The Federal Republic of Yugoslavia was admitted as a member of the UN by General Assembly resolution A/RES/55/12 of 1 November 2000.

13 See note 4 above. The Slovak Republic was admitted on 19 January 1993 as a member state.

14 See note 2 above. The Republic of Slovenia was admitted as a member of the UN by General Assembly resolution A/RES/46/236 of 22 May 1992.

15   See note 6 above. On 13 October 1961, Syria, having resumed its status as an independent state, resumed its separate membership in the United Nations.

16   See note 2 above. By resolution A/RES/47/225 of 8 April 1993, the General Assembly decided to admit as a member of the UN the state being provisionally referred to for all purposes within the UN as "The former Yugoslav Republic of Macedonia," pending settlement of the difference that had arisen over its name.

17   Tanganyika was a member of the UN from 14 December 1961, and Zanzibar was a member from 16 December 1963. Following the ratification on 26 April 1964 of Articles of Union between Tanganyika and Zanzibar, the United Republic of Tanganyika and Zanzibar continued as a single member, changing its name to the United Republic of Tanzania on 1 November 1964.

18   Yemen was admitted to membership in the UN on 30 September 1947 and Democratic Yemen on 14 December 1967. On 22 May 1990, the two countries merged and have since been represented as one member with the name "Yemen."

a few others. Only in 1971, in the era of détente, did the People's Republic assume China's seat in the General Assembly and Security Council. For the first time the UN could claim to represent the overwhelming majority of the world's population.

In comparison to the League of Nations, disarmament and arms limitation in general were less central to the UN. While the League took a more idealistic position that arms reduction could contribute directly to the maintenance of peace, the authors of the UN Charter envisioned the achievement of peace and security through the application of the power of the UN's "policemen" rather than through their disarmament. Disarmament is mentioned in the UN Charter, where it is left in the hands of the Security Council, but early efforts at its achievement—both in nuclear and conventional weapons—were almost a complete failure. A Disarmament Commission was established in 1952; after years of fruitless discussions, it stopped meeting in 1965, only to be revived again in 1978. Special Sessions of the General Assembly were held in 1978 and 1982 to discuss disarmament, and other commissions and committees were created with equally little success, as it was almost impossible to get serious commitments from the superpowers. Beginning in 1969 some negotiations began on arms limitation—the Strategic Arms Limitation Treaties (SALT I and SALT II), followed by the Strategic Arms Reduction Talks (START)—but these were undertaken between the superpowers outside the UN.[4]

Where the UN could make a contribution was in marshalling public opinion in the areas of weapons testing, other kinds of weapons (such as chemical and biological), and banning nuclear weapons from places where there. were none. Treaties were signed banning weapons testing under water and in outer space (1963); banning biological weapons (1972); banning nuclear weapons from Antarctica (1959), Latin America (1967), on the ocean-floor (1971), and outer space and the moon (1967); and creating nuclear-free zones, such as in the South Pacific (1987). These were important achievements but limited because some countries refused to sign—usually the states that did not want to live up to the terms of the treaties. Perhaps the most important was the General Assembly–sponsored Treaty on the Non-Proliferation of Nuclear Weapons (NPT) adopted in 1968, which came into force in 1970. The NPT calls on participants not to transfer to or receive nuclear weapons from other countries, and to pursue negotiations for their limitation and reduction. Most UN members signed the treaty, but many did not, including several states that harboured nuclear ambitions of their own. Until the end of the Cold War, all the efforts of the UN had led to the reduction of very few nuclear weapons, although it could be argued that it had at least facilitated the *process* of disarmament. However, it is hard to disagree with the assessment of three scholars who wrote that "disarmament was always a mirage—visible at a distance but fading away on close approach."[5]

The only significant UN effort in collective security came in Korea, thanks to a unique set of circumstances. Involvement began in 1947 with the creation of the UN Temporary Commission on Korea to supervise the holding of elections in the divided country and hopefully lead to its reunification. Without Soviet support in the North, however, elections were held only in the South (May 1948), and the division of the peninsula was frozen. American efforts to get South Korean UN membership were vetoed by the Soviets. Following the June 1950 invasion of South Korea by the North, the United States brought the question to the Security Council. At that moment the Soviets were boycotting meetings to protest the continued presence of the nationalist Chinese government rather than the new communist one. In their absence, the Security Council passed American-backed resolutions calling for the withdrawal of North Korean forces and authorizing the use of military force to push them back. Forty-five UN members sent troops to Korea, but the war was a UN operation in name only, as the armed forces, the economic and military resources, and the command structure were American. After three years of fighting, an armistice was signed in July 1953, and Korea remained divided.

The Soviets claimed that the Security Council could not pass resolutions without all members being present, but they could not prevent the

Security Council from acting. They also learned their lesson and quickly resumed their seat in the Security Council to block any further action. The Americans and others, meanwhile, turned to the General Assembly as a way to get around Soviet intransigence and supported what became known as the "Uniting for Peace" Resolution (3 November 1950). This stated that if the Security Council failed "to exercise its primary responsibility for the maintenance of international peace and security" in situations when peace was threatened, then the General Assembly "shall consider the matter immediately with a view to making appropriate recommendations to Members for collective measures, including ... the use of armed force."[6] It was a novel attempt to circumvent the Soviet veto, but because the resolution had no binding force, it was never very effective.

Assessments of the UN's role in Korea have been mixed. On one hand, the action of the United States and its allies were successful in forcing the North Koreans back across the 38th parallel and preserving the independence of South Korea. On the other, it pinpointed the inherent problems facing the UN because the Security Council was able to act as it did only because of the absence of the Soviets; it is quite possible that the United States would have acted alone in any case, without the backing of the UN. Since there were no more Security Council boycotts in the future, this first venture in collective security was also the last, at least until after the end of the Cold War. The Security Council remained blocked on most of the central issues in the Cold War, although it still had a small role to play as a place where ambassadors could meet and talk. Beyond that, it made less sense even to meet; in the years following the Korean War, the frequency of Security Council meetings decreased. By the end of the 1950s, it met only a few times each year, and, thanks to other developments, the focus of UN activities began to shift from the Security Council (and collective security) to the General Assembly.

Where the UN did make a significant contribution to peace and security was in the field of peacekeeping. The UN Charter does not specifically discuss peacekeeping; its intent was primarily to deal with the aggression of one state upon another, not the internal conflicts within states. Noninterference and domestic sovereignty reduced the potential for UN action, and the P-5 veto kept it away from crises involving the great powers. But it can be argued that "keeping the peace" is the central mandate of the organization, and there was a place for the UN in conflicts of a secondary nature or in those in which the great powers needed its help. UN peacekeeping was not envisioned in 1944–45, but the need for it soon appeared, and it rapidly evolved into one of the UN's key activities to the point that today peacekeeping is one of the activities most closely associated with the UN in the public's imagination.

The UN's first peacekeepers were really observers sent to different trouble spots to monitor truces, elections, borders, and so on. In 1947, for example, observers were sent to Greece during its civil war to monitor its northern border and to Indonesia to help with the withdrawal of Dutch forces. One of the earliest areas to attract significant UN involvement was the Middle East and, in particular, Palestine, which had been a British mandate territory under the League. The UN supported the division of the territory and the creation of Israel and, following the 1948 Arab-Israeli War, set up the UN Truce Supervision Organization (UNTSO) to monitor the ceasefire. In 1949, following the outbreak of violence that accompanied the partition of India and Pakistan—and the continuing dispute over the Kashmir region—the UN established the UN Military Observer Group in India and Pakistan (UNMOGIP) to oversee the ceasefire.

The birth of what is considered traditional UN peacekeeping, however, occurred during the Suez Crisis, under the leadership of Secretary-General Hammarskjöld. In 1956 the Israelis invaded Egypt, and the British and French intervened in a planned attack to seize the Suez Canal, which the Egyptians had nationalized in 1955. It was blatant aggression and sparked an international crisis in which the British, French, and Israeli governments found themselves the target of considerable condemnation, including from such staunch allies as the United States. The Security Council was powerless, thanks to the vetoes of Britain and France, and it was left to the General Assembly, under the "Uniting for Peace" resolution, to discuss the issue. On the initiative of Lester Pearson, the Canadian Minister of External Affairs, the General Assembly authorized the secretary-general to create a UN military force to intervene to keep the two sides apart and enable the evacuation of the foreign troops. The Egyptian government agreed and the UN Emergency Force (UNEF) was created and sent to Egypt with some 6,000 troops from 10 states.

The traditional concept of UN peacekeepers—the "blue helmets"—was born with the UNEF, and the pattern set down was followed in many subsequent missions: 1) the peacekeepers entered Egyptian territory with the approval of the Egyptian government and remained only as long as it allowed them to; 2) they were there as neutrals and were meant to act that way; 3) the troops were selected from states not directly involved (meaning that generally the great powers did not volunteer forces); and 4) they were to use force only as a last resort and in self-defence. The peacekeepers were there to monitor, facilitate, and report, not to negotiate, solve, or force a solution to the problems in the area.[7] In the case of UNEF, for example, the force was asked to leave in 1967; when it did, hostilities broke out again almost immediately. The peacekeepers were also there because of the tacit approval of the superpowers. They were able to work in those conflicts in which the superpowers stood aside but maintained an interest in a ceasefire if only to prevent further escalation of the conflict.

A considerably different situation emerged in the Congo in the early 1960s. In 1960 the former Belgium colony of the Congo achieved independence and soon fell into civil war, with its province of Katanga seeking independence. On the request of the government of the Congo, the Security Council authorized the creation of the Opération des Nations Unies au Congo (ONUC) and called for the evacuation of all Belgian forces. ONUC peaked at almost 20,000 troops (mainly, but not exclusively, from other African states), which were sent in to stabilize the country from internal secession and foreign intervention. Compared to the experience of the UNEF, ONUC found itself enmeshed in a chaotic situation that was a mixture of regional political struggles, internal rivalries, and Cold War politics. Supporting the central government against the Katanga rebels meant a loss of neutrality, and the ONUC forces became involved in fighting. Before it was over, more than 200 UN and other soldiers were killed, and Secretary-General Hammarskjöld died in a mysterious plane crash. In 1964 a kind of unity was restored to the country, and the UN forces were withdrawn.

The Congo experience left a bad taste in the mouths of many people and established a kind of peacekeeping mission (later to be called "peace enforcement") that was to be avoided. For the next quarter-century, until near the end of the Cold War, most peacekeeping adventures followed the more traditional, Suez-style missions. The 6,500-strong UN force in Cyprus (UNFICYP), for example, was sent in 1964 to act as a buffer force between Greek and Turkish Cypriots when it looked like the situation on the island might degenerate into a full-scale Turkish-Greek war. Several supervisory groups subsequently were sent to the Middle East to separate forces and monitor borders and ceasefires, including in Yemen (1963), Egypt (1973), Syria (1974), and Lebanon (1978). By the end of the 1980s there were a total of 18 UN peacekeeping missions of various sizes.

Like the UNTSO and UNMOGIP missions, UNFICYP and the mission in Lebanon (UNIFIL) became permanent efforts and continue to this day, which only serves to underline the fact that UN peacekeeping in the Cold

War was not about conflict resolution. The missions did at least provide the opportunity for negotiations—but only if the competing sides wished to engage in the process. However, in some places, as in the Middle East, the evacuation of UN troops often led to the return of fighting; in Cyprus, UN intervention froze the status quo so that decades later, a permanent solution is still no closer. And, of course, peacekeeping missions were dispatched only to a minority of conflict areas in the Cold War, those where conditions permitted. Nevertheless, by intervening in troubled areas of the world, maintaining order, and keeping opponents apart, UN peacekeeping undoubtedly saved lives and prevented the potential escalation of local conflicts into larger crises. It was a record of substantial achievement. With the ending of the Cold War, public support for peacekeeping rose, and UN peacekeeping missions took on a new style and vigour.

Because the UN was not able to play a major role as a collective security organization in the Cold War, the superpowers turned, in different ways, to regional defence organizations to fill the void. In the 1950s, the UN and its specialized agencies moved in other directions—dealing with humanitarian issues, the environment, economic development, and peacekeeping—that were of equal importance but not directly related to the Cold War. One of the first was in the field of human rights.

The experience of the war and the revelations of the Holocaust and other horrendous abuses sparked widespread public support for the protection of human rights, and the Charter gave the UN a mandate to act, even if it was not completely clear how it was to achieve its goals. Throughout its history, the UN has had to face the basic contradiction of trying to protect the human rights of individuals from abusive governments when the Charter explicitly forbids it from intervening in the domestic affairs of its members. To make matters more difficult, the great powers, especially the two superpowers, were the most reluctant to give the UN a sweeping mandate in the pursuit of human rights or the enforcement powers to implement them. No state was eager to allow other states to interfere in its affairs; some states were unable to avoid it, but the United States and the Soviet Union could.

There had been strong support at the San Francisco Conference among the smaller powers, the several dozen NGOs, and the Latin American states for the inclusion of human rights provisions—and even of an international bill of rights—in the UN Charter. The great powers responded by agreeing to include general statements on the protection of human rights, but rather than accompany the principles with enforcement powers, the principles were severely restricted by Article 2, which ruled out interference in the domestic affairs of the members. The United States and Soviet Union were uncomfortable allies in the process, as neither supported any kind of binding treaty. It was one thing to criticize other governments for their human rights abuses (attacking each other's human rights record was a common Cold War tactic), but it was quite another to permit external criticism of domestic abuse from colonialism to the Soviet gulag to American racial segregation. There was a difference in tone—the Soviets were critical and suspicious of the whole idea of Western-style individual rights while the Americans tended to rely on delay and technical obstruction—but the goal was the same: the protection of domestic sovereignty against outside interference through the opposition to enforcement measures in human rights agreements.[8]

Nevertheless, the principles were there, they had a broad popular appeal, and political leaders soon embraced at least the rhetoric of human rights. In one of its first acts, the General Assembly and ECOSOC (Article 68) established the Commission on Human Rights (CHR), chaired by Eleanor Roosevelt, the widow of the president, with the goal to produce a legally binding international bill of rights with enforcement provisions. This elusive goal was pursued for more than 30 years and never fully achieved. Politics, great power rivalries, and Cold War tensions were always present, and the original plans were amended several times, usually to place limitations on the extent of human rights protection. For one thing, the members of the CHR were government representatives, not independent participants. In one of its earliest decisions, the CHR announced that it was unable to act upon petitions of human rights abuses from individuals (it had received thousands). Second, the process itself was subdivided. Rather than fashioning a single enforceable and binding bill of rights, it was agreed to first produce a declaration of broad principles and then decide on how to implement them through a covenant that would be ratified by governments. This method had the support of the United States.

Work on the statement of principles proceeded rapidly, and the Universal Declaration of Human Rights (UDHR) was approved on 10 December 1948 (see Appendix 3). In its preamble, the UDHR commits all UN members to the promotion and protection of human rights, which are to be grounded in the fundamental principles of equality and dignity of all humans regardless of race, gender, language, religion, national origin, or birth. Basic rights are listed in 30 articles; the first 22 will be familiar to any reader of the American Constitution and Bill of Rights: "life, liberty and the security of the person," "freedom of thought, conscience and religion," freedom of expression, equal treatment before the law, innocent until proven guilty, freedom of movement, marriage and property rights, and political rights of assembly, and so on. In addition, all slavery is outlawed, as is the use of torture and cruel punishment. The final eight are more social and economic rights: the right to education, work, housing, and medical care; equal pay for equal work; the right to join labour unions; and the right to an adequate standard of living.

There were a few voices in opposition from communist-bloc states that opposed the inclusion of property rights, to American conservatives who were wary of the social rights, to imperialists who worried about the implications of granting equal rights to colonial peoples, but the UDHR became instantly popular with people around the world.[9] It was called the "Magna Carta" of humankind; copies were taped to library walls, and the contents were debated in schools and cafés. Critics were quick to point out that horrible abuses did not disappear with the appearance of the UDHR, but it remains a major achievement in the long struggle for human rights. The UDHR evolved as an accepted part of international law and was embraced by just about everyone; today few government leaders speak against these basic rights even if they do not offer them to the citizens of their own country. Since 1948 everyone has had a standard against which all states can be measured.

The two biggest problems, of course, were that the UDHR was only a declaration and therefore not legally binding and that it included no measures to ensure the implementation of any of the rights it named. Efforts were made to solve these problems and to prepare a binding covenant, but they had much less success. The signing of the UDHR was followed by two decades of commissions, working groups, studies, debates, resolutions, and conventions on human rights, including on the status of refugees (1951), the political rights of women (1952), the treatment of prisoners (1955), and racial discrimination (1965). Each was of value in its own way, but the end results were rather modest. In the heightened tensions of the Cold War, the fundamental divisions remained between the Western bloc support for civil and political rights and the Eastern bloc support for social and economic rights. With the growing number of new representatives from the developing world, concerns were raised about the right of rebellion and self-determination, the right to development, and even the question whether there really was such a thing as a "universal" human right.

After years of painful debate, in 1966 it was agreed to split the proposed covenant into two separate agreements: the International Covenant on Civil and Political Rights and the International Covenant on Economic, Social and Cultural Rights. Even then it took another ten years (1976) to achieve the necessary 35 government ratifications to bring the two covenants into effect. No agreement was ever reached on how to enforce these covenants, and their implementation was left up to each state. Plus, dozens of reservations were made to both covenants, placing limitations on their application and effectiveness.

There are two ways of viewing these developments. One is to see the UDHR and the two covenants as significant progress in the international recognition of human rights and as goals for all states to strive for. Human rights were thrust to the top of the international agenda, new norms of international behaviour were established regardless of the lack of sanctions or enforcement powers, and global awareness of human rights was at an all-time high. The eyes of the world were watching, and no state now wanted to be seen infringing them or to be criticized for denying them. In other words, the proclamation of human rights itself was one more step in the long journey towards recognition and protection of human dignity and freedom as well as an expression of increasing transnational relationships and a reflection of the growth of a global community.

Another way is to look at the level of continuing human rights abuses— the atrocities, genocide, poverty and starvation, use of torture and murder—perpetrated by governments around the world while comfortable UN diplomats and government representatives debated endlessly on the question of human rights. Lofty words were spoken and important documents signed in elaborate ceremonies in historic locations while millions died or were abused at the hands of their own governments. The result was empty promises offered up on the altar of national sovereignty. The pronouncements were toothless proclamations that left the principle of non-interference in the domestic affairs of states intact and the responsibility to protect human rights up to the discretion of each government, in many cases the same governments that were the main offenders and abusers of human rights.

However viewed, the UN was only one part of the international equation on human rights, and its activities did not end with the passage of the two covenants. Work continued in cooperation with governments, NGOs, church groups, relief organizations, and other groups. The campaign for human rights developed into one of the UN's most important projects throughout the Cold War era. In the mid-1960s ECOSOC expanded its mandate to enable it to examine specific human rights violations by states; it still had little power to do anything about them, but it did heighten public awareness by drawing attention to and demanding action upon the most serious abuses.[10]

The growing demands from the developing states in the 1960s for more attention on the right to development and anti-colonialism highlighted the continuing divergence over the concept of human rights between East and West, North and South. The same was true for women's rights, which had been a somewhat languishing focus for the CHR and ECOSOC since the creation of the Commission on the Status of Women in 1946. With the rise of international feminism in the 1970s, the UN was prompted into action, responding in the usual way with a series of commissions, sub-committees, reports and studies, conferences, and resolutions dealing with the problems facing women (and children) around the world. International Women's Year was declared in 1975, and other similar gestures followed, but the success of these efforts was mixed. The barrier of national sovereignty remained; cultural, religious, and historical differences among nations ensured that progress was slow. Nevertheless, the UN helped to turn the international spotlight on issues raised by women's groups—including domestic violence, political rights, and the categorization of rape as a war crime—and reinforced the establishment of norms of international behaviour on women's issues.

The UN began as a club of victors of the Second World War. In its early years the great powers ran the show and made the decisions, with the focus of debate occurring in the Security Council. Things began to change in the 1950s, for two main reasons: first, the Security Council was frozen in the Cold War struggle and lost much of its potential for leadership; second, with decolonization and the growth in membership, largely from Asia and Africa, the General Assembly assumed a far more active role. The veto remained in the hands of the P-5, but by the 1960s the developing world emerged as a power bloc in the UN, and the organization was transformed from a Western-dominated group into a truly diverse and global organization.

The UN did not play a central role in the rapid decolonization of the postwar era. The Trusteeship Council administered fewer than a dozen former mandated territories that were not considered ready for independence, and no one seriously considered the possibility of involving it in the broader decolonization process. Its activities gradually diminished as the territories under its supervision achieved independence or union with other states. The Pacific Islands were the last trustee territories, and all were gone once Palau declared independence in 1994. The Trusteeship Council never played the role that some had envisioned, and it cannot be credited in any way for the wave of decolonization that swept the developing world in the years after the Second World War, but it did fulfill its mandate and contributed to the peaceful transition of its territories from colonies to independent states. Once its territories were gone, the Council suspended its operations and annual meetings, although it is technically still on the books.[11]

Even though the Trusteeship Council played only a minor role in postwar decolonization, the impact of this movement was felt in the UN with the arrival of dozens of new members. Between 1956 and 1980 some 50 states were accepted as UN members. The geography of discourse in the General Assembly began to shift from East-West to North-South, as most of the new members were Asian and African states, with many embracing the non-aligned movement. By the 1960s the developing world constituted a majority of UN membership and could raise new issues, establish priorities, and win votes in the General Assembly. Agendas changed to reflect the new reality, with decolonization, the right of self-determination, and cultural, trade, and economic issues rising to the top. The effect was even felt in the Security Council as it was increased from 11 to 15 members in 1965 to accommodate the rise in UN membership.

For many of these new members, Cold War concerns were of less importance than domestic issues of poverty, aid, and development; thus, economic and social development emerged as one of the UN's prime goals. Development had always been part of the UN's mandate (see Article 55), but most of the early efforts in this regard were focused on the economic rehabilitation of Europe and other areas devastated by the war. By the late 1950s and early 1960s, however, the focus shifted to all those new, developing nations that emerged from the demise of the old empires. As a result, much more attention was directed at ECOSOC and its various committees, where there was no great power veto and the new members could dominate.

The social and economic advancement of the developing world was an enormous undertaking—to help more than half the world's population deal with entrenched poverty, to control the spread of disease, improve literacy rates, establish political stability and democratic institutions, and build an infrastructure that could facilitate and foster industrialization. In response, the UN initiated thousands of projects and campaigns in dozens of countries to provide direct aid, foster industrial growth, improve farming techniques, increase trade, build skills and training, improve health and education facilities, and provide capital for investment. In addition, the specialized agencies contributed in their own ways. For example, the

WHO launched major child-vaccination campaigns in an effort to wipe out malaria and smallpox. In 1963 the FAO introduced a World Food Program to provide food in emergency situations, and UNICEF distributed clothes and food to millions of people around the globe. More generally, the UN launched a technical assistance program in 1949, which was expanded with the creation of the "Special Fund" in 1958. In 1965 it was incorporated into the UN Development Program (UNDP),[12] whose purpose was to help developing states with training, the establishment of domestic institutions and schools, and the transfer of technology. Most of the specialized agencies were involved, and the provision of technical assistance evolved into one of their prime goals.

The UN's efforts were effective but uneven, as there was never enough money to go around. The development program was paid for by voluntary contributions from member governments (including the recipient states in some cases, through matching funds). It is also important to remember that the UN was only one of several participants in development, along with regional development organizations, a growing number of NGOs, and individual states. Indeed, the UN and its specialized agencies provided only a small percentage of total development aid. Many states preferred to oversee their own aid and development policies because they could maintain greater control over how the money was spent or could tie the aid to purchases in their own country.

At the heart of UN development efforts were the Bretton Woods financial institutions. The World Bank in particular came to concentrate on development aid, offering loans to developing countries, usually in combination with loans from other sources. Another body was set up in 1956—the International Finance Corporation—to offer advice and financial aid to private companies to promote domestic investment. To help the very poorest states, the International Development Association was created in 1960 to provide very long-term loans (up to 50 years) at low interest rates. Together these bodies offered tens of billions of dollars in loans and grants to more than 100 states for development purposes—government projects, private businesses and investment, and technical assistance. However, the whole process was criticized for being dominated by the wealthier states, which controlled the institutions, decided how much money they would give and where it would be spent, and often insisted on structural or other regulations in order for the recipient states to qualify for the funds.

While the Bretton Woods institutions were dominated by the powerful developed states, the voice of the developing world was much louder in those institutions where they dominated, such as the General Assembly, UNESCO, and ECOSOC, and it was here that their influence was most strongly felt. Continuing trade and tariff problems led to the staging of the first UN Conference on Trade and Development (UNCTAD) in 1964 in an effort to improve the North-South trade relationship, leading to greater exports from the developing world. UNCTAD evolved into a series of conferences and a semi-permanent organization, producing agreements, policies, plans, and resolutions to improve global trade arrangements but with only limited success. The wealthy states tended to support the existing institutions and the free-market economy, and they did not always respond eagerly to the calls for more aid, lower tariffs, debt relief, grants and loans, and so on. In 1973 the developed states promised to make available 0.7 per cent of their GNP for development assistance, but very few have met that promise.[13]

The developing states demanded more fundamental change, coming together in 1964 as the Group of 77 (G77) to work for the creation of a new economic relationship between North and South. This new group was much more vocal in its criticism of the developed states and in calling for more radical changes to the international economic order. Complaints were made about the strings attached to development loans and the North's use of its economic and tariff policies to ensure the continued underdevelopment of the G77 states and to prevent their transformation into industrial states. Additional support for these views was found in the communist bloc, whose members frequently condemned capitalism and Western imperialism. Development itself took on Cold War overtones.

In 1974 the G77 proclaimed a New International Economic Order (NIEO) with a program of action to negotiate a new international economic structure. Bolstered by rising oil prices, which seemed to promise stronger prices for the developing world's natural resources, the NIEO was meant to take advantage of this new-found strength to establish a more balanced and interdependent relationship between North and South. The results were far less spectacular, as some developing states experienced a massive influx of capital while others were badly hurt by rising oil prices. In addition, the oil crisis produced recession in the North and coincided with the rise of neo-conservatism and a greater reliance on free-market economics in many wealthier nations (in particular, the United States and Britain). In these difficult economic times of rising debts and inflation, the response for many states was deregulation and privatization, and traditional development policies fell out of favour. Conferences continued to be staged, UN declarations were issued to focus international attention on development, and calls for action were made by the General Assembly, but the NIEO never realized its original goals and by the mid-1980s had largely evaporated.[14]

The UN made a positive impact on development in the Cold War era, but there were limitations to its success. It is safe to say that over the course of 40 years, thousands of people lived longer, millions were better off, and many were better educated. The UN and its agencies helped boost agricultural and industrial output in the developing world, international trade between North and South rose dramatically, and global per capita income more than doubled. But at the end of the Cold War the divisions between North and South were greater than ever, and the problems of underdevelopment—poverty, disease, and so on—remained prevalent in a large part of the world. The UN encouraged development but never came close to eliminating many of the symptoms of underdevelopment; in many cases it failed even to keep up with rapid population growth. It is a case of the glass being half empty or half full—the UN could never do enough to make things better, but without it things would have been much worse.

The growing North-South divide inevitably exhibited a political dimension. Many of the developing states joined the non-aligned movement that tried to remain outside the basic Cold War divide between East and West. But the presence of South Africa and, to a lesser degree, Portugal and a few other colonial powers became serious issues in the UN. Beginning in the 1960s, many attempts were made to expel South Africa from the UN and other organizations and, when that failed, to at least isolate that country within the organizations. The Western states, led by the United States, argued that, first, South Africa's membership was a political issue and therefore not suitable for discussion in the technical specialized agencies and, second, that it was better to have South Africa in the UN, where pressure could be applied to improve domestic conditions there. Few states supported South Africa or its policies, but for many African and Asian states its very presence was seen as a tacit acceptance of its government, and the result was endless debates and procedural delays to oust it.

Another source of tension was the Middle East, where the UN was heavily invested in peacekeeping and had passed Security Council Resolution 242 in 1967, which set out the proposed "land for peace" solution to the Arab-Israeli problem. Throughout this period the United States and its allies found themselves increasingly isolated in the UN as the Middle Eastern states and their allies in Asia, Africa, and the Soviet bloc repeatedly denounced Israel and everything it stood for. By the mid-1970s the Palestinian Liberation Organization (PLO) had been granted observer status in the UN and several other organizations, and in 1975 the General Assembly passed Resolution 3379, defining Zionism as "a form of racism and racial discrimination" (it was rescinded in 1991).

Actions such as these reflected the growing tensions in the UN and damaged the organization's prestige, especially in the United States. American criticism, which was growing in the 1970s, surged following the election of President Ronald Reagan in 1980. Reagan was critical of the UN and, with the entrance of the communist Chinese, the presence of the PLO and the persistent attacks on Israel, all the talk about a new economic order, with the Security Council deadlocked and the General Assembly dominated by the anti-American developing states, and all the gratuitous attacks on Yankee imperialism, his criticism turned to hostility.

An example of the growing American disillusion can be seen in the UN's response to the rise of international terrorism, an issue of great concern to the United States and its allies. In the 1970s, the hijacking and sabotage of aircraft, which had largely been a problem in Cuban-American relations in the 1960s, spread to the Middle East and was accompanied by other more violent terrorist acts, from the killing of Israeli athletes at the 1972 Munich Olympic games to the murderous attack on American soldiers in Lebanon in 1983. The ICAO produced three international conventions (The Hague, Tokyo, and Montreal Conventions) to establish legal jurisdiction and extradition in cases of aircraft sabotage and hijacking, but efforts to prompt the UN into effective action largely failed. Even agreeing to a definition of terrorism seemed impossible. While the North demanded immediate action and clear resolutions condemning the acts and those states that harboured terrorists, the South insisted on discussing the "root causes" of terrorism, arguing that some acts might be justified if they were performed in an anti-colonial struggle or against a racist regime.[15] Fruitless debates descended into angry recriminations, and subsequent resolutions were so watered down as to be meaningless.

Americans didn't like the way things were developing at the UN, as evidenced by the increasing frequency of their use of the veto after 1970. Washington threatened to withdraw its support from any part of the UN system that it believed was working contrary to American interests. For example, in 1978 it withdrew from the ILO and, in 1981, announced that it would no longer support any organization that excluded Israel. In its most highly publicized action, in 1984 the United States quit UNESCO, followed by the British in 1985.[16] Running parallel to the G77 proclamation of the NIEO in 1974, UNESCO developed the New World Information and Communication Order (NWICO), which argued that the international media was Western-dominated and owned and too commercial, and called for the "democratization" of the media. To some members this meant state-ownership and the regulation of outside media; to others (usually in the West) it meant state-control, censorship, trade restrictions, and the infringement of the freedom of speech. Western critics charged that UNESCO politicized every issue, was anti-American, wasteful, and too expensive. (The British rejoined UNESCO in 1997; the Americans returned only in 2003.)

The American government also used its financial leverage to secure UN reforms. A handful of developed states had always paid most of the budget of the UN, the specialized agencies, peacekeeping, development aid, and so on, and among these the United States paid the greatest share (and the greatest share in many other international organizations as well). The ceiling on the American contribution had slowly dropped over the years from nearly 40 per cent to about 25 per cent in the early 1970s. But UN expenses were an easy target for critics, and the American government threatened to refuse to pay its share for any UN activities that it did not support. In one instance, it withheld its share of funding a UN office to deal with Palestinian rights.

In most of these cases the withholding of funds was more symbolic than anything else, but a more serious act occurred in 1985 when the American Senate amended the Foreign Relations Act (known as the Kassenbaum Amendment, after Nancy Kassenbaum, a Republican Senator from Kansas), threatening to reduce American payments from 25 per cent to a maximum of 20 per cent unless it agreed to adopt a weighted voting procedure on budgetary matters (meaning that by paying 25 per cent of the budget, the United States would have 25 per cent of the vote).[17] In 1986, Washington paid less than half its assessed $210 million contribution, sparking a major financial crisis and another round of cost-cutting and reductions at the UN. In 1987 the UN agreed to seek consensus on budgetary matters (rather than needing a two-thirds majority), which effectively gave the United States a veto. Nevertheless, at the end of the 1980s the United States was still more than $200 million in arrears. It was not the only member who fell behind, but the withholding of these funds significantly contributed to the UN's ever-present financial difficulties.

With the ending of the Cold War there was some ambivalence about the future of the UN. For some, the thawing of relations between East and West came with the promise of great possibilities for the UN—to assume global leadership in social, cultural, and economic cooperation, and perhaps to take a leading role in peace and security issues—something that it had never been able to do in the past. The future was filled with opportunity, and the UN was well situated to contribute to and benefit from the process of globalization. For others, the internal divisions and weaknesses of the UN were too serious to be overcome. It was an overly bureaucratic and expensive organization that was dominated by the weak and ignored by the strong. For critics, the UN was running out of gas, and, beyond the provision of humanitarian assistance, it likely had little future to play in the development of the international community.[18] Just about everyone saw in the UN what they wanted and measured it against their own, often arbitrary standards and principles. Many called for its reform, but few agreed on what those reforms should be. Others looked to regional and other kinds of international organizations to fill those areas left vacant by the UN and to respond to the problems produced by international stalemate and Cold War animosities.

Notes

1   Roberts and Kingsbury, eds., *United Nations, Divided World*, 10.
2   For a brief review of the careers of these men, see Ryan, *The United Nations and International Politics*, 53–86.
3   Melvern, *The Ultimate Crime*, 94–104.
4   On UN disarmament, see Ziring et al., *The United Nations*, 260–68.
5   Ziring et al., 257.
6   S. Ryan, 41–43.
7   On traditional peacekeeping, see Bellamy et al., *Understanding Peacekeeping*, 95–101.
8   Normand and Zaidi, *Human Rights at the UN*, 237.
9   For the role of the Latin American states in bridging this gap, see Glendon, "The Forgotten Crucible," 27–39; Carozza, "From Conquest to Constitutions," 281–313.
10 For a recent review of the UN record, see Clapham, *Human Rights*, 42–56.
11 S. Ryan, 27; Ziring et al., 306–10.
12 See Murphy, *The United Nations Development Programme*.
13 See Kennedy, *The Parliament of Man*, 126–42.
14 See chapter by Kenneth Dadzie, in Roberts and Kingsbury, 297–326.
15 See chapter by Edward Luck, in Price and Zacher, *The United Nations and Global Security*, 95–108.
16 Imber, *The USA, ILO, UNESCO and IAEA*, 96; S. Ryan, 93.
17 Kilgore, "Cut Down in the Crossfire?" 592–610.
18 See Ruggie, "The United States and the United Nations," 343–56.

5 | Regional and Other International Organizations

States pursue their national interests in international organizations, and sometimes those interests can be better achieved through smaller or more localized organizations established along geographical, regional, cultural, linguistic, or economic lines. These regional or particular organizations cannot do everything, and some problems—dealing with the environment, the spread of disease, disarmament, universal human rights, and so on—might benefit from a global approach. Nevertheless, since the end of the Second World War, the greatest growth in intergovernmental organizations (IGOs) has been among regional organizations, which today constitute the majority of all IGOs.

There were regional and other IGOs before the UN, which has had a regional component since its creation in 1945. Regional voting blocks and informal alliances have always been a part of the UN system (the Latin American bloc, the Western/Eastern blocs, the non-aligned nations, etc.), and many of the specialized agencies established regional offices. For instance, ECOSOC set up four regional economic commissions (Europe, Asia and the Far East, Latin America, and Africa) to help coordinate economic recovery after the war.

Chapter 8 of the UN Charter (see Appendix 2) specifically permits regional organizations to operate, providing they act in ways that are "consistent with the Purposes and Principles of the United Nations" (Article 52). It is clear that the authors of the Charter envisioned regional organizations that would be responsible to and, ultimately, act under the authority of the UN. Enforcement action was to be taken only when authorized by the Security Council, and the UN was to be kept informed regarding actions taken and contemplated. It has not turned out that way completely, as regional organizations have evolved into international actors in their own right and have engaged in myriad functions around the world, including conflict management, economic and trade negotiations, and the protection of human rights. Today, many of these organizations work in cooperation with the UN rather than under its supervision.

It is easy to see why in the last 65 years there has been such rapid growth in regional and more specialized IGOs—it is simpler to organize states that share such characteristics as a common sense of purpose, culture or language, geography, political systems, economic concerns, or anxiety about their security. The outbreak of the Cold War, for example, divided the world into hostile camps, made the creation of universal organizations more difficult, and led directly to a series of regional defence organizations such as the North Atlantic Treaty Organization (NATO) and the Warsaw Pact. In addition, the growth of the non-aligned movement led to the creation of new IGOs, almost in opposition to the major Cold War antagonists. In the developing world, it often made more sense to establish regional organizations—free trade movements, cultural organizations, development organizations—to pursue interests that were not or could not be met by the universal institutions.[1] In many circumstances, states that share a region are better able to understand and respond to the problems of that region. They are more directly involved, more likely to benefit from a solution, and might be more willing to make a contribution to a potential settlement.[2]

At the same time, there is no reason to believe that regional IGOs are inherently more effective or legitimate than universal ones. They are no more democratic just because they comprise states that share territory, culture, or values. "Neighbors are not always impartial," was how one scholar put it,[3] and, while they may be better situated to respond to crises in their own backyards, they have not always proven to be more capable in solving problems than the UN. The African Union has been no more successful in Darfur than the UN; NATO has not been able to pacify Afghanistan; Asian organizations were unable to deal with the financial meltdown of the late 1990s; and so on. And, as one recent study has demonstrated, there is much debate on whether regional organizations are better able to reduce the "legitimacy gap" between leaders and their constituencies.[4]

There are many different kinds of IGOs, and, as human creations, they are imprecise, prone to political interference, and always changing. Even what constitutes a region is unclear.[5] Political decisions allow Turkey into the North Atlantic region as a member of NATO but keep Israel out of Middle Eastern IGOs. Cultural and political differences are given as reasons to exclude states from some organizations, but in others they are overlooked. Most IGOs have major powers as members; some are successful because of their absence. The purpose—and lifespan—of these organizations varies as well. Almost every state is a member of one or more regional IGOs, and many have multiple memberships.

As we saw in the previous chapter, Cold War polarization made effective action by the UN Security Council almost impossible but did not eliminate the desire for security among its members. Reforming the UN to circumvent the Soviet veto was out of the question, although a few did suggest that they be expelled from the UN. However, most people believed that such action would destroy the organization. Forming a regional defence organization seemed to be the best alternative, as Articles 51 and 52 of the Charter permitted.

The United States and its allies began to search for alliances outside the UN to curb the Soviet threat, alliances that would work with (not dispose of) the UN. For example, in 1948 the Brussels Treaty Organization, comprising Belgium, France, Luxembourg, the Netherlands, and Britain, was created as a collective defence organization. It continued to grow with West Germany and Italy joining in 1954, Portugal and Spain in 1990, and Greece in 1995. This strictly European group was overshadowed by the broader negotiations that led to the signing of the 1949 North Atlantic Treaty and the creation of NATO. This was a traditional defence alliance, in which the United States, Canada, and 10 Western European states committed themselves to defend each other against any possible Soviet attack; new members were welcomed in the 1950s, including West Germany, Greece, and Turkey. Although NATO rested on American military strength, all members agreed, according to Article 5 of the Treaty, that "an armed attack against one or more of them in Europe or North America shall be considered an attack against them all" and that if such an attack occurred, then each nation would take "individually and in concert with the other Parties, such action as it deems necessary, including the use of armed force."

The basic structure of NATO includes the North Atlantic Council, with a representative from each member; a secretary-general; and a secretariat operating at its headquarters in Brussels. Military command rests with the Military Committee and the Supreme Headquarters, Allied Powers,

Europe (SHAPE), under the direction of the Supreme Allied Commander. NATO also includes a non-military dimension, rooted in Article 2, which calls for cooperation and the elimination of conflict in economic policies. Nevertheless, defence has always been its key purpose. NATO remained at the heart of the Western alliance for the rest of the Cold War.

At almost the same time, the United States engaged in negotiations for somewhat similar regional defence alliances, although none, other than the Organization of American States (see below), had the strength, unity, and permanence of NATO. In 1954 the South-East Asia Collective Defence Treaty was signed in Manila, establishing the South East Asia Treaty Organization (SEATO). Its council and secretariat were established in Bangkok, but most of its members, other than Thailand and the Philippines, were outside South East Asia (the United States, Britain, France, Pakistan, Australia, and New Zealand). It was created as an anti-communist organization, especially with regards to Indochina, and it disbanded in 1977, following the end of the Vietnam War. Other agreements were signed, but they did not establish full international organizations. In 1951, in the ANZUS Treaty, the United States pledged to protect the security of Australia and New Zealand. In 1955 Iraq, Turkey, Iran, and Pakistan signed the Baghdad Pact, which was renamed the Central Treaty Organization (CENTO) in 1959. Its headquarters were established in Ankara, Turkey, but it was a fairly loose alliance and organization.

The Soviet Union and its allies responded to this activity with the creation of the Warsaw Pact (officially the Warsaw Treaty Organization). Often seen as a response to NATO and, in particular, the entrance of West Germany into NATO, the Warsaw Pact was a defence alliance of Eastern bloc states, including the Soviet Union, Bulgaria, Czechoslovakia, East Germany, Hungary, Poland, Romania, and Albania; despite the name, its headquarters was in Moscow. In the same way that NATO was founded on American military power, the Warsaw Pact was based on the military strength of the Soviet Union, but it was less an organization of equals and more an alliance dominated by its major power. And, in the end, it was invoked only against its own members—in Hungary in 1956 and Czechoslovakia in 1968.

Mention should also be made of the Conference on Security and Co-operation in Europe, established in 1973 to monitor the progress of the Helsinki Accords in which the two Cold War blocs agreed not only to recognize and secure their existing borders but also to a range of cooperative projects in human rights and cultural and educational exchanges. The Conference, with representatives from Europe, the Soviet bloc, and North

America, met regularly to facilitate cooperation and peace in Europe, to help prevent the outbreak of conflicts, and to provide stability for Europe. It was not meant as a replacement for either NATO or the Warsaw Pact, but it was another institution that worked to enhance European security. In 1995, reflecting the changed times after the fall of the Soviet Union, it became the Organization for Security and Co-operation in Europe (OSCE).

The end of the Cold War, the reunification of Germany, and the collapse of the Soviet Union at the start of the 1990s raised questions about the future of these alliances. Many critics asked whether you could still have an alliance with no enemy to defend against. NATO leaders began re-examining Article 2 in search of new roles for the organization to play. Rather than disappearing, NATO expanded, taking in new members—the Czech Republic, Poland, and Hungary in 1999; in 2004, with the entrance of Lithuania, Estonia, Latvia, Slovakia, Romania, and Bulgaria, the membership rose to 26. In addition, NATO launched bombing campaigns in Serbia in 1995 and 1999 and, for the first time, broadened its focus into a humanitarian organization, providing aid and other assistance in Kosovo.[6]

In the aftermath of 9/11, NATO for the first time invoked Article 5 and sent forces outside of Europe to Afghanistan to root out the Taliban. But, faced with the unilateralism of the Bush administration (2001–09) and the appearance of significant differences between Europe and the United States on issues such as the war on terror, missile defence, and the environment, questions are again being raised about NATO's future.

NATO members form the core of the Group of Eight (G8) states that appeared in 1975 in the aftermath of the financial crisis and oil embargo of the early 1970s. It began as the G6, including Japan, Britain, the United States, Germany, France, and Italy, becoming G7 with the entrance of Canada in 1976, and the G8 in 1998 when Russia became a full member. Not a traditional IGO, in that it has no secretariat, secretary-general, constitution, or headquarters, the G8 evolved into a forum for leaders of the most economically powerful states to meet informally each year to discuss joint policies on the major issues of the day, from monetary policy to terrorism to the environment. It also has embraced meetings of government ministers and meetings between members of the group and other states, such as the emerging group of states including China, Brazil, and India. For example, the finance ministers of the 20 largest economies have met as the new G20. The concrete results of the annual G8 summits have been mixed, but the events themselves have attracted both considerable media attention and public protests.

For its part, the Warsaw Pact disbanded in 1991 as its members withdrew and established new governments; many joined the looser intergovernmental Commonwealth of Independent States, created the same year. Security concerns and border issues remained, however, and, in 1996 Russia, China, Kazakhstan, Kyrgyzstan, and Tajikistan established a group known as the Shanghai Five to discuss trade, security, and cultural issues. With the entrance of Uzbekistan in 2001 the group became the Shanghai Cooperation Organization (SCO), with its headquarters in Beijing. Through regular summit meetings of foreign ministers and heads of state, mutual problems are discussed, although respect for each member's sovereignty is a fundamental aspect of the organization. One of its greatest concerns is security, but the SCO is not a NATO-like defence organization; its concerns for security are focused more on internal separatist and terrorist threats, not outside aggression.

The Pan American Union was the first and the largest regional organization in the world, whose history and development was concurrent with that of the League of Nations and the UN. In its early incarnation, the Pan American Union focused on cultural, trade, health, and educational issues, and had less of a significant security or political component. It was not a collective security organization, and when and if security was discussed, it was usually within the context of internal security rather than collective defence against outside aggressors. This is not surprising given the lopsided division of power in the organization, with the United States on one side and the Central and South American republics on the other (and the latter's concerns over American intrusions). And, as one scholar has noted, thanks to the 1823 Monroe Doctrine, the United States "had already assumed responsibility for the security of the hemisphere."[7]

In the years leading up to the outbreak of the Second World War, however, the nature of the organization, its goals, and the concerns of its members began to evolve. In the early 1930s, the American government introduced its "Good Neighbor" policy, removing its military presence from various states in the hemisphere and repudiating the Roosevelt Corollary to the Monroe Doctrine that was used to justify American intervention in the region. American investment still predominated in many parts of the region, and democracy and economic prosperity did not flourish, but the rhetoric of pan-Americanism and non-interference prevailed. Several treaties were negotiated, calling for regional arbitration and the settlement of disputes, such as the Treaty to Avoid or Prevent Conflicts Between the American

States (1923) and the Anti-War Treaty of Non-Aggression and Conciliation (1933). The 1938 Declaration of Lima established new machinery for consultation through the staging of foreign ministers meetings (officially a "Meeting of Consultation of Ministers of Foreign Affairs of the American Republics"), called to discuss specific problems. These meetings were held outside the auspices of the Pan American Union.

The Declaration of Panama issued at the first meeting of foreign ministers in October 1939, just a few months after the war began, proclaimed the solidarity and neutrality of the region, and created a 300-mile neutral zone around the Western Hemisphere (excluding Canada). The Western Hemisphere was united in the war, with the exception of Argentina, which did not declare war until March 1945, and the Latin American states shared many views about the postwar world. The 1945 Mexico City Conference at Chapultepec Castle enabled these states to refine their views, and, as discussed in Chapter Three, they were able to play a significant role at the San Francisco Conference and the founding of the UN.

In the early Cold War years, and reflecting Cold War fears, the Pan American Union was integrated into a new and larger Organization of American States (OAS), which assumed its responsibilities and took on a new security and defence role. On 2 September 1947 the Inter-American Treaty of Reciprocal Assistance (or Rio Treaty) was signed, establishing a collective defence pact for the Western Hemisphere in which an attack on one member was to be considered an attack on all members (although the pact was not technically binding). The signing of the Rio Treaty was followed in 1948 with the 9th International Conference of American States, in Bogotá, Colombia, at which the OAS was created. It was formally established in 1951.

The OAS is similar to other international organizations and has many parallels with the UN. Its goals are to "strengthen the peace and security of the continent"; settle inter-American disputes; defend its members against outside aggression; and promote economic development, social and cultural cooperation, and a host of other functions and activities from the eradication of poverty to the limitation of conventional weapons. Like the UN, the OAS Charter forbids intervention "in matters that are within the international jurisdiction of the Member States" and calls on members to "abstain from intervening in the affairs of another State." However, it contains few enforcement provisions.

The major organs of the organization include the regular Inter-American Conferences to establish basic policies; the "Meeting of Consultation of Foreign Ministers" maintained from the days of the Pan American Union to deal with urgent—especially security and defence—matters; and a Permanent Council, which, unlike the UN Security Council, consists of all members (usually the members' ambassadors in Washington) and has no veto. Important decisions are made based on a two-thirds majority. The old Pan American Union was transformed into the OAS General Secretariat, a secretary-general was selected, and, in 1967 a more formal General Assembly was created. Many other bodies are associated with the OAS, some predating it, and some more closely connected to it than others. The Pan American Health Organization created in 1902, for example, cooperates with the WHO in the Western Hemisphere in its fight against disease, to improve sanitation, and so on; others include the Inter-American Commission on Women (1927), which supports projects dealing with women's human and political rights, equity, and domestic violence. Furthermore, at the 1948 Bogotá conference that created the OAS, the participants adopted the "American Declaration of the Rights and Duties of Man." This human rights declaration influenced and preceded by several months the UN Universal Declaration of Human Rights and was followed by the creation of the Inter-American Commission on Human Rights (IACHR). The IACHR was relatively quiet for many years, but in the 1990s it became more active in monitoring human rights abuses in Haiti, Nicaragua, and elsewhere.

For the Latin American states, the OAS provided a forum for consultation and solidarity in the face of American power. Economic development has always been a goal of the organization, although there was considerable disagreement over the nature and extent of American aid. In 1959 the Inter-American Development Bank (IDB) was set up to oversee lending to Western Hemisphere states and to finance development projects. In addition, like the UN, the OAS established an Economic and Social Council and a Council for Education, Science, and Culture to promote economic and cultural development. In 1993 these latter two bodies were combined into the Inter-American Council for Integral Development (CIDI) to combat poverty and focus the OAS's efforts in economic development. During the Cold War, however, economic development was often overshadowed by the American-inspired anti-communist struggle, as the American government supported a variety of dictators and oppressive regimes in a quest for regional stability. Despite a series of programs and efforts from the OAS, the American government, and various NGOs, poverty, illiteracy, underdevelopment, and unrest persisted throughout the region.

For much of the Cold War, the OAS provided the stage on which tensions between the United States and Latin America were played out, especially over American interventions in the region. American governments considered the OAS a good place to discuss regional economic and political issues and an organization that could be used to attract support for American goals. It didn't always work out that way. The OAS often found itself divided between the United States and the other members over American actions and intervention in Guatemala (1954), the Dominican Republic (1965), Grenada (1983), and Panama (1989). At times the mediating ability and diplomatic pressure of the OAS was effective, but the American support for Britain in the 1982 Falklands War with Argentina seriously divided the organization.

The end of the Cold War had a pronounced affect on the OAS and the whole Western Hemisphere. In 1990, with the increase in democratic governments in Latin America, the OAS established its Unit for Promotion of Democracy to provide information, assistance, and programs to foster democracy. It also provided advice and election monitoring, for example, in Nicaragua in 1990 and 1996, Suriname in 1991, Peru in 1992 and 2000, Paraguay in 1993, and Haiti in 2000. In addition, two other actions were taken to enhance and promote democracy: first, the 1992 Protocol of Washington enables the OAS to suspend members if their governments are overthrown by force; and second, the 1991 General Assembly Resolution 1080 requires the secretary-general to stage a Council meeting within 10 days of an attack or attempted coup on a legitimate member government and then, if warranted, to call a Meeting of Foreign Ministers. These tools permit the OAS to mediate and/or apply diplomatic pressure and economic sanctions to protect its members. Resolution 1080 was used with some success on four occasions in the 1990s: in Haiti (1991) in conjunction with UN efforts to help restore President Aristide following the coup; in Peru (1992) in an effort to persuade President Fujimori to hold fair and free elections; in Guatemala (1993) to support the staging of new elections after the suspension of its Constitution; and in Paraguay (1996) to support the president in his resistance to a potential army seizure of power.

In 1994 the OAS began holding large Summits of the Americas to discuss hemispheric issues, make future plans and policies, and issue declarations on human rights, the environment, sustainable development, and so on. These Conferences have continued to the present day and have become the most public expression of the OAS's activities. Some of the old problems persist—Cuba, for example, has remained suspended since 1962—but much of the division in the Organization has subsided. Indeed, with the entrance of Canada, Jamaica, Trinidad and Tobago, and other Caribbean islands, membership has reached 35 (plus 47 observer states). The OAS now represents almost all the states in the Western Hemisphere and is better positioned to fulfill its goals than ever before. The United States remains the dominant power (and pays most of the bills), but the OAS has helped further regional integration and, as one observer wrote, "now appears to spearhead a vigorous international regime for the defense of democratic rule in the hemisphere."[8]

It should also be remembered that the OAS has not been the only international organization in Latin America; indeed, there were several other regional groups, including the Organization of Central American States (1951), the Latin American Free Trade Association (1960), and the Caribbean Free Trade Area (1968).[9] All these groups dealt with trade and economic issues and promoted regional integration; similar to the OAS, all achieved equally uneven results. The latter group, for example, conducted years of negotiation leading to the establishment of the Caribbean Community (CARICOM) in 1973. Originally with four members (Barbados, Guyana, Jamaica, and Trinidad and Tobago), CARICOM has expanded to 15 and, since 1989, has moved towards the creation of a single market.

The European states were major contributors to the evolution of international organizations, so it is not surprising that some of the largest and most powerful regional organizations are also situated there. Indeed, critics have argued that the League of Nations itself was essentially a European organization, established by Europeans to deal with European problems that remained after the First World War. With its demise, Europeans began to seek other institutions to help preserve the peace of their continent and to re-establish their economies. The years after the Second World War saw the growth of a wide array of international organizations, including pan-European groups; "sub-regional" organizations such as the Nordic Council, which deals only with European issues; the Arctic Council, which includes Canada and the United States and focuses on the managing of Arctic issues; and broader institutions in which the Europeans play a key role, such as NATO and the G8.

Many of the current international organizations appeared at the end of the Second World War and were established to grapple with the emerging security and reconstruction problems of the Cold War era. A good example is the Council of Europe. Created in 1949, it consists of an assembly and

Council of Ministers that meet regularly in Strasbourg, France, to discuss a range of issues, including human rights and development. It also promotes cooperation in cultural and other social activities, but it lacks enforcement power and can make only recommendations to governments. Nevertheless, by 2005 there were 46 members, and the Council had established its own Commissioner for Human Rights.

Several organizations were set up to deal with economic and development problems. One of the most important was the Organization for European Economic Co-operation, established in 1948 to administer Marshall Plan financial aid. It expanded in the 1950s with the entrance of West Germany and, as associate members, Canada and the United States. In 1961 it was renamed the Organization for Economic Co-operation and Development (OECD). More a complex think-tank, global network, and policy forum than an aid/development organization, its goal is to collect and analyze information, to facilitate discussions on economic and trade issues, and to promote economic development and collaboration between its members and, increasingly, between its members and other states. The OECD's council, secretariat, and headquarters are located in Paris, where it stages an annual forum, and its membership has expanded globally to include 30 of the world's richest nations.

The most important European organization is the European Union (EU), which arose from the same circumstances as those mentioned above: the need for economic cooperation to reconstruct Europe at the end of the war; the lingering problem of reconciling and reintegrating Germany into the new Europe and to reduce potential friction between Germany and other states, France especially; and the emergence of the Cold War, which produced new security concerns and the realization that Europe was no longer the same global power that it had been in the past (at least when compared to the new superpowers). Unity was one way to rebuild Europe and to enhance its global position.

The EU began as the European Coal and Steel Community (ECSC), created in 1952 by Belgium, France, West Germany, Italy, Luxembourg, and the Netherlands. The ECSC was hardly a full international organization, and its goal was simply to control the production and marketing of coal and steel in members' countries. But for many it was the first step towards the ultimate achievement of complete European integration, even federation, although early plans to create a European Defence Community fell apart and collapsed in 1954. In 1957, the Treaty of Rome was signed. It was actually two treaties: the European Atomic Energy Community Treaty and the European Economic Community Treaty. The first created Euratom to oversee the use, research, and production of atomic energy in Europe. The second created the European Economic Community (EEC) in1958, a more formal international organization whose goal was to establish a customs union for its members—the removal of tariffs between members and the establishment of a common tariff against the outside world (accomplished by 1968)—and then a full common market with the elimination of other restrictions on trade by standardizing taxation systems, the creation of technical and educational standards, the free movement of peoples, and so on. In addition, the EEC called for movement towards the formation of common European policies for agriculture, fisheries, transport, environmental protection, and other areas. In 1967 the EEC, Euratom, and the European Coal and Steel Community merged into the European Community (EC).

The EC has four main organs: the Commission, the Council of Ministers, the European Parliament, and the Court of Justice. The Commission, situated in Brussels, consists of representatives from each member (although the numbers are slightly weighted in favour of the larger states). It implements European treaties and policies, administers the organization, and proposes policies to further the interests of the whole community. The Council of Ministers includes ministerial representatives from each member (usually the ministers of finance, but other ministers meet if their portfolios are under discussion), with a rotating presidency. It consults with the Commission, decides policy, and is often the most important decision-making body in the EC. The European Parliament, which meets in Strasbourg, France (the secretariat is in Luxembourg), is an assembly representing all member states. At first its members were appointed, but they have been elected since 1979. The Parliament can examine, discuss, and question proposed legislation; although it has some influence, it has no legislative power. The Court of Justice (also in Luxembourg) issues binding decisions on legal issues dealing with the EC, its treaties, and rules. There are also many other institutions and bodies—for example, the European Investment Bank and the Economic and Social Committee—similar to those found in other IGOs.

Membership rose over the decades from the "original six" as Britain, Ireland, and Denmark joined in 1973, Greece in 1981, and Spain and Portugal in 1986. More recently, in 2004, Malta, Cyprus, and several Eastern European states joined; in 2007, Bulgaria and Romania entered, bringing the total membership to 27. Arrangements have been made with other organizations also; for example, in 1973 the EC joined with the European Free Trade Association (EFTA) of Austria, Finland, Norway, Sweden,

Switzerland, and Iceland to create a huge free trade area encompassing all of Western Europe. Other relationships have been negotiated with Asia and North America since the mid-1970s.

In an effort to stabilize the relationship between EC members and their former colonies, two sets of agreements were negotiated. First was the Yaoundé Conventions (1963 and 1967), which established free trade between the EC and their former African colonies. Second was the Lomé Convention, signed in 1975 (and renegotiated several times since), which was broadened to include not only Britain but also the former African, Caribbean, and Pacific (ACP) colonies. The Lomé Convention removed EC tariffs on almost all products from the ACP group and included programs to supply aid, grants, and loans to the former colonies. The Cotonou Agreement (2000) broadened and extended the relationship for 20 years. In the meantime, the ACP Group of States has evolved as a more permanent international organization with a secretariat and summit meetings of heads of state.

Interest in European integration has fluctuated over the years between periods when progress was slow and unity uncertain and others of rapid advancement. The tumultuous years at the end of the Cold War, accompanied by the collapse of the Soviet Union and the reunification of Germany in 1990–91, helped to re-energize enthusiasm for European unity, if only by again heightening concern regarding Europe's security and economic stability. It was during these eventful years that the Treaty of European Unity, known as the Treaty of Maastricht (signed in 1991, came into force in 1993), created the EU and moved Europe towards more complete integration and economic union. In addition to a common trade policy, the EU introduced greater cooperation in defence planning, a common currency, and the implementation of the Common Foreign and Security Policy. There are also plans to introduce a common European citizenship. The euro was launched in 2002 and is now the currency in more than a dozen states.

The EU has emerged as a unique international organization, to the point that some observers suggest that, because of the extent of integration, the creation of European institutions (rather than strictly intergovernmental ones), and the direct connection with the people (not just their governments), it is creating a new level of government above the sovereign state. Indeed, the EU has become an international actor in its own right; it has been granted observer status in many international organizations (including the UN), it participates in the OECD, it spoke for Europe in the General Agreement on Tariffs and Trade (GATT), it has dispatched military and peacekeeping missions to different places (e.g., Bosnia, Democratic Republic of Congo), and it has taken steps towards the formation of a common foreign policy.

The ultimate goal of the EU may be to create a new federation or state of Europe, but efforts in that direction have not yet been completely successful. Europeans do not always vote as one, even in organizations with EU representation (over the war in Iraq, for example), and the two European P-5 members of the Security Council have made no offer to resign their seats in favour of a single EU representative. More seriously, the 2004 "Treaty Establishing a Constitution for Europe" and the Constitution of Europe was stalled in 2005 by the failure of the Dutch and the French to ratify it. It has yet to come into force, and until it does the road to fuller integration is blocked.

Regional organizations in Africa and the Middle East came with a somewhat different set of problems and concerns compared to those in Europe. First, in the years following the Second World War, the African and Middle Eastern states embarked in a process of decolonization and the achievement of independence, and dealing with the legacy of colonialism was a major priority for most organizations. Security, domestic sovereignty, and institution building were natural foci as states established themselves and negotiated new arrangements with their neighbours and former colonial powers. Second, the African and Middle Eastern states faced enormous economic problems, and the lack of financial resources put severe limitations on what their organizations could achieve or pay for. Turning dependence and underdevelopment into independence and economic growth were the major tasks they faced.

The first of the postwar organizations was the League of Arab States, known as the Arab League. Created in Cairo in 1945 (with its headquarters there) by Egypt, Iraq, Lebanon, Saudi Arabia, Syria, Jordan, and Yemen, the Arab League now has more than 20 members, including most of the states of the Middle East and Northern Africa. The Arab League is not a typical regional organization in that, although it is regional in a geographical sense, its membership is defined more by culture and language. In addition, its mandate is largely political in nature. The League provides a forum for debate and the machinery to promote the interest of Arabic-speaking states. It speaks out in support of Arab nationalism and, especially in its early years, worked to support the independence and defend the sovereignty of all Arabic-speaking states. It has been much involved in the long Arab-Israeli dispute and the plight of the Palestinian people—the PLO is a League member.

The League is involved in economic and cultural activities as well, but more attention is paid to economic issues by the Gulf Cooperation Council (GCC), created in 1981 by Bahrain, Kuwait, Oman, Qatar, Saudi Arabia, and the United Arab Emirates. The GCC was established in the wake of the Iran-Iraq War, though neither Iran nor Iraq was invited to be a member, in the fear that it might destabilize the whole Gulf region. The GCC has a military/defence dimension, but its emphasis is on economic policy and mutual assistance. The GCC entered the Greater Arab Free Trade Area with the goal of launching a common market and common currency for the Gulf states.

Although not strictly a regional IGO, the Organization of Petroleum Exporting Countries (OPEC) is often associated with the Gulf states. Created in 1960 by the five oil-producing nations of Iran, Iraq, Kuwait, Saudi Arabia, and Venezuela, OPEC now has 13 full members, six from the Middle East, four from Africa, two from South America, and one from Asia (Indonesia). Its structure is typical of IGOs, with a regular conference of leaders to make major decisions, a board of governors, a secretariat and secretary-general, and various other bodies. Less typical is that it is located in Vienna (moving from Geneva in 1965), for it is rare for an IGO to have its headquarters in a non-member state. OPEC's mandate is to oversee the supply of oil, to set its price, and generally to coordinate the oil policies of its members. OPEC became deeply involved in international politics during the 1973 oil embargo and again during the 1979 Iranian revolution, when prices rose sharply and adversely affected the global economy. In the process it became the target for much criticism as a cartel using its power to bleed the Western economies, while others saw it as an IGO of developing nations that were using their resources for their own benefit.

There was no lack of international organizations in Africa in the post-war era either, as most regions established groups to enhance trade and economic growth. A few were created based on linguistic lines (franco-phone/anglophone), but most arose within geographic areas. The East African Community and the Southern African Customs Union, for example, survived from colonial times although with different names; others included the Central African Customs and Economic Union (1964) and the Economic Community of West African States (1975). In 1989 the states of North Africa—Algeria, Libya, Mauritania, Morocco, and Tunisia—formed the Arab Maghreb Union to promote regional unity and to create a common market. However, internal disputes led to the suspension of its activities. In 1991, in an effort to bring these groups together, the African Economic

Community was created, with a long-term plan to create a pan-African common market. These efforts produced only modest results, and the hoped-for benefits to trade, industrialization, and economic integration did not materialize.

The largest and most important African regional organization was the Organization of African Unity (OAU), established in May 1963 at a conference in Addis Ababa, Ethiopia, which became the seat of its secretariat. Its structure was typical of other international organizations, with an assembly consisting of each member, attended annually by government leaders and heads of state; a council of ministers, usually the state's foreign ministers; a secretariat with an elected secretary-general; and a variety of bureaus and specialized commissions (economic, cultural, technical) to undertake its operations. Eventually 53 African states joined the OAU, and only Morocco left, in 1984, in protest against the membership of the Sahrawi Arab Democratic Republic (the former Western Sahara) in 1982.

The OAU was not a collective security organization; its goal was to foster political and economic cooperation between African states; to work together in the fields of education, science, and technology; and to promote respect for human rights, democratic institutions, and economic development. In addition, the OAU aimed to facilitate the peaceful settlement of disputes between its members and, according to its charter, to "eradicate all forms of colonialism from Africa." It also served as an ideal forum for debating African issues and for negotiating common policies, enabling the African states to coordinate their policies in the UN and other international organizations.

The OAU experienced mixed success in its 40 years of existence; it offered significant support for liberation and anti-colonial movements across the continent, especially in the south—in South Africa, Angola, Namibia, and Rhodesia (Zimbabwe). A Coordinating Committee for the Liberation of Africa was created to facilitate this support for liberation movements, and considerable effort was put into condemning and isolating South Africa economically and politically at home and around the world during the years of apartheid. The OAU states led a direct campaign—with considerable success—to have South Africa ejected or marginalized in other international organizations, in particular the UN and its specialized agencies. At the same time, the OAU offered help on several occasions to mediate border disputes between members, but it was less successful in those areas that attracted outside attention, especially from the superpowers. In addition, the OAU's fundamental criteria of respect for national sovereignty and non-interference limited its ability to intervene in the domestic problems of its members, and, even if the will was there, it lacked sufficient financial resources to do so effectively. Consequently, the OAU had limited ability or inclination to intervene in internal conflicts, human rights abuses, or in civil wars, although it could be argued that, by taking a stand of non-intervention and supporting the territorial integrity and the right of governments to exist, it essentially gave tacit support to the government side in civil wars (for example, in the civil war in Nigeria). The end results were uneven, with, on the one hand, the removal of the colonial powers and racist regimes and the achievement and recognition of sovereignty among its members but, on the other, the establishment and tacit acceptance of many authoritarian, brutal dictatorships and undemocratic governments. The situation sparked references to the OAU as the "Dictators' Club."[10]

In the end the OAU never achieved the kind of internal unity hoped for in 1963, and in July 2002 it was replaced by a new organization—the African Union (AU)—at a conference in Durban, South Africa. Modelled on the EU, the AU is a much broader and more ambitious organization with the goal of economic cooperation, development, and integration in numerous fields, including defence, counter-terrorism, health, and human rights. There are plans for an African parliament, monetary union, and further economic integration. The AU's main organs are similar to the OAU, with an assembly as the main decision-making body, an executive council of foreign ministers, and a commission and chairperson to administer and direct the organization's activities (the OAU secretary-general and staff assumed these positions on an interim basis during the transition in 2002). There are also a handful of Specialized Technical Committees (transportation, financial affairs, health, education, trade, etc.). The AU's headquarters is in Addis Ababa, and its membership comprises almost every state in Africa.

The AU has endorsed a system of collective security and, in 2004, created a 15-member Peace and Security Council, with plans for a standing African military force. Much greater efforts are anticipated in the field of conflict resolution, continental security, and peacekeeping and peacebuilding. Moreover, the strict non-interference policy has been amended, allowing the intervention in another member's domestic affairs in cases of gross crimes against humanity and genocide, embracing a kind of "responsibility to protect" philosophy (see Chapter Seven) for Africa.[11] AU peacekeepers have been sent to several states, including Burundi, Somalia, and the Darfur region of Sudan, but as of yet they have made only a modest impact on the troubled areas of the continent.

The AU has helped the African states move towards more economic liberalism, participated in the promotion and defence of democracy and human rights and in the creation of a common front in the UN and its specialized agencies, and has supported cooperation among its members in areas ranging from cultural activities and festivals to construction projects. All this has led to greater integration into the global economy, making Africa "safer for capitalism."[12] But the task of continental integration is formidable, and the lack of resources still presents a major problem, with many of the AU's members facing intractable problems of poverty, underdevelopment, disease, and political turmoil.

Regional international organizations were slower to emerge in East Asia and the Pacific than in most other areas of the world, although more and more organizations have appeared in recent decades. Most scholars point to the turmoil and diversity of the region to explain this slower growth. The Communist revolution in China, the Korean War, the long Vietnam War, the legacy of European colonialism and Japanese militarism combined with Cold War tensions between the superpowers, plus all the internal strife, the rise of dictatorships, civil wars, and border disputes, worked against the creation of new collaborative institutions. In addition, the diversity of the region—in terms of population size, geography, language, religion, political structures and economic systems, and living standards—all worked against the formation of strong regional organizations. If there was anything that might have fostered a sense of unity, it was a shared concern for independence and the fear of outside—primarily communist—aggression.

It was this concern for sovereignty that led to the creation of the Association of South East Asian Nations (ASEAN) in 1967 by Indonesia, Malaysia, Philippines, Singapore, and Thailand. There are 10 members today: Brunei joined in 1984; Vietnam in 1995; Laos and Myanmar in 1997; and Cambodia in 1999. The major powers of South East Asia (China, Japan, and South Korea) are not members, with the result that ASEAN has evolved as an important channel of communication between the smaller and larger states, and it was one of the few regional organizations not to have a major power in its ranks. But despite this concern for sovereignty and security, ASEAN was not created as a defence or collective security organization, and it was not meant to replace SEATO.

The 1967 Bangkok Declaration created ASEAN with the goal of promoting economic growth and development, social cooperation, and peace and security in the region. Similar in many ways to the OAU/AU more than the

EU, ASEAN is very much an intergovernmental organization. The organization's foundation rests on both the recognition of each member's sovereignty and territorial integrity, and the commitment to non-interference in each other's business. There is little discussion of supranational issues, such as common citizenship, union, or federation, or of a regional identity or culture, or anything that might reduce the absolute sovereignty of its members. Its institutions are similar to other organizations—summit meetings of government leaders, a council of government ministers who meet to discuss specific issues, a secretariat (created in 1976) and secretary-general situated at the Jakarta headquarters, and a variety of subsidiary bodies dealing with specific issues.

At its first summit in Bali in 1976, ASEAN's mandate was broadened. Coming in the wake of the communist victory and reunification in Vietnam, several documents were signed calling for regional cooperation for peace and security, mutual respect, and increased economic and political cooperation. But beyond the preservation of independence and security, ASEAN was not overly successful in sparking significant economic integration or in settling regional disputes. Nevertheless, the rapid economic growth of the whole Pacific Rim in the 1980s breathed new life into the organization, and in 1992 ASEAN launched the ASEAN Free Trade Area (AFTA), which led to the reduction and/or elimination of most tariffs between members.

ASEAN has had even greater success in increasing contacts between its members and the outside world. In 1994 it established the ASEAN Regional Forum (ARF) to bring in other regional partners and states with connections to the region to discuss trade, development, security, and other issues; several trading arrangements were negotiated and connections established with outside international organizations. In 1996, ASEAN itself broadened, with the formation of ASEAN Plus Three—consisting of the ten members plus China, Japan, and South Korea—to promote trade, development, and economic stability in South East Asia. In 2005 a new organization was added to ASEAN, the East Asian Summit, which now comprises 16 states, including India, Australia, and New Zealand. Even more ambitiously, in 2003 ASEAN announced plans to establish the ASEAN Economic Community with the goal of creating a single market and far more political and economic integration. In addition, the new community will have a greater role to play in the areas of governance, democracy, and human rights—all matters that challenge ASEAN's strict non-interference tenet. Consequently, progress has been slow and the goal uncertain; as one scholar wrote, "many ASEAN states remain struggling states, functioning at different levels of political and economic development. If ASEAN started to cast judgment on the internal affairs of its members, it would soon fall apart under the internal pressures. If the organization began to seriously enforce human rights and democratic norms, it would rapidly disintegrate."[13]

ASEAN made some movement into regional dispute settlement—for example, in the early 1990s it cooperated with the UN in settling the civil strife and staging elections in Cambodia, which subsequently became a member— but it has been unable to contribute effectively to the major conflicts, from the war between China and Vietnam and Vietnam's invasion of Cambodia, to dealing with North Korea, to managing the economic crisis of the late 1990s. However, there has been some success, especially economically, and the region is today more democratic, prosperous, and stable than ever before. ASEAN has helped to achieve these goals by providing the forum for discussion and debate that have enabled agreements to be reached and norms to be established. It has been a stabilizing force, one that is increasingly turned to by all the states in the region, including China and Japan.

Many of the ASEAN members also participate in the Asia Pacific Economic Cooperation (APEC) forum, which was founded in 1989 and includes the Pacific Rim states and the United States, Canada, and Australia; it now has more than 20 members. It became a more formal organization in 1993, with the start of regular summit meetings of government leaders and the establishment of a secretariat in Singapore. APEC's mandate is to enhance trade relations between the nations of the Pacific Rim with the ultimate goal of a Pacific free-trade area. It established the machinery to make contacts, discuss trade and other issues, and make economic agreements. However, with the Asian economic crisis of the late 1990s and the serious disputes between members over the future of free trade, the enthusiasm for APEC has weakened on both sides of the Pacific. It also has become a focus for the anti-globalization movement, and several of its summits were accompanied by demonstrations and protests. NGOs, such as the Asia Pacific People's Assembly, have condemned APEC for its leading role in economic globalization.

Empires are not international organizations: they are maintained by force; the members are not sovereign states and usually are not free to leave or join; there rarely is an independent secretariat outside the imperial power's government; and they are hierarchical in structure with no sharing of power, voting, or decision-making. However, in an effort to smooth the transition to independence and to encourage and maintain contact with their former colonies, several attempts were made, with varying success to transform empires into new kinds of international "post-imperial" or "post-decolonization" organizations; for example, the attempt by the government of the Netherlands to create a kind of "Dutch Commonwealth" comprising its former possessions, including Indonesia, collapsed in the 1950s. With the major exception of the British Commonwealth, most of these organizations began with a cultural and social focus and then evolved into more economic and political institutions.

These few "post-imperial" international organizations often share a few characteristics—common language, history and traditions, and economic ties. In most cases, they are dominated by one state (this is often the case in other international organizations as well), usually the former imperial power. As a result, the relationship of the members of the organization is less a web of contacts and interactions than a "hub and spokes" arrangement, with each former colony maintaining bilateral relations with the former imperial power rather than developing new relations with each other. There are exceptions of course, but since these organizations evolved from decaying empires, much of the framework of the imperial relationship remains. At the same time, these organizations probably would not exist without the presence of the former imperial power. For the former imperial states, the new organizations could be used to enhance their international prestige and power and to maintain trade and influence in their former colonies; for the former colonies, membership was a way to enhance their own sovereignty, to promote economic development, and to engage in what has come to be called the North-South dialogue.[14]

The British Empire provides the first and best example. In the late nineteenth and early twentieth centuries, a division appeared between the colonial empire and the "Dominions," the group of settler colonies that had or soon would achieve political and economic autonomy, if not full independence; these included Australia, New Zealand, Canada, Newfoundland, and South Africa. These Dominions refused to be treated as "colonies" in the traditional sense, and a new relationship with the mother country evolved to strengthen the empire through participation and consultation. For many, the future held not independence and a splintering of the empire into independent parts but, rather, the creation of a new global empire—or organization—of equal parts. In 1884 the Imperial Federation League was created in London, branches were established across the empire, and in 1887 the first in a series of Colonial/Imperial Conferences was held to discuss mutual trade and defence issues. In a pattern similar to the Pan American Union, one conference led to another, producing more agreements and interaction, leading to more conferences, integration, and cooperation, and so on.

During the First World War, the equality of the Dominions was officially recognized at an Imperial Conference, and the word "Commonwealth" was introduced to distinguish the Dominions from the colonies. The creation of an Imperial War Cabinet to discuss war aims and the "British Empire Delegation" to speak with one voice at the Versailles Peace Conference and later at the Washington Disarmament Conference seemed to anticipate greater unity. For some, all the talk of a League of Nations was unnecessary and illogical, for the Empire—with its shared language, history, traditions, political systems, values, culture, and so on—made much more sense as an international organization than did the League. The idea of imperial diplomatic unity never materialized, and, in 1931, the Statute of Westminster removed all the remaining colonial trappings on the Dominions. The British Commonwealth that emerged looked much more like an international organization: it comprised a collection of freely associated, equal, and sovereign states, which shared a common head of state and bonds of language and heritage.

Membership in the Commonwealth became part of the process of decolonization through which states travelled on the road to independence and were "rewarded" with membership. Ireland was turned into a Dominion in 1921 and welcomed into the "club," and, although the Irish were never comfortable as a member, they remained inside until 1949. After the Second World War, the membership rose dramatically, first with India, Pakistan, and Ceylon (Sri Lanka) and then, in the 1960s, dozens of others, including many African, Caribbean, and Pacific island states. An agreed-upon formula allowed a state to assume complete independence but remain in the Commonwealth by recognizing the British monarch only as head of the Commonwealth—even the word "British" was dropped.

The newly independent states tended to choose to remain in this decentralized and looser organization, seeing in membership some of the same benefits as membership in the UN and other international organizations. For many, it represented a recognition of sovereignty, not the loss of sovereignty, and as a member they were at the table to discuss trade, foreign aid, cultural and technical exchanges, and migration issues; they could be a part of a process for international change and progress. The Commonwealth also had the advantage of being off-bounds for the United States and the Soviet Union, providing a greater sense of freedom and a broader stage for everyone else in an organization not dominated by the superpowers. Perhaps most important, the Commonwealth became a prime vehicle for the negotiation of aid and development policies. In the 1950s, for example, Commonwealth foreign ministers established the Colombo Plan for Cooperative Economic Development in an effort to end poverty and promote economic and technical development in South East Asia. The Colombo Plan was gradually expanded to include non-Commonwealth states, and the infusion of American money was also welcomed as it became part of the larger anti-communist effort.

In 1965 the Commonwealth became more like other international organizations with the appointment of a secretary-general and the creation of the Commonwealth Secretariat, which helped organize Commonwealth meetings, enhanced cooperation between members, and acted as a clearing house for information. Commonwealth conferences and the meetings of prime ministers—named the Commonwealth Heads of Government Meetings in the 1970s—were revived, and many voluntary associations were created, including the Commonwealth Air Transport Council, the Commonwealth Agricultural Bureau, the Commonwealth Science Council, and the popular Commonwealth Games sporting event, which took over from the earlier Empire Games.

There were divisions and problems in the organization throughout the postwar period, from the shock over British actions in the Suez Crisis in 1956, which seriously damaged North-South relations, to the Nigerian civil war and the ongoing tensions between India and Pakistan that led to Pakistan's exit and the entrance of Bangladesh into the organization. The Commonwealth also refused to recognize and, in conjunction with the UN, imposed sanctions following Rhodesia's 1965 unilateral declaration of independence. The greatest tensions, however, arose over the issue of South Africa; its presence in the organization poisoned relations between the "new" and the "old" members and threatened to destroy the idea of a multiracial and diverse Commonwealth. South Africa's exit from the organization in 1961 was followed by the entrance of many more members, including Sierra Leone, Tanganyika and Zanzibar (united as Tanzania in 1964), Uganda, Kenya, Zambia, and Malawi. But South Africa remained a major issue, and the matter of sanctions against the apartheid regime was a constant issue at Commonwealth meetings. The Commonwealth took an increasingly hard line against South Africa, introducing sanctions on arms sales, air services, and oil exports, and in the 1980s the sanctions issue became a major sore point between a majority of members and the Thatcher government in Britain.

The Commonwealth survived, however, welcoming back as members Pakistan in 1989 and South Africa in 1994, although Zimbabwe left in 2003. New members continued to arrive; for example, Namibia joined in 1990 (joining the UN and OAU at the same time), and by the end of the century there were 54 members. While many maintain the British monarch as head of state, a majority are now independent republics, and several have their own monarchies. Many of its members have tiny populations, and as Britain moves closer into Europe and other regional organizations develop and attract support, the future relevance of the Commonwealth remains uncertain.[15]

The French and Belgian governments were facing many similar problems in their rapid decolonization following the Second World War, and in several regions—Indochina, Algeria, Congo—it was an unpleasant experience. But like the British, the French desired to maintain contact and influence in their former colonies, while the newly independent states saw advantages for trade, development, cultural connections, and so on in that relationship as well. As a result, by the 1950s some voices were raised in support of a French-speaking international organization, loosely modelled on the British example, which would foster relations among French-speaking communities around the world. French-speaking journalists, universities, and other groups began organizing in the 1960s. More specific discussions occurred from 1967, and in 1970, on the urging of the leaders of several African states, l'Agence de Coopération Culturelle et Technique (ACCT) was born. It is now universally known as la Francophonie.

Inevitably, comparisons are made between la Francophonie and the Commonwealth, and while there are parallels, there are also significant differences. While the Commonwealth focuses on the relationship with the British monarchy, la Francophonie is committed to the French language and its membership is open to all states with a connection to French culture and language, including many states that were not French colonies, such as Belgium (and its former colonies), Switzerland, and Luxembourg. Other members include Cambodia, Canada, and Haiti, as well as more than 20 African states such as Gabon, Congo, Ivory Coast, Madagascar, Mali, Mauritius, Senegal, Rwanda, Burundi, and Niger. French need not be the first language in a state for it to qualify for membership; only an historical or cultural connection to the language is necessary. Consequently, in several member states—Vietnam, Romania, and Bulgaria, for example—only a small minority of the population actually speaks French; the 1999 meeting included observers from Albania, Macedonia, and Poland.

In the 1980s la Francophonie followed the example of the Commonwealth and launched a series of summit meetings of heads of governments, the first being held in Paris in 1986. The summits, held every two years, became the central element in the organization, and in 1991 a permanent council of all members was created. In 1995, the ACCT, renamed the Agence intergouvernementale de la Francophonie, became the secretariat. In 2005, the organization adopted a new charter and officially renamed itself the Organisation internationale de la Francophonie. At the 1997 summit in Hanoi, former UN Secretary-General Boutros Boutros-Ghali was elected the first secretary-general of la Francophonie, with a mandate to speak for the organization and to champion the French language and culture. During his term from 1997 to 2002, Boutros-Ghali helped raise the organization's profile, but as an Egyptian (Egypt was only an associate member of la Francophonie) and as a person whose mother tongue was Arabic (although he was fluent in both French and English), he seemed to personify some of the inherent weaknesses of both la Francophonie and the French language at the end of the twentieth century.

With the staging of regular large summits of government leaders, la Francophonie inevitably moved beyond cultural, linguistic, educational, and scientific and technical issues, taking stands on human rights, economic development, and environmental and political questions. At the 1991 summit in Chaillot, France, for example, the Chaillot Declaration called for action and progress to promote democracy and human rights, and the themes of human rights and democracy have remained on the agenda ever since. Critics were quick to question this commitment; in 1999, before the summit in Moncton, Canada, Amnesty International listed 32 of la Francophonie's members as human rights abusers.[16] Observers quickly pointed out that similar charges could be made with respect not only to the Commonwealth and the OAS but, for that matter, the UN itself.

La Francophonie has become more politicized, and it continues today with some 55 members; both it and the Commonwealth have a larger membership than the original UN. Moreover, since it was created after the process of decolonization had largely been accomplished when France already had established close post-independence ties with its former colonies, la Francophonie was spared the internal strife experienced in the Commonwealth over Rhodesia, South Africa, Suez, and so on. It was also able to avoid the angry disputes over membership. In stark contrast to the Commonwealth, no state has felt compelled to quit la Francophonie, leading one analyst to conclude that the French "were poor colonizers, but effective post-colonial managers."[17]

Mention should also be made of two other post-imperial or cultural organizations: the oldest, the Organization of Iberian-American States for Education, Science and Culture, or OEI (from the Organización de Estados Iberoamericanos para la Educación, la Ciencia y la Cultura); and the newest, the Community of Portuguese Language Countries, or CPLP (from the Communidade dos Países de Língua Portuguesa). The OEI began informally in the 1950s to increase cooperation and contact between the Iberian states and Latin America and to promote education and linguistic cooperation; by the 1980s it had become a more formal organization and began holding summits of government leaders in 1991. With both Spain and Portugal as members, along with almost 20 states from Latin America, part of its mandate is to promote the use of both Spanish and Portuguese; in more recent years, it has taken positions on more political and economic issues.

The CPLP, modelled loosely on la Francophonie and the Commonwealth, was created in 1996 with its headquarters in Lisbon. It consists of Portugal, Brazil, and the former Portuguese colonies in Africa, including Angola, Mozambique, Cape Verde, Guinea-Bissau, and São Tomé and Príncipe. In 2002, East Timor joined, bringing the total membership to eight. Like other cultural organizations, CPLP has a secretariat and executive secretary, a council, and regular conferences for both government leaders and foreign ministers. All members have Portuguese as an official language, and the organization's goal is to promote the use of Portuguese and improve cultural ties and economic, social, technical, and scientific cooperation between members. There is a political dimension as well, and the organization has become involved in some election monitoring (in East Timor, for example) and in aid and economic development programs, especially help from Portugal and Brazil for Portuguese-language education.

By the 1990s there were calls within the UN itself for the regional organizations to be more involved in preventive diplomacy, peacemaking and peacekeeping, reconstruction and development, and so on. Thus, a much closer relationship has developed. High-level meetings between various groups have been held, and some policies have been coordinated; for example, the UN Security Council has worked with the AU for the provision of peacekeeping forces for Darfur.[18] The trend is likely to continue. So long as the benefits of membership outweigh the costs, regional IGOs will remain— in balance with and an indispensable part of the world of international organizations.

Notes

1 See Pentland, "The Regionalization of World Politics," 599–630.
2 Hettne and Söderbaum, "The UN and Regional Organization in Global Security," 230.
3 Nye, *Peace in Parts*, 130.
4 Hoffmann and Van Der Vleuten, eds. *Closing or Widening the Gap?*, 1–11.
5 Hemmer and Katzenstein, "Why Is There No NATO in Asia?" 575.
6 Huysmans, "Shape-shifting NATO," 599–618.
7 Ball, *The OAS in Transition*, 10.
8 Boniface, "Is There a Democratic Norm in the Americas," 366.
9 Armstrong et al., *From Versailles to Maastricht*, 227–30.
10 BBC News website, http://news.bbc.co.uk/2/hi/africa/country_profiles.
11 Powell and Tieku, "The African Union's New Security Agenda," 937–52.
12 See chapter by Philip Nel, "Making Africa Safe for Capitalism: US Policy and Multilateralism in Africa," in Foot et al., *US Hegemony and International Organizations*, 192.
13 Narine, "From Conflict to Collaboration," 18.
14 Srinivasan, *The Rise, Decline, and Future of the British Commonwealth*, 83–106.
15 See Mayall, "Democratizing the Commonwealth," 379–92.
16 Jennifer Ditchburn, "International Attention to Focus on Moncton," *The Globe and Mail* (Toronto), 30 August 1999: A3.
17 Srinivasan, 104.
18 Ramcharan, *Preventive Diplomacy at the UN*, 194–208.

6 | The World of International NGOs

Organizations are not the sole prerogative of the state. For as long as there have been intergovernmental organizations (IGOs) and, for that matter, states and governments, there have been non-governmental organizations (NGOs). For many of the same reasons that governments have banded together in organizations, individuals and groups within civil society have come together to form organizations to further their interests.

There is a tremendous variety of NGOs, as they can contain and encompass any individual or group of people who choose to work alone or in combination with others to attain a goal however defined by those involved. They can be academic, scientific, financial, humanitarian, sports-related, religious, professional—any group that exists outside of government. There are no official rules for NGOs, and all attempts to categorize them are filled with exceptions. They vary in shape and size and in their commitment and principles; some are very public in their activities and use of the media, while others work quietly behind the scenes; some are local, others are universal in nature; some claim to speak on behalf of other people (and animals, the environment, outer space, etc.), while others speak only for themselves; some are charities that rely on individual contributions, while others are dependent on government or corporate sources of revenue, and still others get funds from both sources; and some exist on practically nothing, while others are well funded with budgets that rival the GDP of small nations. Increasingly they have formed "transnational federations" comprising national chapters that share a global ideology and image.[1]

The diversity has produced a variety of new names, including GONGOs (government-organized NGOs), QUANGOs (quasi-autonomous NGOs), PINGOs (public-interest NGOs), DONGOS (donor-organized NGOs), BINGOs (business and industry NGOs), and the very small single-person "suitcase" NGOs. Many advocate democracy but are hardly democratic themselves; many overlap with each other, such as aid and humanitarian NGOs, or those dealing with the rights of women and children, or those concerned with the environment. Occasionally, NGOs duplicate their activities, leading to tensions, especially when they hold diametrically opposed views, for example, on abortion rights or development projects.

Nevertheless, it is worthwhile to make some generalizations about NGOs and, for the purposes of this book, transnational or international NGOs (INGOs). Generally speaking, NGOs and INGOs are voluntary non-profit organizations (although there are many business federations and associations of manufacturers, etc.), and they work outside of government and do not seek power or office in states (although they often try to influence those in power). As a result, political parties, criminal organizations, and violent or revolutionary groups are usually not considered to be NGOs. An NGO, wrote one scholar, "is any non-profit-making, non-violent, organised group of people who are not seeking government office. An international NGO... can be any non-violent, organised group of individuals or organizations from more than one country."[2]

There is considerable debate regarding the nature of NGOs, ranging from those who see them as harbingers and instruments of a new transnational civil society that will ultimately undermine state sovereignty, to those who conceptualize them as "benign parasites," living independent from but within society, to those who argue that they are merely the tools of powerful states and a new form of Western colonialism.[3] There is more agreement on what they do and how they act: NGOs lobby governments, international organizations, other groups, and so on; they launch direct action campaigns; they protest and focus public attention; they research and study, collect information, and write pamphlets, reports, and books; they advise governments, IGOs, the media, and the public; and they help to set agendas, and monitor and implement policies initiated by governments and international organizations.

As mentioned in Chapter One, NGOs have been around long time, although there were not very many of them until the late nineteenth century. Some professional associations, women's groups, intellectual societies, workers' unions, charities, and religions, as well as organizations that worked to ban prostitution and the opium trade, could loosely be described as NGOs. No one can be certain which was first. One of the earliest examples of a standard NGO is the London Committee for the Abolition of the Slave Trade (1787), which sparked an anti-slavery movement that broadened into international form with the creation of Anti-Slavery Societies in Britain and the United States in the early nineteenth century. Another was the Young Men's Christian Association, launched in Britain in 1844 and spreading to seven countries by 1854. The creation of the International Committee of the Red Cross in 1863, with national Red Cross Societies appearing in Europe and the United States, is another example, although because of the involvement of governments in its operations, it is not a typical INGO.

INGOs exhibited several common characteristics. They emerged in a context conducive to their growth, generally in wealthier states with established liberal democratic governments and a growing middle class. NGOs need people with time and money at their disposal, with the relative freedom to speak what they believe and to act the way they want, and with the freedom and ability to communicate with others, to organize, and to travel. They also need to be able to raise money and have access to funds from donors— individuals, foundations, or government. Likewise, the more educated middle classes developed a greater awareness of the outside world and concern over the problems sparked by industrialization and underdevelopment. In addition, NGOs flourished in an environment that provided the necessary transportation and communications infrastructure—from trains, telephones, newspapers, and automobiles at the end of the nineteenth century to airplanes, television, and the Internet at the turn of the twenty-first. Not surprisingly, for the most part, NGOs first appeared in Europe and North America, while the fewest appeared in the colonized world, among the poorest and least developed states, and in the communist bloc. Only since the 1970s have NGOs begun to appear in large numbers in Asia and Africa.[4]

The number of NGOs increased so greatly in the early twentieth century that the Union of International Associations was formed just before the outbreak of the First World War, which interrupted its activities. However, in 1929 the Federation of International Institutions was created to serve as a kind of umbrella organization for NGOs. Between the wars, League of Nations Societies appeared in many states (along with the International Federation of League of Nations Societies), and many more NGOs were formed in conjunction with the League. Article 24 of the League Covenant announced that all existing "international bureaus" (with their consent) and all future international bureaus "shall be placed under the direction of the League." The NGOs played a relatively small role in League affairs, although they were given some limited representation on a few League committees if and when the committee discussed an issue of direct relevance to a specific NGO. Other organizations, such as the International Labour Organization, gave others, such as the International Federation of Trade Unions, a much more direct role. Outside the League, new NGOs appeared across Europe and the Western Hemisphere, including such groups as the Save the Children Fund, the Associated Country Women of the World, the National Geographic Society, various Institutes for International Affairs, and dozens of charities, sports committees, and professional associations. At the turn of the century there were around 100 INGOs; by 1939, there were an estimated 700.[5]

As noted in Chapter Three, 42 NGOs attended the San Francisco Conference and, in addition to having some influence on the human rights provisions, they were given formal recognition in the UN Charter. Article 71 states that ECOSOC "may make suitable arrangements for consultation with non-governmental organizations which are concerned with matters within its competence," and in the early postwar era ECOSOC's Committee on Non-Governmental Organizations began to grant "consultative status" to a variety of NGOs. There were conditions for consultative status: the NGOs had to be non-profit and non-violent; they had to represent a broader group or more general goal (such as human rights) rather than a specific thing or person; and, with a few exceptions, they had to be international in nature. Three levels or NGO categories were established: those with a broad interest in UN activities; those with specific competence in a particular area of UN work; and those interested in informing public opinion on issues.[6]

Consultative status meant that NGOs could attend ECOSOC meetings and request items to be placed on its agenda for discussion. They also had access to UN documents and, more indirectly, access to UN buildings, where they could lobby state representatives and UN employees for their cause. They could be turned to for their knowledge, expertise, and experience, but they could not formulate resolutions or vote in any proceedings. In other words, NGOs got a voice and input—and influence—but no decision-making power. Moreover, they had no access to the General Assembly or Security Council, although a largely ceremonial exception was made twice, giving observer status in the General Assembly to the International Committee of the Red Cross in 1990 and the International Federation of Red Cross and Red Crescent Societies in 1994.[7] NGOs were relegated to the "soft" areas of UN work such as culture, development assistance, and human rights, and largely excluded from the "hard" economic and security issues; this situation has changed only slightly over 65 years. Nevertheless, Paul Kennedy has called their history part of the "story of the United Nations with the Great Powers left out,"[8] and today there are several thousand NGOs officially recognized by the UN.

Most INGO activity, however, even for those registered with ECOSOC, occurred outside the UN. Development and humanitarian agencies predated the UN and continued to grow in number in the postwar era. Oxfam, CARE International, Save the Children Fund, and numerous church and missionary groups focused on the delivery of food, medicine, and social welfare services around the world; others provided family planning and adoption services. World Vision, a Christian humanitarian NGO, was created in 1951 during the Korean War, and it expanded globally in the 1960s and 1970s with a particular focus on its child sponsorship campaign. In 1971, as a result of their experiences in the civil war in Nigeria, a small group of French doctors launched Médecins Sans Frontières (MSF), or Doctors Without Borders, to provide free supplies, medical treatment, and training to those in desperate need. Some of the earliest missions were dispatched to disaster areas in the wake of earthquakes and hurricanes, but MSF workers quickly moved into war-torn areas where they often became outspoken witnesses to atrocities, putting their own safety at risk. MSF won the Nobel Peace Prize in 1999. Members of other humanitarian assistance NGOs also found themselves in increasingly dangerous crises in Somalia, Darfur, Cambodia, El Salvador, and many other places. Although governments and UN agencies came to rely on their expertise and experience, they found themselves remaining in violent situations longer than they might have done in the past.

At first these NGOs offered direct relief assistance but over time a more collaborative, self-help approach evolved as humanitarian organizations worked with emerging nations for their social and economic development. More emphasis was placed on "sustainable" development, but the definition of that term varied from group to group. Differences of opinion have appeared in cases ranging from carbon emissions to the rain forests to baby seals where development interests clashed with those of environmentalists, animal rights groups, and others. NGOs appeared in the developing world as well, but the field was dominated by Western states; by the 1990s about half of all relief aid money went through eight NGOs: Oxfam, CARE International, Save the Children Fund, MSF, World Vision International, CIDSE (Coopération internationale pour le développement et la solidarité), Eurostep, and the Association of Protestant Development Organizations in Europe.[9]

The emerging peace and disarmament—"ban the bomb"— movement was a natural attraction for NGOs, and dozens of groups organized, marched and protested, and raised public awareness of the dangers of the arms race, radioactive fall-out, and nuclear war. Scientists and researchers, pacifists, students, women and men joined such NGOs as the Women's International League for Peace and Freedom, which was created in The Hague in 1915; the Stockholm International Peace Research Institute (1966); and International Physicians for the Prevention of Nuclear War, which was awarded the 1985 Nobel Peace Prize. Grassroots movements appeared in Japan, Britain, the United States, and many other countries. Two NGO committees were organized at the UN—the NGO Committee on Disarmament in New York and the NGO Special Committee on Disarmament in Geneva—to support, promote, and encourage disarmament activities and to distribute information to a broad network of international disarmament NGOs.[10] Although no NGOs have been seated at the negotiating table with the superpowers, they have been constant observers and critics of the disarmament process, and by helping to raise international awareness, they undoubtedly help to influence and raise public support for disarmament.

Most of these NGOs were in one way or another involved with human rights issues; indeed, the struggle for basic human rights was a natural focus for many NGOs, especially following the signing of the Universal Declaration of Human Rights (UDHR) in 1948. Governments were unlikely to hold themselves accountable for their actions or publicize their human rights abuses, so NGOs were the ideal vehicle to monitor and report on the implementation of the UDHR. They could promote human rights, encourage public support, and, occasionally, lobby—or shame—governments into action. The focus for much early activity was naturally the UN Human Rights Commission, although there were difficulties from the very start. Politics was always involved (for example, over membership on the Commission and over which states were to be investigated); until 1967 it was forbidden even to mention by name a state that abused human rights. Countries vied for membership on the Commission, in some cases for negative reasons—as a way to prevent attacks on themselves, to discredit the information provided by the NGOs, and even to ensure that the Commission itself remained ineffective. Nevertheless, the NGOs learned to walk the fine line between providing information and attacking states directly, and they were able to play an effective role in publicizing flagrant human rights abuses.[11]

There was a wide variety of human rights NGOs, often with different methods and goals; they have been both religious and secular, universal and regional, student or trade union based, concentrated on protecting the rights of minorities and refugees, and so on. The most prominent is Amnesty International, founded in 1961 by British lawyer Peter Benenson. Started as a letter-writing campaign to free two jailed Portuguese students, Amnesty International has grown into a global organization with chapters in more than 150 states. Its mandate has broadened from freeing prisoners of conscience into a more universal promotion of human rights, with campaigns against torture, the death penalty, and political executions or "disappearances." No state is free of its scrutiny and, by the time it was awarded the Nobel Peace Prize in 1977, Amnesty International had worked to free thousands of political prisoners around the world.

In 1978, following the signing of the Helsinki Accords (1975), which partly aimed to guarantee human rights in the Eastern bloc, Helsinki Watch was set up in the United States to monitor the application of the Accords. It expanded through the establishment of chapters to monitor other regions and emerged as Human Rights Watch in 1988. Its method was, according to its website, "naming and shaming" of abusive governments to publicize abuses and to pressure governments for change.[12] Since 1978 Human Rights Watch has launched campaigns for the rights of women and against the use of child soldiers.

Other examples of human rights NGOs reveal their scope and diversity, such as the German-based anti-corruption NGO, Transparency International (1993); the Committee to Protect Journalists, set up by American journalists in 1981 in an effort to protect their colleagues and to protest abuses against journalists; and No Peace Without Justice, an NGO launched in Italy in 1993 to support the creation of the International Criminal Court and to promote human rights and justice around the world.

Perhaps the greatest NGO growth has been in the general area of environmentalism. Some of the earliest NGOs were conservationist organizations, such as the International Union for Conservation of Nature and Natural Resources, but they did not receive much international attention. With the publication of Rachel Carson's *Silent Spring* in 1962 and the growing public awareness of the ills of modern life from air pollution and pesticide use to oil spills and the destruction of the ozone layer, hundreds of new NGOs appeared and the modern environmental movement was born. Similar to other groups, environmental NGOs varied from local groups fighting to preserve their neighbourhoods to universal organizations trying to save the planet. Their techniques were similar, however, and included lobbying, monitoring, protesting, informing, and publicizing.

One of the oldest, the American-based Sierra Club, was founded in 1892 as an association that worked primarily for the creation and preservation of national parks; in the 1970s it expanded into a universal conservation NGO. Others range from the World Conservation Union, started in 1948 as a conservation group with input from both NGOs and government agencies, to Pollution Probe, a group founded by Canadian students in 1969 to lobby for action on pollution issues like acid rain. The variety of groups is highlighted by two of the largest: the World Wildlife Fund (WWF—also known as the World Wide Fund for Nature) and Greenpeace. The WWF is a Swiss-based and fairly research-focused environmental NGO, founded in 1961, which raises money and has initiated hundreds of projects globally, in particular to protect endangered animal species. In the 1960s it launched a major campaign to save elephants through the banning of the ivory trade and was instrumental in the signing of the African Convention on the Conservation of Nature and Natural Resources in 1968.[13] Greenpeace, formed in 1971 in Canada, is very much more an activist environmental group that relies on direct action and civil disobedience to pursue its goals by working against nuclear testing, whaling, the seal hunt, the destruction of the rain forest, wasteful logging practices, and global warming. Members of Greenpeace have often put themselves in harm's way to attract international attention to a worthy cause; in 1985 one of its members was killed when the Greenpeace ship *Rainbow Warrior* was sunk by the French secret service to prevent it from interfering in French nuclear testing in the South Pacific.

The UN was late coming to the environmental movement, which is missing altogether from the UN Charter. Change came in the 1970s, however, especially with the 1972 Stockholm Conference on the Human Environment called to discuss pollution, insecticide use, and nuclear testing. The result was the UN Environment Program (UNEP) to collect information and study environmental issues, educate the public about the problems of pollution, and monitor environmental changes. The Stockholm Conference was a landmark for a couple of reasons. First, it exposed a North-South division between those who advocated strong action against polluting states and those who argued that environmentalism was "a rich state's disease" and that severe regulations would hinder economic growth among developing nations.[14] Second, there were some 200 environmental NGOs in attendance as observers and unofficial participants, and, although no NGO signed any declaration, resolution, or agreement, a kind of precedent was established making it difficult to exclude NGOs from future UN conferences.

The number of NGOs grew rapidly in the 1960s according to historian Paul Kennedy because of the mass mobilization of that decade—the public protests and demands for reforms, civil rights, and women's rights—along with the widespread cynicism, especially among young people, regarding traditional political parties. Many people began searching for alternative forms of action and protest, and this led to the creation of thousands of NGOs, all trying to change or reform public policy in some way, shape, or form.[15] Moreover, the rate of growth did not level off in the 1970s and 1980s; on the contrary, NGO numbers rose even faster. The *Yearbook of International Organizations* (edition 36, 1999/2000) lists a total of 1,718 NGOs in 1964; in 1972 that number had grown to 3,733; in 1978 it was 9,521; by 1985 it had boomed to 20,634. The numbers have continued to rise, reaching 36,054 in 1995 and 43,958 in 1999.

The NGO explosion wasn't confined to the Western states, either. Decolonization, the movement towards democracy and more open societies, and the end of the Cold War all proved helpful for the growth of NGOs in the developing world. Many NGOs were launched through North-South collaboration as groups in the developing states aligned themselves with outside organizations, such as Greenpeace and Amnesty International. The Climate Action Network, for example, a global network of more than 450 environmental NGOs (with a special focus on climate change), established branches all over the world, including regional groups in Latin America, Africa, South Asia, and South East Asia. Indians for Collective Action was set up in 1965 by Indian students in the United States to provide aid for their homeland. Africare, established in the United States in 1970 through the collaboration between Africans and African Americans, evolved into a major aid and economic development NGO particularly involved in HIV/AIDs prevention and education. Another example is Breadline Africa (1993), established through the collaborative efforts of Africans and Europeans.

Even greater was the explosive growth of indigenous NGOs in Asia and Africa in the 1980s, although it was not uniform and tended to rise and fall regionally, reflecting the uneven development of democratic societies, the variety of postcolonial situations and the lingering effects of colonialism, the advent of autocratic dictatorships, and the level of internal strife and civil wars on these continents. Human rights, pro-democracy, and community-based organizations appeared by the hundreds and varied greatly in size and influence. Examples include the Constitutional Rights Project, created in Nigeria in 1990, which was set up to promote human rights, working through the legal system and giving assistance to the victims of human rights abuses; the

African Human Rights Heritage (1992), which established chapters across Africa; and the Asian Human Rights Commission, an umbrella organization that promotes democracy, human rights, gender equality, and various UN programs. The Africa Commission of Health and Human Rights Promoters was launched in 1989, with branches in several African states; it works in cooperation with the WHO to provide health assistance and to promote human rights. Aid and development organizations multiplied as well, ranging from relatively small groups like Mahashakti Seva Kendra (1992), a women's organization set up after the disastrous Bhopal chemical spill to work in the areas affected by the gas; to Planact (1985), a South African think-tank of professionals committed to development aid projects; to BRAC (Bangladesh Rural Advancement Committee), an economic development NGO, which was set up in 1972, following the war for independence, to assist refugees returning from India and which has evolved into a more general aid organization and one of the largest anti-poverty NGOs in Asia.

A similar situation emerged behind the Iron Curtain. Charter 77, for example, was established by a group of Czechoslovakian intellectuals (including future president Vaclav Hável) in 1977 to promote human rights, political freedom, and democracy, and to ensure Soviet compliance with the Helsinki Accords. The end of the Cold War sparked a rush of new NGOs in Eastern Europe and the former Soviet bloc. Groups like the Black Sea University Foundation in Romania; the Centre for Economic Development in Bulgaria, a think-tank on economic and public policy issues; the Civic Initiative Center in Georgia, a pro-democracy NGO that promotes education and community involvement and projects; and in Latvia The Movement of Youth, which promotes youth exchanges, visits, and study groups. Like the NGOs in Asia and Africa, dozens of these new groups immediately sought consultative status with ECOSOC and the UN.

The growth in the number of NGOs was not a temporary phenomenon; indeed, it accelerated, radically transforming the role they played in the international system. NGOs were embraced and even promoted by governments and intergovernmental international organizations who realized that they were well-organized and cost-effective agencies with access to all parts of the globe; they were filled with talented and experienced people who were committed to their particular cause and ready to act; they often were better informed about the problems in different regions than many governments and IGOs; and they were often working in ways that paralleled the work of governments and IGOs. As a result, governments and IGOs increasingly turned to NGOs to undertake tasks on their behalf, for example, to provide services, or to gather information, or to rally public opinion behind a specific issue. A much closer relationship evolved as more and more funding was made available for NGOs to carry out these tasks, and even more NGOs were launched. As one scholar put it, "given the billions of dollars of international funding now available to NGOs in all corners of the globe, it would have been more surprising if there had been *no* explosive growth of NGOs in the 1980s and 1990s."[16]

NGOs found a prominent role and voice—and international spotlight—in the series of global UN conferences that were frequent and popular in the 1980s and, especially, in the 1990s. There were several conferences on women's rights, the largest in Beijing in 1995; others were staged focusing on children (New York, 1990) and education (Thailand, 1990), food (Rome, 1996), the environment (Rio, 1992), climate change (Kyoto, 1997), human rights (Vienna, 1993), and population and development (Cairo, 1994). Here NGOs could lobby in the hallways, provide information to governments big and small, access the international media to get their message across, stage parallel events, and observe and, in some cases, participate in the official discussions.

At the Earth Summit Conference in Rio de Janeiro in 1992 (officially the UN Conference on the Environment and Development), for example, there were almost 1,500 NGOs in attendance. The conference itself was, in many ways, prompted by the work of environmental NGOs, which focused increased international attention on the problem of greenhouse gases. Some conference participants were both government representatives and members of NGOs; other NGOs were invited to contribute to a variety of working groups; and, in general, the NGOs were farther ahead on the issue of climate change than most governments and likely accelerated the pace of negotiations, which produced the Earth Charter and road map for future action.[17] In 1993, at the World Conference on Human Rights in Vienna, 171 governments met "upstairs" while representatives from 1,529 NGOs met "downstairs" where, despite the opposition from many states (often the worst human rights abusers), they were able to defend the concept of "universal" human rights and help give the final push to the creation of the new post of UN High Commissioner for Human Rights to coordinate the UN's activities.[18] Similarly, in Kyoto in 1997, dozens of NGOs lobbied successfully for the inclusion in the Kyoto Accords of stronger commitments on reductions of carbon dioxide emissions.

One of the greatest successes for INGOs was the movement against anti-personnel landmines in the 1990s (there were millions of landmines all over the world, killing and injuring tens of thousands of people each year). More than 1,000 NGOs were involved in the campaign, united under an umbrella organization, the International Campaign to Ban Landmines. An anti-landmine media campaign was launched with support from a host of politicians, musicians, and Hollywood celebrities; the resulting international wave of opposition helped kick-start what became known as the "Ottawa Process," which led to 122 states signing the Ottawa Convention (1997), officially the Convention on the Prohibition of the Use, Stockpiling, Production and Transfer of Anti-Personnel Mines and on Their Destruction. Under the Convention each signatory state was to remove and destroy its existing landmines, to provide aid for those hurt by landmines, and to cease manufacturing landmines. The United States and several other landmine-producing states have not signed the Convention, but a new international norm regulating landmines has been established.[19] It was a relatively rare example of NGOs having a significant impact on what is usually considered a "hard" military and security issue.

The Ottawa Convention and Kyoto Accords were the culmination of a process of cooperation between governments, IGOs, and NGOs. NGOs had come in from the cold, first as invited guests and then as "partners" with governments and IGOs. No longer was it a question whether or not they would be able to make themselves heard on important issues and at international conferences (and not just ECOSOC conferences); they now expected to be there and to have a seat at or near the negotiating table.[20] Collaboration replaced confrontation; consultation and contribution were assumed; participation on UN committees (dealing with the AIDS crisis, for example) became more common; taking on the task of implementing decisions (especially in the areas of economic development and humanitarian assistance) became more frequent. And not just for the UN and its specialized agencies; other large IGOs, such as the EU and the OAS, also opened their doors and welcomed the NGOs as "partners."

By 1992 more than $8 billion for development assistance was channelled through NGOs, approximately 13 per cent of the global total; in 2000 most of the $1 billion budget of the UN High Commissioner for Refugees was dispensed through NGOs. Conversely, public-sector funding, which accounted for only 1.5 per cent of NGO budgets in 1970, by the end of the century accounted for approximately 40 per cent.[21] The IMF and WTO have limited involvement with NGOs, but the World Bank developed a very close working relationship with them and regularly included them in Bank-financed development projects. In 1973–88, NGOs were connected to only 6 per cent of all World Bank projects; by the early 1990s that percentage had grown to 30 per cent; by the end of the century NGOs were involved in 50 per cent of Bank projects. Outside the UN system, states, private foundations, and other IGOs were channelling their money through NGOs as well; for example, by 1995 the EU was funnelling 15–20 per cent of its foreign aid via NGOs.[22]

At the turn of the century the relationship between NGOs and the UN was closer than ever before. In 1999, the UN Department of Economic and Social Affairs, NGO Section, launched a new program to enhance the relationship and collaboration between the UN and NGOs, and in 2001 it inaugurated new regional networks of NGOs, especially in Africa, Asia and the Pacific, Eastern Europe, and Latin America. The benefits from the new arrangement flowed both ways; on the one hand, increasing access and influence of regional NGOs in ECOSOC and the UN Development Program and, on the other, improving the implementation of UN programs and initiatives in the different regions.[23]

This appeared to be a win-win situation, with the NGOs gaining access to the decision-makers and being able to influence directly decisions in the fields they knew best. The NGOs were also going to be there afterwards, to help implement UN decisions and conference resolutions, and to monitor the actions of governments and IGOs to ensure compliance. This meant that the powerful would be held accountable; it also meant more funding for NGOs and, ultimately, more NGOs. From the perspective of governments and IGOs, they benefited from the dedication, experience, knowledge, and expertise of the NGOs in implementing policies and overseeing programs. Bringing them in as partners was a good way to mute potential criticism (from the NGOs), and it moved them off the street to the conference table, integrating them into the negotiation process as allies.

New problems and concerns about the relationship arose, naturally enough. Questions of NGO legitimacy and accountability were asked with increasing frequency. NGOs were criticized for their lack of transparency, as many claimed to represent universal standards but were themselves unregulated, unrepresentative in nature, and relatively secretive about their operations. Could they really claim to speak on behalf of "the people"? These concerns even prompted the creation of another NGO—NGOWatch—in 2003, by the conservative American Enterprise Institute. NGOWatch condemned the lack of accountability of NGOs that were now receiving huge amounts of American foreign aid money and worked (without much success) to reduce their influence. To offset some of this criticism several

INGOs produced the Accountability Charter, which by 2009 has been signed by many of the largest NGOs, including Amnesty International, Greenpeace, Oxfam, Transparency International, and dozens more.[24]

Other critics suggested that many NGOs had been co-opted by (primarily Western) governments and IGOs in their pursuit of "partnership," access, and contracts (where raising money became a goal in itself rather than the means to an end) and that by accepting government funds, NGOs had become the tool of those governments in the pursuit of their foreign policy interests. This made their claims of neutrality and impartiality less convincing and, in the worst cases, made NGO staff in the field potential targets of attack. Still others noted financing deals where NGOs—on both the right and left—received secret funding to help others pursue political objectives. Most of all, critics pointed to the competition, tension, and duplication created by hundreds of NGOs competing for scarce resources and government contracts, a process that often produced confusion, tension, and, ultimately, failure in the field. In 1995, for example, there were more than 200 humanitarian assistance NGOs working in Goma, in the Democratic Republic of the Congo (formerly Zaire); in 1996 another 240 NGOs were at work in Bosnia. Were they really that cost-effective and better able to provide development aid than governments or the traditional international organizations? Or did they cause more problems than they solved?[25]

NGOs are not going away; they, along with IGOs, multinational corporations, media empires, unions, religions, and other groups, as well as sovereign states, are part of the process of global integration that has been occurring in the past decades. In many ways, NGOs represent and express internationally the interests of civil society, speaking for that part of international society not represented by state organizations. They have become "fully-fledged actors in international governance,"[26] as advisers, administrators, advocates, and monitors for people and causes, working on behalf of governments, IGOs, and themselves. In the process they now employ millions of people worldwide, their budgets are valued in the billions of dollars, they provide much of the world's humanitarian assistance, and they often find themselves on the frontlines of the world's trouble spots.

They have not, however, supplanted governments and are unlikely to do so in the future. Despite their growth in numbers and influence, they still are not the decision-makers in the international community, and to note their rise is not to suggest the demise of the sovereign state. It can be argued, conversely, that ultimate success for an NGO—especially one focused on development, human rights, disarmament, or environmentalism—logically leads to *its* demise. With no cause to fight for, there would be no reason to continue. Neither will happen, of course, and the collaboration among states, IGOs, and NGOs is likely to continue and grow through the twenty-first century, especially if the future brings greater connections, integration, and interdependence among the peoples of the world.

Notes

1 Weiss and Gordenker, eds. *NGOs, the UN, and Global Governance*, 28.
2 Willetts, *"The Conscience of the World,"* 5.
3 Heins, *Nongovernmental Organizations in International Society*, 1–4.
4 Boli and Thomas, ed. *Constructing World Culture*, 53–60.
5 See chapter by Bill Seary, "The Early History," in Willetts, *The Conscience of the World*, 15–30.
6 Willetts, "From 'Consultative Arrangements' to 'Partnership,'" 192.
7 Willetts, *"The Conscience of the World,"* 41–45.
8 Kennedy, *The Parliament of Man*, 207.
9 Simmons, "Learning to Live with NGOs," 92.
10 Boothby, *The United Nations and Disarmament*, 29–30.
11 Gaer, "Reality Check," 389–404.
12 www.hrw.org.
13 Iriye, *Global Community*, 118–19.
14 Ryan, *The United Nations and International Politics*, 149–50.
15 Kennedy, 216.
16 Reimann, "A View from the Top," 63.
17 Mathews, "Power Shift," 55.
18 Gaer, 396–98.
19 Price, "Reversing the Gun Sights," 613–44.
20 Willetts, "From 'Consultative Arrangements' to 'Partnership,'" 191–92.
21 Simmons, 87, 94; Cooley and Ron, "The NGO Scramble," 10.
22 Reimann, 49–51.
23 UN Department of Economic and Social Affairs, NGO Division, "High Level Consultation and Regional Capacity Building Workshop To Launch the UN-NGO-Informal regional Network in Eastern Europe," Aide Memoire, n.d.
24 See www.ingoaccountabilitycharter.org.
25 Cooley and Ron, 10; Collingwood, "Non-governmental Organisations," 440–49; Bebbington et al., eds., *Can NGOs Make a Difference?*, 12–13; see chapter by Michael Maren, "Nongovernmental Organizations and International Development Bureaucracies," in Carpenter, ed., *Delusions of Grandeur*, 227–37.
26 Ripinsky and Van Den Bossche, *NGO Involvement in International Organizations*, 1.

7 | The UN in the Modern Era

The end of the Cold War, the reunification of Germany, and the collapse of the Soviet Union were moments in history that seemed to change everything. The relaxation of international tensions, the removal of old barriers, the increasing spirit of friendship and cooperation, and the rise of democratic governments around the world all hinted at the dawn of a new era of peace and international collaboration. As the world stepped back from the brink of nuclear confrontation, new words—interdependence, integration, democratization, economic liberalism, and multilateralism—were substituted in place of the old ideological denunciations.[1] The rapidity of change, the revolution in communications, the growth of international trade, the spread of democracy across Eastern Europe, Asia, and Latin America were all forces that fell under the broader word "globalization." Globalization was in the air, even if the moment didn't last.

For the UN, its specialized agencies, the regional organizations and NGOs, and international organizations in general, the easing of Cold War tensions presented an opportunity for cooperation only dreamed of since the late 1940s. With the removal of the old antagonisms, the possibility of cooperation in the Security Council was much greater; with the removal of the Cold War lens through which so many international disputes were viewed, a clearer, more nuanced understanding of the problems in the world would surely be possible; and in the absence of the divisive tactics and mutual suspicions of competing superpowers, it was believed that concerted international action would be faster, more focused, and effective.

There were encouraging signs, even before the fall of the Berlin Wall. In 1987, the Security Council passed a unanimous resolution calling for a cease-fire in the Iran-Iraq War, which had dragged on for seven years; the following year, when both sides agreed to stop fighting, the UN sent in a small mission to monitor the situation. In 1988, the UN helped facilitate negotiations in Afghanistan to enable the Soviets to extricate themselves from a disastrous situation without loss of face. That same year, UN officials helped negotiate an agreement for the independence of Namibia, a small West African nation that had for years been torn by internal strife. The UN established a peacekeeping force, the UN Transition Assistance Group (UNTAG), in South-West Africa to oversee the withdrawal of foreign troops and to monitor the election of a new government in 1990. Namibia was soon one of the newest UN members.

The new era of cooperation was also revealed in the lead-up to the 1991 Gulf War. The Iraqi invasion and annexation of Kuwait in the summer of 1990 presented the clearest form of aggression and unleashed a flurry of activity at the UN. The international community condemned the invasion, and the United States, in particular, was determined to oust Iraq from Kuwait by whatever means necessary. Over the fall of 1990 several Security Council resolutions were passed imposing sanctions and demanding an Iraqi withdrawal; when these did not work, it called on UN members to contribute forces and to "use all necessary means" to force the Iraqis out. The Americans could count on the support of the British and French, and the Soviets and Chinese went along, but considerable pressure was put on other governments; in exchange for their support, the United States forgave Egypt its $14 billion debt, gave Turkey $8 billion in military aid, and arranged a World Bank loan for Iran.[2]

The American-led military force launched its attack on 15 January 1991 and very quickly liberated Kuwait, although it did not cross into Iraq to depose Saddam Hussein. But the end of the fighting was only the start for UN involvement in Iraq. The UN Iraq-Kuwait Observer Mission was established to monitor the Iraqi-Kuwait border; relief operations were launched; and several teams of monitors and inspectors were dispatched to Iraq to oversee humanitarian assistance, to help with refugees, and to search for chemical and other weapons of mass destruction. Various sanctions were maintained against Hussein's regime, including a "no-fly zone" in northern Iraq, and the Iraqi people suffered for many years under them.

The UN received a boost in prestige from its role in the Gulf War, although its actions provoked some mixed feelings then and afterwards. For many observers, the UN had responded to clear aggression and acted the way it was supposed to: meetings were held, negotiation attempts were made, resolutions were passed, and ultimately the will of the international community prevailed and an aggressor was forced to retreat. This was collective security in action, setting a precedent for a new way of doing business in the post–Cold War world. Others were less confident, noting that the military mission was designed, commanded, and directed from Washington, not New York, and that the United States had used its influence on the UN to gain international sanction for what it intended to do in any event. The victory in the Gulf, therefore, was not the harbinger of future UN activity but, rather, the first demonstration of post–Cold War American unilateralism, now that the United States was the sole remaining superpower.

Nothing better symbolized the new mood, however, than the January 1992 Security Council meeting at which all the members were represented by their respective heads of state and government. The meeting was "an unprecedented recommitment, at the highest political level, to the Purposes and Principles of the Charter"[3] and seemed to augur well for future consensus and cooperation among the world's leading powers. At that meeting the leaders turned to the new Secretary-General, Boutros Boutros-Ghali, to prepare a report about the future of the UN, especially in the areas of peace and security. The Egyptian-born and multilingual Boutros-Ghali was a former law professor and government official, with wide support from the states in the developing world, who took over from Javier Pérez de Cuéllar as secretary-general just a few weeks earlier.

Boutros-Ghali's report—*An Agenda for Peace*—advocated a more active and dynamic UN and Security Council. Its optimism for the future was based on the assumption that the end of the Cold War had removed the major roadblock to international cooperation. The report focused on four areas—preventive diplomacy, peacemaking, peacekeeping, and peacebuilding—which, as the names suggest, dealt with crises at different stages from early detection and prevention to what was referred to as "post-conflict peacebuilding." Several proposals were offered, including dispute resolution techniques, the use of early warning systems, the revitalization of all UN institutions and the International Court of Justice, and the request for the permanent availability of armed forces for use at the discretion of the Security Council. State sovereignty was left untouched, but the report also hinted at the possibility that in some extreme cases the Security Council should act even without the consent of the concerned states. It was a bold and optimistic document, and although it never formed the basis of a Security

Council resolution, it did serve as a loose blueprint for future UN action. It also appeared at the beginning of a decade that would see an enormous expansion of UN peacekeeping activities. The promise of cooperation, consensus, and of a shared sense of purpose, however, would not be realized.

The UN embarked on a more ambitious program of action in the following years. One of the most important areas—and in many ways a direct consequence of the ending of the Cold War—was in electoral assistance. With the collapse of the Soviet Union, many former Soviet satellite states moved to establish democratic governments, as did other states when their Cold War conflicts were resolved. The UN was well placed to facilitate this process in that it could provide skilled individuals to help supervise, organize, and monitor elections and its established neutrality and impartiality gave an element of legitimacy to the elections themselves.

In 1992 the General Assembly established a small Electoral Assistance Unit (EAU) in the Department of Political Affairs. Its mandate was to provide electoral assistance in various forms from limited technical support to broad supervision and organization (registration, ballot counting, verification, etc.). To allay any fears of intervention in domestic affairs of any state, the EAU involved itself only on request from governments, meaning that it could not act through the invitation of a particular political party or group. It also worked in conjunction with several other international organizations, including the OAS, EU, OAU, the Commonwealth, and la Francophonie. Some electoral assistance was provided even before its creation in Namibia, as noted above, and in Nicaragua in 1990. Other assistance was provided to Angola (1992), Cambodia (1993), El Salvador (1993–94), Mozambique (1994), Armenia (1995), Mali (1997), Nigeria, (1998–99), Nepal (1999), South Africa (1999), East Timor (1999), and Tanzania (2000). The number of missions has declined in recent years, in part because the need for international assistance has diminished as many states have made the transition to democratic government.[4]

Other kinds of peacekeeping also grew rapidly in the early post–Cold War years. Between 1987 and 1992 13 missions were established, and by 1992 an estimated 528,000 personnel had served under the UN flag, at a cost of more than 800 lives and more than $8 billion.[5] The list of UN acronyms lengthened, but the missions varied in size from a few observers to thousands. In Haiti, for example, the elected government was overthrown in a military coup in 1991 and the UN worked with the OAS and the American government to obtain the return of President Aristide. However, the small UN Mission in Haiti (UNMIH) sent to Port-au-Prince in 1993 to train the police and military was kept on board its ship by an angry mob. Aristide was returned to power in 1994, but only after the Security Council authorized the American government to forcibly remove the coup leaders. Conversely, in Cambodia the UN almost completely took over the running of the country in advance of the 1993 elections.

Unfortunately, fewer and fewer of these new missions were of the traditional variety of peacekeeping, with the UN sending in the blue helmets (with the involved states' permission) to keep two states apart. Increasingly, the UN was brought into civil wars and other internal disputes, often without the acquiescence of all sides, and into what were now referred to as "failed states," where government control itself was absent. The UN's will and dedication were clear, but its financial resources were quickly stretched to the limit. The crises in Somalia, Rwanda, and Yugoslavia each in their own way tested the limits of UN intervention.

With the end of the Cold War a process of disintegration began in the republic of Yugoslavia with the appearance of several independence movements in Croatia, Macedonia, Slovenia, Montenegro, and Bosnia and Herzegovina. Serbia wished to maintain the core of the former Yugoslavia; in 1991 fighting erupted between Serbia and various separatist movements. The problem was compounded by the diversity of the newly independent areas, and, thanks to a mixture of ancient hatreds, ethnic rivalries, and the intermingling of populations, determining the borders of the new states was bitterly contested and marred by the appearance of "ethnic cleansing." It was an ugly situation; very quickly the former republic slid into chaos as Europe experienced its worst fighting since the end of the Second World War.

The UN became involved in 1992, but as the situation on the ground shifted quickly, its forces were criticized for being unprepared, under-equipped, and slow—and even unwilling—to respond. International sanctions were applied against Serbia, and the UN Protection Force for Yugoslavia (UNPROFOR) was inserted to keep different factions apart, especially to protect the Bosnian Muslims, or Bosniaks. Several other UN missions were dispatched to different parts of the region before the fighting was over, and humanitarian aid and help for the growing number of refugees and displaced people were provided in UN-protected "safe areas." Nevertheless, Serb military action continued, and thousands of Bosnian Muslims were murdered in Srebrenica and elsewhere. The Security Council was divided on how to respond, with the Russians least enthusiastic for action against the Serbs, and in August 1995 NATO intervened with a series of bombing strikes against Serb targets. Negotiations began in

FIGURE 7.1 List of Operations, UN Peacekeeping, 1948–2009

Acronym	Mission Name	Start Date	Closing Date
UNTSO	UN Truce Supervision Organization	May 1948	Present
UNMOGIP	UN Military Observer Group in India and Pakistan	January 1949	Present
UNEF I	First United Nations Emergency Force	November 1956	June 1967
UNOGIL	United Nations Observation Group in Lebanon	June 1958	December 1958
ONUC	United Nations Operation in the Congo	July 1960	June 1964
UNSF	United Nations Security Force in West New Guinea	October 1962	April 1963
UNYOM	United Nations Yemen Observation Mission	July 1963	September 1964
UNFICYP	United Nations Peacekeeping Force in Cyprus	March 1964	Present
DOMREP	Mission of the Representative of the Secretary-General in the Dominican Republic	May 1965	October 1966
UNIPOM	United Nations India-Pakistan Observation Mission	September 1965	March 1966
UNEF II	Second United Nations Emergency Force	October 1973	July 1979
UNDOF	United Nations Disengagement Observer Force	June 1974	Present
UNIFIL	United Nations Interim Force in Lebanon	March 1978	Present
UNGOMAP	UN Good Offices Mission in Afghanistan and Pakistan	May 1988	March 1990
UNIIMOG	United Nations Iran-Iraq Military Observer Group	August 1988	February 1991
UNAVEM I	United Nations Angola Verification Mission I	January 1989	June 1991
UNTAG	United Nations Transition Assistance Group	April 1989	March 1990
ONUCA	United Nations Observer Group in Central America	November 1989	January 1992
UNIKOM	United Nations Iraq-Kuwait Observation Mission	April 1991	October 2003
MINURSO	United Nations Mission for the Referendum in Western Sahara	April 1991	Present
UNAVEM II	United Nations Angola Verification Mission II	June 1991	February 1995
ONUSAL	United Nations Observer Mission in El Salvador	July 1991	April 1995
UNAMIC	United Nations Advance Mission in Cambodia	October 1991	March 1992
UNPROFOR	United Nations Protection Force	February 1992	March 1995
UNTAC	United Nations Transitional Authority in Cambodia	March 1992	September 1993
UNOSOM I	United Nations Operation in Somalia I	April 1992	March 1993
ONUMOZ	United Nations Operation in Mozambique	December 1992	December 1994
UNOSOM II	United Nations Operation in Somalia II	March 1993	March 1995
UNOMUR	United Nations Observer Mission Uganda-Rwanda	June 1993	September 1994
UNOMIG	United Nations Observer Mission in Georgia	August 1993	June 2009
UNOMIL	United Nations Observer Mission in Liberia	September 1993	September 1997
UNMIH	United Nations Mission in Haiti	September 1993	June 1996
UNAMIR	United Nations Assistance Mission for Rwanda	October 1993	March 1996
UNASOG	United Nations Aouzou Strip Observer Group	May 1994	June 1994
UNMOT	United Nations Mission of Observers in Tajikistan	December 1994	May 2000

Acronym	Mission Name	Start Date	Closing Date
UNAVEM III	United Nations Angola Verification Mission III	February 1995	June 1997
UNCRO	United Nations Confidence Restoration Operation in Croatia	May 1995	January 1996
UNPREDEP	United Nations Preventive Deployment Force	March 1995	February 1999
UNMIBH	United Nations Mission in Bosnia and Herzegovina	December 1995	December 2002
UNTAES	United Nations Transitional Administration for Eastern Slavonia, Baranja, and Western Sirmium	January 1996	January 1998
UNMOP	United Nations Mission of Observers in Prevlaka	January 1996	December 2002
UNSMIH	United Nations Support Mission in Haiti	July 1996	July 1997
MINUGUA	United Nations Verification Mission in Guatemala	January 1997	May 1997
MONUA	United Nations Observer Mission in Angola	June 1997	February 1999
UNTMIH	United Nations Transition Mission in Haiti	August 1997	December 1997
MIPONUH	United Nations Civilian Police Mission in Haiti	December 1997	March 2000
	UN Civilian Police Support Group	January 1998	October 1998
MINURCA	United Nations Mission in the Central African Republic	April 1998	February 2000
UNOMSIL	United Nations Observer Mission in Sierra Leone	July 1998	October 1999
UNMIK	United Nations Interim Administration Mission in Kosovo	June 1999	Present
UNAMSIL	United Nations Mission in Sierra Leone	October 1999	December 2005
UNTAET	United Nations Transitional Administration in East Timor	October 1999	May 2002
MONUC	United Nations Organization Mission in the Democratic Republic of the Congo	November 1999	Present
UNMEE	United Nations Mission in Ethiopia and Eritrea	July 2000	July 2008
UNMISET	United Nations Mission of Support in East Timor	May 2002	May 2005
UNMIL	United Nations Mission in Liberia	September 2003	Present
UNOCI	United Nations Operation in Côte d'Ivoire	April 2004	Present
MINUSTAH	United Nations Stabilization Mission in Haiti	June 2004	Present
ONUB	United Nations Operation in Burundi	June 2004	December 2006
UNMIS	United Nations Mission in the Sudan	March 2005	Present
UNMIT	United Nations Integrated Mission in Timor-Leste	August 2006	Present
UNAMID	African Union–United Nations Hybrid Operation in Darfur	July 2007	Present
MINURCAT	United Nations Mission in the Central African Republic and Chad	September 2007	Present

Source: "UN peacekeeping missions," www.un.org/en/peacekeeping/list.shtml.
© United Nations, 2008. Reproduced with permission.

December 1995 under American auspices, leading to the Dayton Accords that brought the war to an end. UNPROFOR was replaced by the NATO Peace Implementation Force (I-FOR). As noted in Chapter Five, this mission was a new departure for NATO, taking it into the area of peacekeeping and humanitarian assistance.

Within a few years more conflict erupted, this time in the Serbian province of Kosovo, where fighting broke out between Serbian forces and the Kosovo Liberation Army, representing the Albanian-Kosovar population, which wanted independence for the province. In 1998, when the Serbian government launched another "ethnic cleansing" campaign against the ethnic Albanians, more calls were made for international intervention. The Security Council remained divided, and, as in 1995, it was NATO that launched bombing attacks, without Security Council approval, against Serbian targets until the Serb military withdrew. Thousands more people were killed and displaced from their homes, and NATO responded with more humanitarian assistance. In 2008, following a referendum, Kosovo declared its independence.

While these events were unfolding in Europe, Somalia, already a poor African country, in 1991 slipped into civil war and almost complete anarchy with warring factions, separatist groups, and a mounting humanitarian crisis. Hundreds died every day and millions more were threatened while the infrastructure of the state collapsed. In response, the Security Council authorized the creation of the UN Operation in Somalia, or UNOSOM I, in 1992, to oversee delivery of aid and to protect the aid workers. When this initial measure proved totally inadequate given the extent of famine and chaos, a second larger and more heavily armed force was created, the Unified Task Force (UNITAF), which was given responsibility for humanitarian assistance, the protection of key sites, and to arrange a ceasefire and ultimately disarm the factions; it was superseded by UNOSOM II in 1993. Miscommunication, disagreement over the goals, and the general expansion of the mission hampered the undertaking, and fighting broke out between UN forces and one of the warring factions. Before it was over, hundreds of Somalis and 23 Pakistani and 18 American soldiers were killed. The UN forces were withdrawn in 1995.

At the end of the mission, accusations flew in an angry dispute between Washington and New York over the responsibility for the disaster. Secretary-General Boutros-Ghali was the target for considerable American criticism, but there was enough blame to go around. Phrases like "Somalia syndrome" and "crossing the Mogadishu line" were thrown about with promises from the Clinton administration never again to put American forces in such confused, open-ended, and untenable situations. It was an unfortunate turn of events, not only because Somalia remained in disarray but also because the American retreat from peacekeeping occurred at the very moment that focused international action might have helped save the lives of thousands of people in Rwanda.

The UN Assistance Mission to Rwanda (UNAMIR) was established in 1993 following the negotiation of a ceasefire between the Hutu-dominated government and Tutsi rebels of the Rwandan Patriotic Front. The mission, commanded by Canadian General Roméo Dallaire, received a limited mandate to monitor the ceasefire and help rebuild the country. UNAMIR was completely unprepared to respond effectively to the situation in April 1994 when the death of the Rwandan president in an airplane crash sparked a Hutu-led campaign of mass murder against the Tutsi-Rwandans. Coming in the wake of the Somali disaster, there was little international enthusiasm to increase the UN's commitment, and Dallaire's warnings of a potential genocide and requests for reinforcements went largely unheeded in New York. The Security Council sidestepped the question of labelling the Tutsi killing as genocide, which would have mandated action, and the members, including the United States, were reluctant to intervene in any significant way. Those who did act only removed their personnel from the country. In the end, close to 800,000 Rwandans were killed in only a few weeks, and more than 2 million refugees fled into neighbouring states. Facing another humanitarian catastrophe and only after most of the killing had ceased, the UN reinforced UNAMIR to provide assistance to the refugees and to help with reconstruction. The UN mission was withdrawn in April 1996.

The UN emerged from these disasters with its reputation tarnished as never before. In hindsight, there was probably far too much optimism about the future of the UN and its ability to do all things and to enhance its role in the international community. The end of the Cold War did not produce world peace; indeed, it sparked and/or coincided with the appearance of dozens of new conflicts that, ironically, without the Cold War veneer were harder to comprehend, let alone resolve. The spread of ethnic and other intra-state conflicts, violent independence movements, and international terrorism made the world more dangerous than ever and placed an impossible burden on the UN and its agencies. On top of it all, no one wanted to spend their "peace dividend" on the UN or its operations, and the organization experienced a relentless and apparently permanent financial crisis throughout the post–Cold War era.

The road travelled by the UN was paved with good intentions, but its experience exposed important problems. For one thing, the mandates themselves were often unclear so that "mission creep" was a consistent problem, as operations were regularly broadened beyond their original mandates. Peacemaking rather than peacekeeping was now the norm, exposing the UN forces to increased violence and confusion over their expected role. To make matters worse, in several cases reports were made of criminal activity and abuse—from trading aid for sex to the murder and torture of civilians—perpetrated by UN forces in the field. For another, the Security Council, which held ultimate responsibility for the missions, was often divided on what to do, from the split between Russia and the rest over Serbia to Rwanda where there was little agreement other than a shared desire to limit involvement. The lack of unity in the Security Council reflected the divisions among the P-5 and the fluctuation in their support for the different missions. In particular, American support shifted dramatically from the high generated by the victory in the Gulf in 1991 to a low with the death of American soldiers in Somalia in 1993. At the time that the world faced genocide in Rwanda, the Clinton administration and American public opinion were moving away from support for involvement. Finally, none of the major powers was willing to provide the financial and human resources necessary to conduct successfully the breadth of missions now being assigned to the UN. As UN official Shashi Tharoor explained, if the UN was to be an international fire brigade, then the world "will have to do better than the present system, under which the fire breaks out, the aldermen on the Security Council agree it needs to be put out, and the fire chief is then sent out to hire firemen, rent fire trucks, find hoses of the right length, and look for sources of water to put into them"[6]

One concrete outcome of these horrific events, however, was the creation of several international criminal tribunals. In 1993, the Security Council established the International Criminal Tribunal for the former Yugoslavia (ICTFY) and later the International Criminal Tribunal for Rwanda (ICTR) to bring war criminals and murderers to trial. The ICTFY indicted more than 100 individuals for war crimes, including former Yugoslav president Slobodan Milošević, who cheated justice by dying in his cell in 2006, and Bosnian Serb leader Radovan Karadžić, who was arrested in 2008. That same year, three Rwandan military leaders were also found guilty of genocide and war crimes and given life sentences. Similar tribunals, courts, and investigative panels have been created for Cambodia, Lebanon, East Timor, and Sierra Leone. In the latter case Charles Taylor, the former president of Liberia, was arrested for war crimes committed in Sierra Leone.

As international support rose for a permanent criminal court, the Rome Statute established the International Criminal Court (ICC) in 1998. Although the ICC was not endorsed or supported by the United States and several other states, including China, Sudan, and Libya, it received the required ratifications and came into existence in 2002. Since then, it has slowly begun to take action. Dozens of warrants for war crimes were issued for Joseph Krony, the Ugandan guerrilla leader of the Lord's Resistance Army, and a few other military leaders in Uganda for their involvement in murder, rape, and the forced abduction of thousands of children. The ICC also issued more than 50 warrants for crimes against humanity against two Sudanese individuals, a government minister and militia leader, but they have not yet surrendered to the court. In 2009, war crime charges were laid against Sudanese President Omar al-Bashir.

Condemnation of the UN rose dramatically in the wake of the failures in Yugoslavia, Somalia, and Rwanda and only added to the unease created by its never-ending financial troubles. The revival of Republican fortunes in the American Congress in 1994 meant that the criticism would only grow. The Clinton administration blamed Secretary-General Boutros-Ghali for the disaster in Somalia and vetoed his renewal for a second term; in January 1997, Kofi Annan of Ghana became secretary-general. Annan rose through the ranks of the UN and was partly educated in the United States, and his intelligence and charisma helped him become one of the most popular men to hold that post.

The organization that Annan inherited was in many ways active and vigorous. Interaction and collaboration between the UN, the regional organizations, and NGOs were expanding rapidly; the large summit conferences of the 1980s and 1990s, on the environment, women's rights, and so on, were public expressions of the growing convergence of international society; and increasingly issues such as peace and security, disarmament, human rights, and economic development were being folded into the broader and increasingly popular term "human security." There was progress in the creation of the ICC, the landmines convention, and the Kyoto Protocol, and in the negotiation of human rights conventions such as the Convention on the Rights of the Child (1989) and the Declaration on the Right to Development (1986). Despite considerable debate between universalism and cultural relativism, there was a growing acceptance of women's rights as *human* rights.[7] These declarations and conventions were landmark achievements, even if they were weakened in an effort to attract broad support and lacked enforcement provisions. But they could not mask the reality that millions still suffered serious human rights abuses and millions more children died every year from preventable causes. As two scholars wrote about the relationship between ideals and outcomes, it "is hard to argue that the dramatic advance in commitments on paper has been matched by even marginal improvements in human rights conditions."[8]

This was also the era of globalization—the opening of markets and access to capital, free trade, deregulation, privatization, the decline of state control over the economy, and the rise in power of transnational corporations. The IMF and World Bank were always dominated by the United States and its allies, and in the post–Cold War era the forces of economic liberalism were triumphant with the creation of the WTO in 1995. The WTO was independent of the UN and quickly began to establish international economic rules and regulations and to settle disputes.

The economic climate widened the divisions between North and South, rich and poor, developed and underdeveloped. For the poorer states, aid from the international financial organizations came with more strings attached and was frequently criticized as a form of neo-colonialism. The World Bank increasingly insisted on economic reforms—liberalization, tariff reductions, changes to currency and interest rates, opening of markets, the removal of state subsidies and services, and in some cases legal and political reforms—in order for developing states to qualify for aid. Economic recession and the debt crises in the 1980s, meanwhile, left the poorer states in a vulnerable position and at the mercy of the Western-dominated international financial organizations. By 1994, for example, aid comprised 16.3 per cent of GNP of sub-Saharan African nations (up from 3.4 per cent in 1980) and in 34 states (mostly in Africa) aid made up more than 10 per cent of GNP.[9] This level of economic dependence gave the financial organizations considerable leverage, and the gap between North and South, exposed during the debates over the New International Economic Order in the 1970s, grew larger than ever before. The divisions were seen not only in economic issues but also in the field of human rights, on political and security issues, and throughout the UN and the specialized agencies.

The century ended on an ambitious note, however. At the UN Summit meeting in 2000, Secretary-General Annan introduced the UN's Millennium Development Goals to be achieved over 15 years. The goals were honourable, if difficult to achieve, and included the eradication of extreme poverty, the reduction of infant mortality by two-thirds, halting the spread of HIV/ AIDS and malaria, gender equality, and the achievement of universal primary education. Benchmarks were set out to measure progress, and the target date (2015) was far enough into the future to permit some optimistic thinking about the chances for success. Some progress has been made, but as 2015 approaches the goals are far from being realized.

The terrorist attacks of 11 September 2001 shocked the UN, like everyone else, and its response was immediate. In the wave of international sympathy for the United States, few opposed dramatic action against the 9/11 perpetrators. The attacks were condemned as threats to international peace and security, and the Security Council invoked the Americans' right of self-defence to hunt down the terrorists. NATO soon followed with its UN-mandated mission in Afghanistan—its first operation outside of Europe.

Relations between the UN and the Bush administration soon declined, however, as the latter's disdain for the organization was barely concealed. Things only worsened as the United States moved to topple Saddam Hussein in Iraq. The Security Council passed multiple resolutions—for example, demanding that Iraq comply with weapons inspectors—and set deadlines for compliance, but it did not sanction military action. The Bush administration sought the approval of the Security Council for its planned attack on Iraq, citing the existence of weapons of mass destruction there, an Iraqi connection to the 9/11 terrorists, and the fact that Hussein had disregarded earlier Security Council resolutions. When it became clear that the United States could not attract a majority of the Security Council, it withdrew its resolution and, in 2003, launched its attack without Security Council authorization.

It was a low point for many UN supporters. As one observer pointed out, those who supported the American invasion condemned the UN for not backing the United States, while those opposed to the invasion condemned the UN for failing to stop it.[10] Worse, perhaps, the UN—ignored and bypassed by Washington—was seen as irrelevant and impotent in the face of American unilateralism. In May 2003, however, the Security Council responded to American requests to establish a mission in Iraq to help rebuild the country and to provide humanitarian assistance. The new endeavour turned to disaster when a truck-bomb exploded outside the UN's Baghdad headquarters in August, killing 22 UN officials. The tragedy was only heightened by the realization that, in the eyes of many people, the UN was regarded merely as a tool of the Americans in Iraq. The remaining UN personnel were removed, although a few did return in 2005 to help during the Iraqi election. But relations between the UN and the Bush administration did not improve; indeed, in August 2005 President Bush appointed John Bolton as UN ambassador, and he proved to be extremely critical, dismissive, and needlessly antagonistic to the UN and its operations. Bolton's and Annan's terms came to an end at the end of 2006.

The deterioration of relations with Washington was not the only concern for the UN in the new century. The legacy of Rwanda, Bosnia, Kosovo, Somalia, and elsewhere suggested the need for a re-examination of the UN's role in peacekeeping, humanitarian intervention, and conflict prevention. Given the disasters of the 1990s, many believed that new answers were needed for the old questions about the intersection of state sovereignty and human rights and concerning the point where the rights of the individual trumped the sovereignty of the state.

In 2000, Secretary-General Annan established a small panel to investigate the future of UN peacekeeping, and the resulting Brahimi Report, named after the panel's chair, Lakhdar Brahimi of Algeria, offered a blueprint for reform. Many recommendations were made—better organization, clearer instructions, more funding and support—but the thrust of the report called for more vigorous action in peacekeeping and a greater commitment to protect the victims in crisis situations. UN missions now arrived in volatile and violent situations, where there was no peace to keep. Therefore, it was necessary to distinguish between peacekeeping and peacebuilding missions; in the latter case, it might be necessary to take dramatic action to protect civilians without prior UN authorization. A number of these recommendations were introduced, including the creation of the UN Peacebuilding Commission in 2005.[11]

Another step was taken with the establishment of the International Commission on Intervention and State Sovereignty established at the Millennium Summit in 2000. The Commission's 2001 report—*The Responsibility to Protect*—argued that there were limitations to state sovereignty ("sovereignty is not a license to kill" is how one of the authors later put it[12]), and in cases where the state fails to protect its citizens or is actively harming its own population, the international community was obliged to assume that responsibility; in such cases "the principle of non-intervention yields to the international responsibility to protect."[13] There were numerous conditions to be met before any intervention would be considered legitimate, intervention was to be a last resort and only in extreme cases, and great emphasis was placed on conflict prevention and rebuilding after a crisis, but it was the challenge to state sovereignty that received the most attention. For many critics, especially in Asia, Africa, and Latin America, there were questions raised about how and when the responsibility to protect, or R2P as it came to be called, would be invoked and under what circumstances, as well as fears that it would just be another way for rich developed states to intervene in poorer developing states.[14]

R2P was endorsed by the General Assembly at the 2005 World Summit, but its implementation has been slow, and peacekeeping efforts at the turn of the century experienced mixed results. New missions totalling more than 40,000 personnel were dispatched to Congo, Sierra Leone, Ethiopia, and East Timor to supervise the implementation of ceasefires, to help with reconstruction and training, and to monitor elections.[15] In 2003, 15,000 peacekeepers were dispatched to Liberia, an African state long mired in civil war and near complete collapse. The mission (UNOMIL) helped with reconstruction and was given a stronger mandate to protect citizens. It remained in Liberia to help supervise elections in 2005.[16]

Much less success was experienced in Darfur, the western region of Sudan, where a 2003 uprising was suppressed by both government forces and a quasi-guerilla militia force that undertook a brutal campaign of violence, murder, and rape in what appeared to be more a case of ethnic cleansing than an effort to weed out "rebels." In the process, hundreds of thousands were killed, and more than 2 million people were forced from their homes. The response of the UN and other international organizations was hardly robust. On the Security Council, the Americans and, to a lesser degree, the British were focused on Iraq and had less time for Darfur, while the Chinese—the major purchaser of Sudanese oil and weapons supplier to Sudan—were opposed to any kind of intervention. The AU proved to be more willing to act, although it remained concerned about violating Sudanese sovereignty. The African Union Mission in Sudan (AMIS) sent some 7,000 troops in 2004. The signing of a peace agreement in 2005 was followed by the deployment of a joint UN-AU mission in Darfur (UNAMID) in 2006. Despite the missions, the Security Council resolutions condemning the Sudanese government, and the embracing of R2P, the human catastrophe continues. With respect to the major powers, two observers wrote, "their actions and inactions add up to a tale of self-interest and risk aversion masked by ethical posturing; of prevarication and procrastination in the face of a supreme humanitarian emergency."[17]

There have always been competing views of the UN and its missions, commissions, agencies, declarations, resolutions, and conventions. From the hope for the future of humankind to the handmaiden of the Western imperial powers, from a bastion of collective security to an impotent debating society, the UN has meant different things to different people at different times. But for millions of people around the world, the UN represents tangible aid and assistance, better health, education, and drinking water. Its conventions have established norms adopted by virtually all nations, and although they are not always followed, they represent the basic building blocks for a better international society. Moreover, the peacekeeping efforts of the UN and the regional organizations have saved thousands of lives and allowed negotiations for peace to proceed. In times of need, these institutions are turned to for help by the states that comprise the international community.

At the same time, many of those same states have proven reluctant to pay their assessments to enable the UN to continue operating. And, however much a beacon of hope in the world, the UN has also been mired in financial crisis and has suffered severe cutbacks, a very public scandal over the selling of Iraqi oil for food, and allegations of sexual harassment at its headquarters. It has consistently failed to measure up to its own standards, for example, in establishing gender equality. The creation of a new Human Rights Council in 2006 was designed to make it more difficult for states with bad human rights records to become members, but the original promise has not been fulfilled. It has been a difficult time in UN history, and many serious challenges awaited Ban Ki-Moon, the former South Korean foreign minister, when he became secretary-general in 2007.

The issue of UN reform is very much in the air, as it has been for most of the organization's history. There is constant pressure to do more for less, and to be more responsive, accountable, transparent, robust, and so on. Complaints about the Security Council—that the P-5 are a remnant of the Second World War and no longer reflect global realities—are common, especially from those who want P-5 status for themselves. Some want to enlarge the P-5; others want to amend their powers and remove the veto. Equally, tensions between great and small powers remain, and today the UN can do as little about the Russians in Chechnya, the Chinese in Tibet, or the Americans in Iraq as it could in earlier times in other places. The role and influence of the United States is great but not always positive, making the relationship between New York and Washington perhaps more important than ever before.

Secretary-General Dag Hammarskjöld is reported to have said that the UN was not created to bring us to heaven but, rather, to "save us from hell."[18] Membership is not qualified by a state's human rights record or the presence of a democratic government or free institutions; indeed, some of the most unpleasant dictatorships have been and remain members. The tensions between state sovereignty and human rights enforcement remain, but the UN does bring people together, sets priorities and goals, provides plans and procedures for action, and lends a degree of legitimacy to international action around the world. As former UN official Ramesh Thakur wrote, the United Nations "is at once the symbol of humanity's collective aspirations for a better life in a safer world for all, a forum for negotiating the terms of converting the collective aspirations into a common programme of action and the principal international instrument for the realisation of the aspirations and the implementation of the plans. On balance, the world has been a better and safer place with the UN than would have been the case without it."[19]

Much the same can be said for international organizations in general. They provide international fora for debate; they provide international exposure to issues that affect millions of people; they provide aid, assistance, education, and information, as well as energy and determination. International organizations focus attention on problems, offer potential solutions, and take action in places and areas ignored by others. And today, more than ever, global problems—in the environment, international trade and economic development, human rights, health, agriculture and food, criminal activity, and so on—will require global solutions, and international organizations will help to fill this void.

International organizations are not going away, and their numbers continue to grow. They have not replaced the sovereign state nor are they likely to, but today it is hard to imagine anyone grappling with a broad international issue without the help from an international organization of some kind. International organizations, wrote historian Akira Iriye, "have proved quite successful in reconciling differences because their only weapons are ideas, a sense of commitment, and voluntary service. They have not spent billions on arms, nor have they engaged in mass killing. They are civilized societies, and so they have a mission to turn the world into a civilized community."[20]

Notes

1 Mingst and Karns, *The United Nations in the Post-Cold War Era*, 6–7.
2 Ryan, *The United Nations and International Politics*, 103.
3 United Nations, *An Agenda for Peace.*
4 Ludwig, *UN Electoral Assistance.*
5 *An Agenda for Peace.*
6 Meisler, *Kofi Annan*, 70.
7 Guerrina and Zalewski, "Negotiating Difference/Negotiating Rights," 5–6; Hochstetler et al., "Sovereignty in the Balance," 600.
8 Normand and Zaidi, *Human Rights at the UN*, 322.
9 Williams, "Aid and Sovereignty," 565–68.
10 Thakur, *The United Nations, Peace, and Security*, 4.
11 "Report of the Panel on United Nations Peace Operations," A/55/305—S/2000/809; Hanhimäki, *The United Nations*, 87–89.
12 Evans, *The Responsibility to Protect*, 11.
13 International Development Research Centre, *The Responsibility to Protect.*
14 Welsh et al., "The Responsibility to Protect," 508–10.
15 Bellamy et al., *Understanding Peacekeeping*, 278–79.
16 Lebor, *"Complicity with Evil,"* 218–19.
17 Black and Williams, "Darfur's Challenge to International Society," 2.
18 Urquhart, *Hammarskjöld*, 48.
19 Thakur, 2.
20 Iriye, *Global Community*, 193.

The Covenant of the League of Nations (including Amendments)

THE HIGH CONTRACTING PARTIES, In order to promote international co-operation and to achieve international peace and security by the acceptance of obligations not to resort to war, by the prescription of open, just and honourable relations between nations, by the firm establishment of the understandings of international law as the actual rule of conduct among Governments, and by the maintenance of justice and a scrupulous respect for all treaty obligations in the dealings of organized peoples with one another, Agree to this Covenant of the League of Nations.

Article 1

1. The original Members of the League of Nations shall be those of the Signatories which are named in the Annex to this Covenant and also such of those other States named in the Annex as shall accede without reservation to this Covenant. Such accession shall be effected by a Declaration deposited with the Secretariat within two months of the coming into force of the Covenant. Notice thereof shall be sent to all other Members of the League.

2. Any fully self-governing State, Dominion or Colony not named in the Annex may become a Member of the League if its admission is agreed to by two-thirds of the Assembly, provided that it shall give effective guarantees of its sincere intention to observe its international obligations, and shall accept such regulations as may be prescribed by the League in regard to its military, naval and air forces and armaments.

3. Any Member of the League may, after two years' notice of its intention so to do, withdraw from the League, provided that all its international obligations and all its obligations under this Covenant shall have been fulfilled at the time of its withdrawal.

Article 2

The action of the League under this Covenant shall be effected through the instrumentality of an Assembly and of a Council, with a permanent Secretariat.

Article 3

1. The Assembly shall consist of Representatives of the Members of the League.

2. The Assembly shall meet at stated intervals and from time to time as occasion may require at the Seat of the League or at such other place as may be decided upon.

3. The Assembly may deal at its meetings with any matter within the sphere of action of the League or affecting the peace of the world.

4. At meetings of the Assembly each Member of the League shall have one vote, and may have not more than three Representatives.

Article 4

1. The Council shall consist of Representatives of the Principal Allied and Associated Powers, together with Representatives of four other Members of the League. These four Members of the League shall be selected by the Assembly from time to time in its discretion. Until the appointment of the Representatives of the four Members of the League first selected by the Assembly, Representatives of Belgium, Brazil, Spain and Greece shall be members of the Council.

2. With the approval of the majority of the Assembly, the Council may name additional Members of the League whose Representatives shall always be members of the Council; the Council, with like approval may increase the number of Members of the League to be selected by the Assembly for representation on the Council.

2 bis. The Assembly shall fix by a two-thirds' majority the rules dealing with the election of the non-permanent Members of the Council, and particularly such regulations as relate to their term of office and the conditions of re-eligibility.

3. The Council shall meet from time to time as occasion may require, and at least once a year, at the Seat of the League, or at such other place as may be decided upon.

4. The Council may deal at its meetings with any matter within the sphere of action of the League or affecting the peace of the world.

5. Any Member of the League not represented on the Council shall be invited to send a Representative to sit as a member at any meeting of the Council during the consideration of matters specially affecting the interests of that Member of the League.

6. At meetings of the Council, each Member of the League represented on the Council shall have one vote, and may have not more than one Representative.

Article 5

1. Except where otherwise expressly provided in this Covenant or by the terms of the present Treaty, decisions at any meeting of the Assembly or of the Council

shall require the agreement of all the Members of the League represented at the meeting.

2. All matters of procedure at meetings of the Assembly or of the Council, including the appointment of Committees to investigate particular matters, shall be regulated by the Assembly or by the Council and may be decided by a majority of the Members of the League represented at the meeting.

3. The first meeting of the Assembly and the first meeting of the Council shall be summoned by the President of the United States of America.

Article 6

1. The permanent Secretariat shall be established at the Seat of the League. The Secretariat shall comprise a Secretary General and such secretaries and staff as may be required.

2. The first Secretary General shall be the person named in the Annex; thereafter the Secretary General shall be appointed by the Council with the approval of the majority of the Assembly.

3. The secretaries and staff of the Secretariat shall be appointed by the Secretary General with the approval of the Council.

4. The Secretary General shall act in that capacity at all meetings of the Assembly and of the Council.

5. The expenses of the League shall be borne by the Members of the League in the proportion decided by the Assembly.

Article 7

1. The Seat of the League is established at Geneva.

2. The Council may at any time decide that the Seat of the League shall be established elsewhere.

3. All positions under or in connection with the League, including the Secretariat, shall be open equally to men and women.

4. Representatives of the Members of the League and officials of the League when engaged on the business of the League shall enjoy diplomatic privileges and immunities.

5. The buildings and other property occupied by the League or its officials or by Representatives attending its meetings shall be inviolable.

Article 8

1. The Members of the League recognize that the maintenance of peace requires the reduction of national armaments to the lowest point consistent with national safety and the enforcement by common action of international obligations.

2. The Council, taking account of the geographical situation and circumstances of each State, shall formulate plans for such reduction for the consideration and action of the several Governments.

3. Such plans shall be subject to reconsideration and revision at least every ten years.

4. After these plans shall have been adopted by the several Governments, the limits of armaments therein fixed shall not be exceeded without the concurrence of the Council.

5. The Members of the League agree that the manufacture by private enterprise of munitions and implements of war is open to grave objections. The Council shall advise how the evil effects attendant upon such manufacture can be prevented, due regard being had to the necessities of those Members of the League which are not able to manufacture the munitions and implements of war necessary for their safety.

6. The Members of the League undertake to interchange full and frank information as to the scale of their armaments, their military, naval and air programs and the condition of such of their industries as are adaptable to war-like purposes.

Article 9

A permanent Commission shall be constituted to advise the Council on the execution of the provisions of Articles 1 and 8 and on military, naval and air questions generally.

Article 10

The Members of the League undertake to respect and preserve as against external aggression the territorial integrity and existing political independence of all Members of the League. In case of any such aggression or in case of any threat or danger of such aggression the Council shall advise upon the means by which this obligation shall be fulfilled.

Article 11

1. Any war or threat of war, whether immediately affecting any of the Members of the League or not, is hereby declared a matter of concern to the whole League, and the League shall take any action that may be deemed wise and effectual to safeguard the peace of nations. In case any such emergency should arise the Secretary General shall on the request of any Member of the League forthwith summon a meeting of the Council.

2. It is also declared to be the friendly right of each Member of the League to bring to the attention of the Assembly or of the Council any circumstance whatever affecting international relations which threatens to disturb international peace or the good understanding between nations upon which peace depends.

Article 12

1. The Members of the League agree that, if there should arise between them any dispute likely to lead to a rupture they will submit the matter either to arbitration or judicial settlement or to enquiry by the Council, and they agree in no case to resort to war until three months after the award by the arbitrators or the judicial decision, or the report by the Council.

2. In any case under this Article the award of the arbitrators or the judicial decision shall be made within a reasonable time, and the report of the Council shall be made within six months after the submission of the dispute.

Article 13

1. The Members of the League agree that whenever any dispute shall arise between them which they recognize to be suitable for submission to arbitration or judicial settlement and which cannot be satisfactorily settled by diplomacy, they will submit the whole subject-matter to arbitration or judicial settlement.

2. Disputes as to the interpretation of a treaty, as to any question of international law, as to the existence of any fact which if established would constitute a breach of any international obligation, or as to the extent and nature of the reparation to be made for any such breach, are declared to be among those which are generally suitable for submission to arbitration or judicial settlement.

3. For the consideration of any such dispute, the court to which the case is referred shall be the Permanent Court of International Justice, established in accordance with Article 14, or any tribunal agreed on by the parties to the dispute or stipulated in any convention existing between them.

4. The Members of the League agree that they will carry out in full good faith any award or decision that may be rendered, and that they will not resort to war against a Member of the League which complies therewith. In the event of any failure to carry out such an award or decision, the Council shall propose what steps should be taken to give effect thereto.

Article 14

The Council shall formulate and submit to the Members of the League for adoption plans for the establishment of a Permanent Court of International Justice. The Court shall be competent to hear and determine any dispute of an international character which the parties thereto submit to it. The Court may also give an advisory opinion upon any dispute or question referred to it by the Council or by the Assembly.

Article 15

1. If there should arise between Members of the League any dispute likely to lead to a rupture, which is not submitted to arbitration or judicial settlement in accordance with Article 13, the Members of the League agree that they will submit the matter to the Council. Any party to the dispute may effect such submission by giving notice of the existence of the dispute to the Secretary General, who will make all necessary arrangements for a full investigation and consideration thereof.

2. For this purpose the parties to the dispute will communicate to the Secretary General, as promptly as possible, statements of their case with all the relevant facts and papers, and the Council may forthwith direct the publication thereof.

3. The Council shall endeavour to effect a settlement of the dispute, and if such efforts are successful, a statement shall be made public giving such facts and explanations regarding the dispute and the terms of settlement thereof as the Council may deem appropriate.

4. If the dispute is not thus settled, the Council either unanimously or by a majority vote shall make and publish a report containing a statement of the facts of the dispute and the recommendations which are deemed just and proper in regard thereto.

5. Any Member of the League represented on the Council may make public a statement of the facts of the dispute and of its conclusions regarding the same.

6. If a report by the Council is unanimously agreed to by the members thereof other than the Representatives of one or more of the parties to the dispute, the Members of the League agree that they will not go to war with any party to the dispute which complies with the recommendations of the report.

7. If the Council fails to reach a report which is unanimously agreed to by the members thereof, other than the Representatives of one or more of the parties to the dispute, the Members of the League reserve to themselves the right to take such action as they shall consider necessary for the maintenance of right and justice.

8. If the dispute between the parties is claimed by one of them, and is found by the Council, to arise out of a matter which by international law is solely within the domestic jurisdiction of that party, the Council shall so report, and shall make no recommendation as to its settlement.

9. The Council may in any case under this Article refer the dispute to the Assembly. The dispute shall be so referred at the request of either party to the dispute, provided that such request be made within fourteen days after the submission of the dispute to the Council.

10. In any case referred to the Assembly, all the provisions of this Article and of Article 12 relating to the action and powers of the Council shall apply to the action and powers of the Assembly, provided that a report made by the Assembly, if concurred in by the Representatives of those Members of the League represented on the Council and of a majority of the other Members of the League, exclusive in each case of the Representatives of the parties to the dispute, shall have the same force as a report by the Council concurred in by all the members thereof other than the Representatives of one or more of the parties to the dispute.

Article 16

1. Should any Member of the League resort to war in disregard of its covenants under Articles 12, 13 or 15, it shall ipso facto be deemed to have committed an act of war against all other members of the League, which hereby undertake immediately to subject it to the severance of all trade or financial relations, the prohibition of all intercourse between their nationals and the nationals of the covenant-breaking State, and the prevention of all financial, commercial or personal intercourse between the nationals of the covenant-breaking State and the nationals of any other State, whether a Member of the League or not.

2. It shall be the duty of the Council in such case to recommend to the several Governments concerned what effective military, naval or air force the Members of the League shall severally contribute to the armed forces to be used to protect the covenants of the League.

3. The Members of the League agree, further, that they will mutually support one another in the financial and economic measures which are taken under this Article, in order to minimize the loss and inconvenience resulting from the above measures, and that they will mutually support one another in resisting any special measures aimed at one of their number by the covenant-breaking State, and that they will take the necessary steps to afford passage through their territory to the

forces of any of the Members of the League which are co-operating to protect the covenants of the League.

4. Any Member of the League which has violated any covenant of the League may be declared to be no longer a Member of the League by a vote of the Council concurred in by the Representatives of all the other Members of the League represented thereon.

Article 17

1. In the event of a dispute between a Member of the League and a State which is not a Member of the League, or between States not Members of the League, the State or States not Members of the League shall be invited to accept the obligations of membership in the League for the purposes of such dispute, upon such conditions as the Council may deem just. If such invitation is accepted, the provisions of Articles 12 to 16 inclusive shall be applied with such modifications as may be deemed necessary by the Council.

2. Upon such invitation being given the Council shall immediately institute an inquiry into the circumstances of the dispute and recommend such action as may seem best and most effectual in the circumstances.

3. If a State so invited shall refuse to accept the obligations of membership in the League for the purposes of such dispute, and shall resort to war against a Member of the League, the provisions of Article 16 shall be applicable as against the State taking such action.

4. If both parties to the dispute when so invited refuse to accept the obligations of membership in the League for the purposes of such dispute, the Council may take such measures and make such recommendations as will prevent hostilities and will result in the settlement of the dispute.

Article 18

Every treaty or international engagement entered into hereafter by any Member of the League shall be forthwith registered with the Secretariat and shall as soon as possible be published by it. No such treaty or international engagement shall be binding until so registered.

Article 19

The Assembly may from time to time advise the reconsideration by Members of the League of treaties which have become inapplicable and the consideration of international conditions whose continuance might endanger the peace of the world.

Article 20

1. The Members of the League severally agree that this Covenant is accepted as abrogating all obligations or understandings inter se which are inconsistent with the terms thereof, and solemnly undertake that they will not hereafter enter into any engagements inconsistent with the terms thereof.

2. In case any Member of the League shall, before becoming a Member of the League, have undertaken any obligations inconsistent with the terms of this

Covenant, it shall be the duty of such Member to take immediate steps to procure its release from such obligations.

Article 21

Nothing in this Covenant shall be deemed to affect the validity of international engagements, such as treaties of arbitration or regional understandings like the Monroe doctrine, for securing the maintenance of peace.

Article 22

1. To those colonies and territories which as a consequence of the late war have ceased to be under the sovereignty of the States which formerly governed them and which are inhabited by peoples not yet able to stand by themselves under the strenuous conditions of the modern world, there should be applied the principle that the well-being and development of such peoples form a sacred trust of civilization and that securities for the performance of this trust should be embodied in this Covenant.

2. The best method of giving practical effect to this principle is that the tutelage of such peoples should be entrusted to advanced nations who by reason of their resources, their experience or their geographical position can best undertake this responsibility, and who are willing to accept it, and that this tutelage should be exercised by them as Mandatories on behalf of the League.

3. The character of the mandate must differ according to the stage of the development of the people, the geographical situation of the territory, its economic conditions and other similar circumstances.

4. Certain communities formerly belonging to the Turkish Empire have reached a stage of development where their existence as independent nations can be provisionally recognized subject to the rendering of administrative advice and assistance by a Mandatory until such time as they are able to stand alone. The wishes of these communities must be a principal consideration in the selection of the Mandatory.

5. Other peoples, especially those of Central Africa, are at such a stage that the Mandatory must be responsible for the administration of the territory under conditions which will guarantee freedom of conscience and religion, subject only to the maintenance of public order and morals, the prohibition of abuses such as the slave trade, the arms traffic and the liquor traffic, and the prevention of the establishment of fortifications or military and naval bases and of military training of the natives for other than police purposes and the defence of territory, and will also secure equal opportunities for the trade and commerce of other Members of the League.

6. There are territories, such as South-West Africa and certain of the South Pacific Islands, which, owing to the sparseness of their population, or their small size, or their remoteness from the centres of civilization, or their geographical contiguity to the territory of the Mandatory, and other circumstances, can be best administered under the laws of the Mandatory as integral portions of its territory, subject to the safeguards above mentioned in the interests of the indigenous population.

7. In every case of mandate, the Mandatory shall render to the Council an annual report in reference to the territory committed to its charge.

8. The degree of authority, control, or administration to be exercised by the Mandatory shall, if not previously agreed upon by the Members of the League, be explicitly defined in each case by the Council.

9. A permanent Commission shall be constituted to receive and examine the annual reports of the Mandatories and to advise the Council on all matters relating to the observance of the mandates.

Article 23

Subject to and in accordance with the provisions of international conventions existing or hereafter to be agreed upon, the Members of the League:

1. will endeavour to secure and maintain fair and humane conditions of labour for men, women, and children, both in their own countries and in all countries to which their commercial and industrial relations extend, and for that purpose will establish and maintain the necessary international organizations;

2. undertake to secure just treatment of the native inhabitants of territories under their control;

3. will entrust the League with the general supervision over the execution of agreements with regard to the traffic in women and children, and the traffic in opium and other dangerous drugs;

4. will entrust the League with the general supervision of the trade in arms and ammunition with the countries in which the control of this traffic is necessary in the common interest;

5. will make provision to secure and maintain freedom of communications and of transit and equitable treatment for the commerce of all Members of the League. In this connection, the special necessities of the regions devastated during the war of 1914–1918 shall be borne in mind;

6. will endeavour to take steps in matters of international concern for the prevention and control of disease.

Article 24

1. There shall be placed under the direction of the League all international bureaux already established by general treaties if the parties to such treaties consent. All such international bureaux and all commissions for the regulation of matters of international interest hereafter constituted shall be placed under the direction of the League.

2. In all matters of international interest which are regulated by general convention but which are not placed under the control of international bureaux or commissions, the Secretariat of the League shall, subject to the consent of the Council and if desired by the parties, collect and distribute all relevant information and shall render any other assistance which may be necessary or desirable.

3. The Council may include as part of the expenses of the Secretariat the expenses of any bureau or commission which is placed under the direction of the League.

Article 25

The Members of the League agree to encourage and promote the establishment and co-operation of duly authorized voluntary national Red Cross organizations having as purposes the improvement of health, the prevention of disease and the mitigation of suffering throughout the world.

Article 26

1. Amendments to this Covenant will take effect when ratified by the Members of the League whose Representatives compose the Council and by a majority of the Members of the League whose Representatives compose the Assembly.

2. No such amendments shall bind any Member of the League which signifies its dissent therefrom, but in that case it shall cease to be a Member of the League.

The Charter of the United Nations

Introductory Note

The Charter of the United Nations was signed on 26 June 1945, in San Francisco, at the conclusion of the UN Conference on International Organization, and came into force on 24 October 1945. The Statute of the International Court of Justice is an integral part of the Charter.

Amendments to Articles 23, 27, and 61 of the Charter were adopted by the General Assembly on 17 December 1963 and came into force on 31 August 1965. A further amendment to Article 61 was adopted by the General Assembly on 20 December 1971 and came into force on 24 September 1973. An amendment to Article 109, adopted by the General Assembly on 20 December 1965, came into force on 12 June 1968.

The amendment to Article 23 enlarges the membership of the Security Council from 11 to 15. The amended Article 27 provides that decisions of the Security Council on procedural matters shall be made by an affirmative vote of nine members (formerly seven) and on all other matters by an affirmative vote of nine members (formerly seven), including the concurring votes of the five permanent members of the Security Council.

The amendment to Article 61, which entered into force on 31 August 1965, enlarged the membership of the Economic and Social Council from 18 to 27. The subsequent amendment to that Article, which entered into force on 24 September 1973, further increased the membership of the Council from 27 to 54.

The amendment to Article 109, which relates to the first paragraph of that Article, provides that a General Conference of Member States for the purpose of reviewing the Charter may be held at a date and place to be fixed by a two-thirds vote of the members of the General Assembly and by a vote of any nine members (formerly seven) of the Security Council. Paragraph 3 of Article 109, which deals with the consideration of a possible review conference during the tenth regular session of the General Assembly, has been retained in its original form in its reference to a "vote, of any seven members of the Security Council," the paragraph having been acted upon in 1955 by the General Assembly, at its tenth regular session, and by the Security Council.

Charter of the United Nations

WE THE PEOPLES OF THE UNITED NATIONS DETERMINED to save succeeding generations from the scourge of war, which twice in our lifetime has brought untold sorrow to mankind, and to reaffirm faith in fundamental human rights, in the dignity and worth of the human person, in the equal rights of men and women and of nations large and small, and to establish conditions under which justice and respect for the obligations arising from treaties and other sources of international law can be maintained, and to promote social progress and better standards of life in larger freedom,

AND FOR THESE ENDS to practice tolerance and live together in peace with one another as good neighbours, and to unite our strength to maintain international peace and security, and to ensure, by the acceptance of principles and the institution of methods, that armed force shall not be used, save in the common interest, and to employ international machinery for the promotion of the economic and social advancement of all peoples,

HAVE RESOLVED TO COMBINE OUR EFFORTS TO ACCOMPLISH THESE AIMS.

Accordingly, our respective Governments, through representatives assembled in the city of San Francisco, who have exhibited their full powers found to be in good and due form, have agreed to the present Charter of the United Nations and do hereby establish an international organization to be known as the United Nations.

Chapter I: Purposes and Principles

Article 1

The Purposes of the United Nations are:

1. To maintain international peace and security, and to that end: to take effective collective measures for the prevention and removal of threats to the peace, and for the suppression of acts of aggression or other breaches of the peace, and to bring about by peaceful means, and in conformity with the principles of justice and international law, adjustment or settlement of international disputes or situations which might lead to a breach of the peace;

2. To develop friendly relations among nations based on respect for the principle of equal rights and self-determination of peoples, and to take other appropriate measures to strengthen universal peace;

3. To achieve international co-operation in solving international problems of an economic, social, cultural, or humanitarian character, and in promoting and encouraging respect for human rights and for fundamental freedoms for all without distinction as to race, sex, language, or religion; and

4. To be a centre for harmonizing the actions of nations in the attainment of these common ends.

Article 2

The Organization and its Members, in pursuit of the Purposes stated in Article 1, shall act in accordance with the following Principles.

1. The Organization is based on the principle of the sovereign equality of all its Members.

2. All Members, in order to ensure to all of them the rights and benefits resulting from membership, shall fulfil in good faith the obligations assumed by them in accordance with the present Charter.

3. All Members shall settle their international disputes by peaceful means in such a manner that international peace and security, and justice, are not endangered.

4. All Members shall refrain in their international relations from the threat or use of force against the territorial integrity or political independence of any state, or in any other manner inconsistent with the Purposes of the United Nations.

5. All Members shall give the United Nations every assistance in any action it takes in accordance with the present Charter, and shall refrain from giving assistance to any state against which the United Nations is taking preventive or enforcement action.

6. The Organization shall ensure that states which are not Members of the United Nations act in accordance with these Principles so far as may be necessary for the maintenance of international peace and security.

7. Nothing contained in the present Charter shall authorize the United Nations to intervene in matters which are essentially within the domestic jurisdiction of any state or shall require the Members to submit such matters to settlement under the present Charter; but this principle shall not prejudice the application of enforcement measures under Chapter VII.

Chapter II: Membership

Article 3

The original Members of the United Nations shall be the states which, having participated in the United Nations Conference on International Organization at San Francisco, or having previously signed the Declaration by United Nations of 1 January 1942, sign the present Charter and ratify it in accordance with Article 110.

Article 4

1. Membership in the United Nations is open to all other peace-loving states which accept the obligations contained in the present Charter and, in the judgment of the Organization, are able and willing to carry out these obligations.

2. The admission of any such state to membership in the United Nations will be effected by a decision of the General Assembly upon the recommendation of the Security Council.

Article 5

A Member of the United Nations against which preventive or enforcement action has been taken by the Security Council may be suspended from the exercise of the rights and privileges of membership by the General Assembly upon the rec- ommendation of the Security Council. The exercise of these rights and privileges may be restored by the Security Council.

Article 6

A Member of the United Nations which has persistently violated the Principles contained in the present Charter may be expelled from the Organization by the General Assembly upon the recommendation of the Security Council.

Chapter III: Organs

Article 7

1. There are established as the principal organs of the United Nations: a General Assembly, a Security Council, an Economic and Social Council, a Trusteeship Council, an International Court of Justice, and a Secretariat.

2. Such subsidiary organs as may be found necessary may be established in accordance with the present Charter.

Article 8

The United Nations shall place no restrictions on the eligibility of men and women to participate in any capacity and under conditions of equality in its princi- pal and subsidiary organs.

Chapter IV: The General Assembly

COMPOSITION

Article 9

1. The General Assembly shall consist of all the Members of the United Nations.

2. Each Member shall have not more than five representatives in the General Assembly.

FUNCTIONS AND POWERS

Article 10

The General Assembly may discuss any questions or any matters within the scope of the present Charter or relating to the powers and functions of any organs provided for in the present Charter, and, except as provided in Article 12, may make recommendations to the Members of the United Nations or to the Security Council or to both on any such questions or matters.

Article 11

1. The General Assembly may consider the general principles of co-operation in the maintenance of international peace and security, including the principles governing disarmament and the regulation of armaments, and may make recommendations with regard to such principles to the Members or to the Security Council or to both.

2. The General Assembly may discuss any questions relating to the maintenance of international peace and security brought before it by any Member of the United Nations, or by the Security Council, or by a state which is not a Member of the United Nations in accordance with Article 35, paragraph 2, and, except as provided in Article 12, may make recommendations with regard to any such questions to the state or states concerned or to the Security Council or to both. Any such question on which action is necessary shall be referred to the Security Council by the General Assembly either before or after discussion.

3. The General Assembly may call the attention of the Security Council to situations which are likely to endanger international peace and security.

4. The powers of the General Assembly set forth in this Article shall not limit the general scope of Article 10.

Article 12

1. While the Security Council is exercising in respect of any dispute or situation the functions assigned to it in the present Charter, the General Assembly shall not make any recommendation with regard to that dispute or situation unless the Security Council so requests.

2. The Secretary-General, with the consent of the Security Council, shall notify the General Assembly at each session of any matters relative to the maintenance of international peace and security which are being dealt with by the Security Council and shall similarly notify the General Assembly, or the Members of the United Nations if the General Assembly is not in session, immediately the Security Council ceases to deal with such matters.

Article 13

1. The General Assembly shall initiate studies and make recommendations for the purpose of:

a. promoting international co-operation in the political field and encouraging the progressive development of international law and its codification;

b. promoting international co-operation in the economic, social, cultural, educational, and health fields, and assisting in the realization of human rights and fundamental freedoms for all without distinction as to race, sex, language, or religion.

2. The further responsibilities, functions and powers of the General Assembly with respect to matters mentioned in paragraph 1 (b) above are set forth in Chapters IX and X.

Article 14

Subject to the provisions of Article 12, the General Assembly may recommend measures for the peaceful adjustment of any situation, regardless of origin, which it deems likely to impair the general welfare or friendly relations among nations, including situations resulting from a violation of the provisions of the present Charter setting forth the Purposes and Principles of the United Nations.

Article 15

1. The General Assembly shall receive and consider annual and special reports from the Security Council; these reports shall include an account of the measures that the Security Council has decided upon or taken to maintain international peace and security.

2. The General Assembly shall receive and consider reports from the other organs of the United Nations.

Article 16

The General Assembly shall perform such functions with respect to the international trusteeship system as are assigned to it under Chapters XII and XIII, including the approval of the trusteeship agreements for areas not designated as strategic.

Article 17

1. The General Assembly shall consider and approve the budget of the Organization.

2. The expenses of the Organization shall be borne by the Members as apportioned by the General Assembly.

3. The General Assembly shall consider and approve any financial and budgetary arrangements with specialized agencies referred to in Article 57 and shall examine the administrative budgets of such specialized agencies with a view to making recommendations to the agencies concerned.

VOTING

Article 18

1. Each member of the General Assembly shall have one vote. Decisions of the General Assembly on important questions shall be made by a two thirds majority of the members present and voting. These questions shall include: recommendations with respect to the maintenance of international peace and security, the election of the non-permanent members of the Security Council, the election of the members of the Economic and Social Council, the election of members of the Trusteeship Council in accordance with paragraph 1 (c) of Article 86, the admission of new Members to the United Nations, the suspension of the rights and privileges of membership, the expulsion of Members, questions relating to the operation of the trusteeship system, and budgetary questions.

2. Decisions on other questions, including the determination of additional categories of questions to be decided by a two-thirds majority, shall be made by a majority of the members present and voting.

Article 19

A Member of the United Nations which is in arrears in the payment of its financial contributions to the Organization shall have no vote in the General Assembly if the amount of its arrears equals or exceeds the amount of the contributions due from it for the preceding two full years. The General Assembly may, nevertheless, permit such a Member to vote if it is satisfied that the failure to pay is due to conditions beyond the control of the Member.

PROCEDURE

Article 20

The General Assembly shall meet in regular annual sessions and in such special sessions as occasion may require. Special sessions shall be convoked by the Secretary-General at the request of the Security Council or of a majority of the Members of the United Nations.

Article 21

The General Assembly shall adopt its own rules of procedure. It shall elect its President for each session.

Article 22

The General Assembly may establish such subsidiary organs as it deems necessary for the performance of its functions.

Chapter V: The Security Council

COMPOSITION

Article 23

1. The Security Council shall consist of fifteen Members of the United Nations. The Republic of China, France, the Union of Soviet Socialist Republics, the United Kingdom of Great Britain and Northern Ireland, and the United States of America shall be permanent members of the Security Council. The General Assembly shall elect ten other Members of the United Nations to be non-permanent members of the Security Council, due regard being specially paid, in the first instance to the contribution of Members of the United Nations to the maintenance of international peace and security and to the other purposes of the Organization, and also to equitable geographical distribution.

2. The non-permanent members of the Security Council shall be elected for a term of two years. In the first election of the non-permanent members after the increase of the membership of the Security Council from eleven to fifteen, two of the four additional members shall be chosen for a term of one year. A retiring member shall not be eligible for immediate re-election.

3. Each member of the Security Council shall have one representative.

FUNCTIONS AND POWERS

Article 24

1. In order to ensure prompt and effective action by the United Nations, its Members confer on the Security Council primary responsibility for the maintenance of international peace and security, and agree that in carrying out its duties under this responsibility the Security Council acts on their behalf.

2. In discharging these duties the Security Council shall act in accordance with the Purposes and Principles of the United Nations. The specific powers granted to the Security Council for the discharge of these duties are laid down in Chapters VI, VII, VIII, and XII.

3. The Security Council shall submit annual and, when necessary, special reports to the General Assembly for its consideration.

Article 25

The Members of the United Nations agree to accept and carry out the decisions of the Security Council in accordance with the present Charter.

Article 26

In order to promote the establishment and maintenance of international peace and security with the least diversion for armaments of the world's human and economic resources, the Security Council shall be responsible for formulating, with the assistance of the Military Staff Committee referred to in Article 47, plans to be submitted to the Members of the United Nations for the establishment of a system for the regulation of armaments.

VOTING

Article 27

1. Each member of the Security Council shall have one vote.

2. Decisions of the Security Council on procedural matters shall be made by an affirmative vote of nine members.

3. Decisions of the Security Council on all other matters shall be made by an affirmative vote of nine members including the concurring votes of the permanent members; provided that, in decisions under Chapter VI, and under paragraph 3 of Article 52, a party to a dispute shall abstain from voting.

PROCEDURE

Article 28

1. The Security Council shall be so organized as to be able to function continuously. Each member of the Security Council shall for this purpose be represented at all times at the seat of the Organization.

2. The Security Council shall hold periodic meetings at which each of its members may, if it so desires, be represented by a member of the government or by some other specially designated representative.

3. The Security Council may hold meetings at such places other than the seat of the Organization as in its judgment will best facilitate its work.

Article 29

The Security Council may establish such subsidiary organs as it deems necessary for the performance of its functions.

Article 30

The Security Council shall adopt its own rules of procedure, including the method of selecting its President.

Article 31

Any Member of the United Nations which is not a member of the Security Council may participate, without vote, in the discussion of any question brought before the Security Council whenever the latter considers that the interests of that Member are specially affected.

Article 32

Any Member of the United Nations which is not a member of the Security Council or any state which is not a Member of the United Nations, if it is a party to a dispute under consideration by the Security Council, shall be invited to participate, without vote, in the discussion relating to the dispute. The Security Council shall lay down such conditions as it deems just for the participation of a state which is not a Member of the United Nations.

Chapter VI: Pacific Settlement of Disputes

Article 33

1. The parties to any dispute, the continuance of which is likely to endanger the maintenance of international peace and security, shall, first of all, seek a solution by negotiation, enquiry, mediation, conciliation, arbitration, judicial settlement, resort to regional agencies or arrangements, or other peaceful means of their own choice.

2. The Security Council shall, when it deems necessary, call upon the parties to settle their dispute by such means.

Article 34

The Security Council may investigate any dispute, or any situation which might lead to international friction or give rise to a dispute, in order to determine whether the continuance of the dispute or situation is likely to endanger the maintenance of international peace and security.

Article 35

1. Any Member of the United Nations may bring any dispute, or any situation of the nature referred to in Article 34, to the attention of the Security Council or of the General Assembly.

2. A state which is not a Member of the United Nations may bring to the attention of the Security Council or of the General Assembly any dispute to which it is a party if it accepts in advance, for the purposes of the dispute, the obligations of pacific settlement provided in the present Charter.

3. The proceedings of the General Assembly in respect of matters brought to its attention under this Article will be subject to the provisions of Articles 11 and 12.

Article 36

1. The Security Council may, at any stage of a dispute of the nature referred to in Article 33 or of a situation of like nature, recommend appropriate procedures or methods of adjustment.

2. The Security Council should take into consideration any procedures for the settlement of the dispute which have already been adopted by the parties.

3. In making recommendations under this Article the Security Council should also take into consideration that legal disputes should as a general rule be referred by the parties to the International Court of Justice in accordance with the provisions of the Statute of the Court.

Article 37

1. Should the parties to a dispute of the nature referred to in Article 33 fail to settle it by the means indicated in that Article, they shall refer it to the Security Council.

2. If the Security Council deems that the continuance of the dispute is in fact likely to endanger the maintenance of international peace and security, it shall decide whether to take action under Article 36 or to recommend such terms of settlement as it may consider appropriate.

Article 38

Without prejudice to the provisions of Articles 33 to 37, the Security Council may, if all the parties to any dispute so request, make recommendations to the parties with a view to a pacific settlement of the dispute.

Chapter VII: Action with Respect to Threats to the Peace, Breaches of the Peace, and Acts of Aggression

Article 39

The Security Council shall determine the existence of any threat to the peace, breach of the peace, or act of aggression and shall make recommendations, or decide what measures shall be taken in accordance with Articles 41 and 42, to maintain or restore international peace and security.

Article 40

In order to prevent an aggravation of the situation, the Security Council may, before making the recommendations or deciding upon the measures provided for in Article 39, call upon the parties concerned to comply with such provisional measures as it deems necessary or desirable. Such provisional measures shall be without prejudice to the rights, claims, or position of the parties concerned. The Security Council shall duly take account of failure to comply with such provisional measures.

Article 41

The Security Council may decide what measures not involving the use of armed force are to be employed to give effect to its decisions, and it may call upon the Members of the United Nations to apply such measures. These may include complete or partial interruption of economic relations and of rail, sea, air, postal, telegraphic, radio, and other means of communication, and the severance of diplomatic relations.

Article 42

Should the Security Council consider that measures provided for in Article 41 would be inadequate or have proved to be inadequate, it may take such action by air, sea, or land forces as may be necessary to maintain or restore international peace and security. Such action may include demonstrations, blockade, and other operations by air, sea, or land forces of Members of the United Nations.

Article 43

1. All Members of the United Nations, in order to contribute to the maintenance of international peace and security, undertake to make available to the Security Council, on its call and in accordance with a special agreement or agreements, armed forces, assistance, and facilities, including rights of passage, necessary for the purpose of maintaining international peace and security.

2. Such agreement or agreements shall govern the numbers and types of forces, their degree of readiness and general location, and the nature of the facilities and assistance to be provided.

3. The agreement or agreements shall be negotiated as soon as possible on the initiative of the Security Council. They shall be concluded between the Security Council and Members or between the Security Council and groups of Members and shall be subject to ratification by the signatory states in accordance with their respective constitutional processes.

Article 44

When the Security Council has decided to use force it shall, before calling upon a Member not represented on it to provide armed forces in fulfilment of the obligations assumed under Article 43, invite that Member, if the Member so desires, to participate in the decisions of the Security Council concerning the employment of contingents of that Member's armed forces.

Article 45

In order to enable the United Nations to take urgent military measures, Members shall hold immediately available national air-force contingents for combined international enforcement action. The strength and degree of readiness of these contingents and plans for their combined action shall be determined within the limits laid down in the special agreement or agreements referred to in Article 43, by the Security Council with the assistance of the Military Staff Committee.

Article 46

Plans for the application of armed force shall be made by the Security Council with the assistance of the Military Staff Committee.

Article 47

1. There shall be established a Military Staff Committee to advise and assist the Security Council on all questions relating to the Security Council's military requirements for the maintenance of international peace and security, the employment and command of forces placed at its disposal, the regulation of armaments, and possible disarmament.

2. The Military Staff Committee shall consist of the Chiefs of Staff of the permanent members of the Security Council or their representatives. Any Member of the United Nations not permanently represented on the Committee shall be invited by the Committee to be associated with it when the efficient discharge of the Committee's responsibilities requires the participation of that Member in its work.

3. The Military Staff Committee shall be responsible under the Security Council for the strategic direction of any armed forces placed at the disposal of the Security Council. Questions relating to the command of such forces shall be worked out subsequently.

4. The Military Staff Committee, with the authorization of the Security Council and after consultation with appropriate regional agencies, may establish regional subcommittees.

Article 48

1. The action required to carry out the decisions of the Security Council for the maintenance of international peace and security shall be taken by all the Members of the United Nations or by some of them, as the Security Council may determine.

2. Such decisions shall be carried out by the Members of the United Nations directly and through their action in the appropriate international agencies of which they are members.

Article 49

The Members of the United Nations shall join in affording mutual assistance in carrying out the measures decided upon by the Security Council.

Article 50

If preventive or enforcement measures against any state are taken by the Security Council, any other state, whether a Member of the United Nations or not, which finds itself confronted with special economic problems arising from the carrying out of those measures shall have the right to consult the Security Council with regard to a solution of those problems.

Article 51

Nothing in the present Charter shall impair the inherent right of individual or collective self-defence if an armed attack occurs against a Member of the United Nations, until the Security Council has taken measures necessary to maintain international peace and security. Measures taken by Members in the exercise of this right of self-defence shall be immediately reported to the Security Council and shall not in any way affect the authority and responsibility of the Security Council under the present Charter to take at any time such action as it deems necessary in order to maintain or restore international peace and security.

Chapter VIII: Regional Arrangements

Article 52

1. Nothing in the present Charter precludes the existence of regional arrangements or agencies for dealing with such matters relating to the maintenance of international peace and security as are appropriate for regional action provided that such arrangements or agencies and their activities are consistent with the Purposes and Principles of the United Nations.

2. The Members of the United Nations entering into such arrangements or constituting such agencies shall make every effort to achieve pacific settlement of local disputes through such regional arrangements or by such regional agencies before referring them to the Security Council.

3. The Security Council shall encourage the development of pacific settlement of local disputes through such regional arrangements or by such regional agencies either on the initiative of the states concerned or by reference from the Security Council.

4. This Article in no way impairs the application of Articles 34 and 35.

Article 53

1. The Security Council shall, where appropriate, utilize such regional arrangements or agencies for enforcement action under its authority. But no enforcement action shall be taken under regional arrangements or by regional agencies without the authorization of the Security Council, with the exception of measures against any enemy state, as defined in paragraph 2 of this Article, provided for pursuant to Article 107 or in regional arrangements directed against renewal of aggressive policy on the part of any such state, until such time as the Organization may, on request of the Governments concerned, be charged with the responsibility for preventing further aggression by such a state.

2. The term enemy state as used in paragraph 1 of this Article applies to any state which during the Second World War has been an enemy of any signatory of the present Charter.

Article 54

The Security Council shall at all times be kept fully informed of activities undertaken or in contemplation under regional arrangements or by regional agencies for the maintenance of international peace and security.

Chapter IX: International Economic and Social Cooperation

Article 55

With a view to the creation of conditions of stability and well-being which are necessary for peaceful and friendly relations among nations based on respect for the principle of equal rights and self-determination of peoples, the United Nations shall promote:

a. higher standards of living, full employment, and conditions of economic and social progress and development;

b. solutions of international economic, social, health, and related problems; and international cultural and educational cooperation; and

c. universal respect for, and observance of, human rights and fundamental freedoms for all without distinction as to race, sex, language, or religion.

Article 56

All Members pledge themselves to take joint and separate action in co-operation with the Organization for the achievement of the purposes set forth in Article 55.

Article 57

1. The various specialized agencies, established by intergovernmental agreement and having wide international responsibilities, as defined in their basic instruments, in economic, social, cultural, educational, health, and related fields, shall be brought into relationship with the United Nations in accordance with the provisions of Article 63.

2. Such agencies thus brought into relationship with the United Nations are hereinafter referred to as specialized agencies.

Article 58

The Organization shall make recommendations for the co-ordination of the policies and activities of the specialized agencies.

Article 59

The Organization shall, where appropriate, initiate negotiations among the states concerned for the creation of any new specialized agencies required for the accomplishment of the purposes set forth in Article 55.

Article 60

Responsibility for the discharge of the functions of the Organization set forth in this Chapter shall be vested in the General Assembly and, under the authority of the General Assembly, in the Economic and Social Council, which shall have for this purpose the powers set forth in Chapter X.

Chapter X: The Economic and Social Council

COMPOSITION

Article 61

1. The Economic and Social Council shall consist of fifty-four Members of the United Nations elected by the General Assembly.

2. Subject to the provisions of paragraph 3, eighteen members of the Economic and Social Council shall be elected each year for a term of three years. A retiring member shall be eligible for immediate re-election.

3. At the first election after the increase in the membership of the Economic and Social Council from twenty-seven to fifty-four members, in addition to the members elected in place of the nine members whose term of office expires at the end of that year, twenty seven additional members shall be elected. Of these twenty-seven additional members, the term of office of nine members so elected shall expire at the end of one year, and of nine other members at the end of two years, in accordance with arrangements made by the General Assembly.

4. Each member of the Economic and Social Council shall have one representative.

FUNCTIONS AND POWERS

Article 62

1. The Economic and Social Council may make or initiate studies and reports with respect to international economic, social, cultural, educational, health, and related matters and may make recommendations with respect to any such matters to the General Assembly to the Members of the United Nations, and to the specialized agencies concerned.

2. It may make recommendations for the purpose of promoting respect for, and observance of, human rights and fundamental freedoms for all.

3. It may prepare draft conventions for submission to the General Assembly, with respect to matters falling within its competence.

4. It may call, in accordance with the rules prescribed by the United Nations, international conferences on matters falling within its competence.

Article 63

1. The Economic and Social Council may enter into agreements with any of the agencies referred to in Article 57, defining the terms on which the agency concerned shall be brought into relationship with the United Nations. Such agreements shall be subject to approval by the General Assembly.

2. It may co-ordinate the activities of the specialized agencies through consultation with and recommendations to such agencies and through recommendations to the General Assembly and to the Members of the United Nations.

Article 64

1. The Economic and Social Council may take appropriate steps to obtain regular reports from the specialized agencies. It may make arrangements with the Members of the United Nations and with the specialized agencies to obtain reports on the steps taken to give effect to its own recommendations and to recommendations on matters falling within its competence made by the General Assembly.

2. It may communicate its observations on these reports to the General Assembly.

Article 65

The Economic and Social Council may furnish information to the Security Council and shall assist the Security Council upon its request.

Article 66

1. The Economic and Social Council shall perform such functions as fall within its competence in connection with the carrying out of the recommendations of the General Assembly.

2. It may, with the approval of the General Assembly, perform services at the request of Members of the United Nations and at the request of specialized agencies.

3. It shall perform such other functions as are specified elsewhere in the present Charter or as may be assigned to it by the General Assembly.

VOTING

Article 67

1. Each member of the Economic and Social Council shall have one vote.

2. Decisions of the Economic and Social Council shall be made by a majority of the members present and voting.

PROCEDURE

Article 68

The Economic and Social Council shall set up commissions in economic and social fields and for the promotion of human rights, and such other commissions as may be required for the performance of its functions.

Article 69

The Economic and Social Council shall invite any Member of the United Nations to participate, without vote, in its deliberations on any matter of particular concern to that Member.

Article 70

The Economic and Social Council may make arrangements for representatives of the specialized agencies to participate, without vote, in its deliberations and in those of the commissions established by it, and for its representatives to participate in the deliberations of the specialized agencies.

Article 71

The Economic and Social Council may make suitable arrangements for consultation with nongovernmental organizations which are concerned with matters within its competence. Such arrangements may be made with international organizations and, where appropriate, with national organizations after consultation with the Member of the United Nations concerned.

Article 72

1. The Economic and Social Council shall adopt its own rules of procedure, including the method of selecting its President.

2. The Economic and Social Council shall meet as required in accordance with its rules, which shall include provision for the convening of meetings on the request of a majority of its members.

Chapter XI: Declaration Regarding Non-Self-Governing Territories

Article 73

Members of the United Nations which have or assume responsibilities for the administration of territories whose peoples have not yet attained a full measure of self-government recognize the principle that the interests of the inhabitants of these territories are paramount, and accept as a sacred trust the obligation to promote to the utmost, within the system of international peace and security established by the present Charter, the well-being of the inhabitants of these territories, and, to this end:

a. to ensure, with due respect for the culture of the peoples concerned, their political, economic, social, and educational advancement, their just treatment, and their protection against abuses;

b. to develop self-government, to take due account of the political aspirations of the peoples, and to assist them in the progressive development of their free political institutions, according to the particular circumstances of each territory and its peoples and their varying stages of advancement;

c. to further international peace and security;

d. to promote constructive measures of development, to encourage research, and to cooperate with one another and, when and where appropriate, with specialized international bodies with a view to the practical achievement of the social, economic, and scientific purposes set forth in this Article; and

e. to transmit regularly to the Secretary-General for information purposes, subject to such limitation as security and constitutional considerations may require, statistical and other information of a technical nature relating to economic, social, and educational conditions in the territories for which they are respectively responsible other than those territories to which Chapters XII and XIII apply.

Article 74

Members of the United Nations also agree that their policy in respect of the territories to which this Chapter applies, no less than in respect of their metropolitan areas, must be based on the general principle of good-neighborliness, due account being taken of the interests and wellbeing of the rest of the world, in social, economic, and commercial matters.

Chapter XII: International Trusteeship System

Article 75

The United Nations shall establish under its authority an international trusteeship system for the administration and supervision of such territories as may be placed there under by subsequent individual agreements. These territories are hereinafter referred to as trust territories.

Article 76

The basic objectives of the trusteeship system, in accordance with the Purposes of the United Nations laid down in Article 1 of the present Charter, shall be:

a. to further international peace and security;

b. to promote the political, economic, social, and educational advancement of the inhabitants of the trust territories, and their progressive development towards self-government or independence as may be appropriate to the particular circumstances of each territory and its peoples and the freely expressed wishes of the peoples concerned, and as may be provided by the terms of each trusteeship agreement;

c. to encourage respect for human rights and for fundamental freedoms for all without distinction as to race, sex, language, or religion, and to encourage recognition of the interdependence of the peoples of the world; and

d. to ensure equal treatment in social, economic, and commercial matters for all Members of the United Nations and their nationals, and also equal treatment for the latter in the administration of justice, without prejudice to the attainment of the foregoing objectives and subject to the provisions of Article 80.

Article 77

1. The trusteeship system shall apply to such territories in the following categories as may be placed there under by means of trusteeship agreements:

a. territories now held under mandate;

b. territories which may be detached from enemy states as a result of the Second World War; and

c. territories voluntarily placed under the system by states responsible for their administration.

2. It will be a matter for subsequent agreement as to which territories in the foregoing categories will be brought under the trusteeship system and upon what terms.

Article 78

The trusteeship system shall not apply to territories which have become Members of the United Nations, relationship among which shall be based on respect for the principle of sovereign equality.

Article 79

The terms of trusteeship for each territory to be placed under the trusteeship system, including any alteration or amendment, shall be agreed upon by the states directly concerned, including the mandatory power in the case of territories held under mandate by a Member of the United Nations, and shall be approved as provided for in Articles 83 and 85.

Article 80

1. Except as may be agreed upon in individual trusteeship agreements, made under Articles 77, 79, and 81, placing each territory under the trusteeship system, and until such agreements have been concluded, nothing in this Chapter shall be construed in or of itself to alter in any manner the rights whatsoever of any states or any peoples or the terms of existing international instruments to which Members of the United Nations may respectively be parties.

2. Paragraph 1 of this Article shall not be interpreted as giving grounds for delay or postponement of the negotiation and conclusion of agreements for placing mandated and other territories under the trusteeship system as provided for in Article 77.

Article 81

The trusteeship agreement shall in each case include the terms under which the trust territory will be administered and designate the authority which will exercise the administration of the trust territory. Such authority, hereinafter called the administering authority, may be one or more states or the Organization itself.

Article 82

There may be designated, in any trusteeship agreement, a strategic area or areas which may include part or all of the trust territory to which the agreement applies, without prejudice to any special agreement or agreements made under Article 43.

Article 83

1. All functions of the United Nations relating to strategic areas, including the approval of the terms of the trusteeship agreements and of their alteration or amendment shall be exercised by the Security Council.

2. The basic objectives set forth in Article 76 shall be applicable to the people of each strategic area.

3. The Security Council shall, subject to the provisions of the trusteeship agreements and without prejudice to security considerations, avail itself of the assistance of the Trusteeship Council to perform those functions of the United Nations under the trusteeship system relating to political, economic, social, and educational matters in the strategic areas.

Article 84

It shall be the duty of the administering authority to ensure that the trust territory shall play its part in the maintenance of international peace and security. To this end the administering authority may make use of volunteer forces, facilities, and assistance from the trust territory in carrying out the obligations towards the Security Council undertaken in this regard by the administering authority, as well as for local defence and the maintenance of law and order within the trust territory.

Article 85

1. The functions of the United Nations with regard to trusteeship agreements for all areas not designated as strategic, including the approval of the terms of the trusteeship agreements and of their alteration or amendment, shall be exercised by the General Assembly.

2. The Trusteeship Council, operating under the authority of the General Assembly shall assist the General Assembly in carrying out these functions.

Chapter XIII: The Trusteeship Council

COMPOSITION

Article 86

1. The Trusteeship Council shall consist of the following Members of the United Nations:

a. those Members administering trust territories;

b. such of those Members mentioned by name in Article 23 as are not administering trust territories; and

c. as many other Members elected for three-year terms by the General Assembly as may be necessary to ensure that the total number of members of the Trusteeship Council is equally divided between those Members of the United Nations which administer trust territories and those which do not.

2. Each member of the Trusteeship Council shall designate one specially qualified person to represent it therein.

FUNCTIONS AND POWERS

Article 87

The General Assembly and, under its authority, the Trusteeship Council, in carrying out their functions, may:

a. consider reports submitted by the administering authority;

b. accept petitions and examine them in consultation with the administering authority;

c. provide for periodic visits to the respective trust territories at times agreed upon with the administering authority; and

d. take these and other actions in conformity with the terms of the trusteeship agreements.

Article 88

The Trusteeship Council shall formulate a questionnaire on the political, economic, social, and educational advancement of the inhabitants of each trust territory, and the administering authority for each trust territory within the competence of the General Assembly shall make an annual report to the General Assembly upon the basis of such questionnaire.

VOTING

Article 89

1. Each member of the Trusteeship Council shall have one vote.

2. Decisions of the Trusteeship Council shall be made by a majority of the members present and voting.

PROCEDURE

Article 90

1. The Trusteeship Council shall adopt its own rules of procedure, including the method of selecting its President.

2. The Trusteeship Council shall meet as required in accordance with its rules, which shall include provision for the convening of meetings on the request of a majority of its members.

Article 91

The Trusteeship Council shall, when appropriate, avail itself of the assistance of the Economic and Social Council and of the specialized agencies in regard to matters with which they are respectively concerned.

Chapter XIV: The International Court of Justice

Article 92

The International Court of Justice shall be the principal judicial organ of the United Nations. It shall function in accordance with the annexed Statute, which is based upon the Statute of the Permanent Court of International Justice and forms an integral part of the present Charter.

Article 93

1. All Members of the United Nations are *ipso facto* parties to the Statute of the International Court of Justice.

2. A state which is not a Member of the United Nations may become a party to the Statute of the International Court of Justice on conditions to be determined in each case by the General Assembly upon the recommendation of the Security Council.

Article 94

1. Each Member of the United Nations undertakes to comply with the decision of the International Court of Justice in any case to which it is a party.

2. If any party to a case fails to perform the obligations incumbent upon it under a judgment rendered by the Court, the other party may have recourse to the Security Council, which may, if it deems necessary, make recommendations or decide upon measures to be taken to give effect to the judgment.

Article 95

Nothing in the present Charter shall prevent Members of the United Nations from entrusting the solution of their differences to other tribunals by virtue of agreements already in existence or which may be concluded in the future.

Article 96

1. The General Assembly or the Security Council may request the International Court of Justice to give an advisory opinion on any legal question.

2. Other organs of the United Nations and specialized agencies, which may at any time be so authorized by the General Assembly, may also request advisory opinions of the Court on legal questions arising within the scope of their activities.

Chapter XV: The Secretariat

Article 97

The Secretariat shall comprise a Secretary-General and such staff as the Organization may require. The Secretary-General shall be appointed by the General Assembly upon the recommendation of the Security Council. He shall be the chief administrative officer of the Organization.

Article 98

The Secretary-General shall act in that capacity in all meetings of the General Assembly, of the Security Council, of the Economic and Social Council, and of the Trusteeship Council, and shall perform such other functions as are entrusted to him by these organs. The Secretary-General shall make an annual report to the General Assembly on the work of the Organization.

Article 99

The Secretary-General may bring to the attention of the Security Council any matter which in his opinion may threaten the maintenance of international peace and security.

Article 100

1. In the performance of their duties the Secretary-General and the staff shall not seek or receive instructions from any government or from any other authority external to the Organization. They shall refrain from any action which might reflect on their position as international officials responsible only to the Organization.

2. Each Member of the United Nations undertakes to respect the exclusively international character of the responsibilities of the Secretary-General and the staff and not to seek to influence them in the discharge of their responsibilities.

Article 101

1. The staff shall be appointed by the Secretary-General under regulations established by the General Assembly.

2. Appropriate staffs shall be permanently assigned to the Economic and Social Council, the Trusteeship Council, and, as required, to other organs of the United Nations. These staffs shall form a part of the Secretariat.

3. The paramount consideration in the employment of the staff and in the determination of the conditions of service shall be the necessity of securing the highest standards of efficiency, competence, and integrity. Due regard shall be paid to the importance of recruiting the staff on as wide a geographical basis as possible.

Chapter XVI: Miscellaneous Provisions

Article 102

1. Every treaty and every international agreement entered into by any Member of the United Nations after the present Charter comes into force shall as soon as possible be registered with the Secretariat and published by it.

2. No party to any such treaty or international agreement which has not been registered in accordance with the provisions of paragraph 1 of this Article may invoke that treaty or agreement before any organ of the United Nations.

Article 103

In the event of a conflict between the obligations of the Members of the United Nations under the present Charter and their obligations under any other international agreement, their obligations under the present Charter shall prevail.

Article 104

The Organization shall enjoy in the territory of each of its Members such legal capacity as may be necessary for the exercise of its functions and the fulfilment of its purposes.

Article 105

1. The Organization shall enjoy in the territory of each of its Members such privileges and immunities as are necessary for the fulfilment of its purposes.

2. Representatives of the Members of the United Nations and officials of the Organization shall similarly enjoy such privileges and immunities as are necessary for the independent exercise of their functions in connection with the Organization.

3. The General Assembly may make recommendations with a view to determining the details of the application of paragraphs 1 and 2 of this Article or may propose conventions to the Members of the United Nations for this purpose.

Chapter XVII: Transitional Security Arrangements

Article 106

Pending the coming into force of such special agreements referred to in Article 43 as in the opinion of the Security Council enable it to begin the exercise of its responsibilities under Article 42, the parties to the Four-Nation Declaration, signed at Moscow, 30 October 1943, and France, shall, in accordance with the provisions of paragraph 5 of that Declaration, consult with one another and as occasion requires with other Members of the United Nations with a view to such joint action on behalf of the Organization as may be necessary for the purpose of maintaining international peace and security.

Article 107

Nothing in the present Charter shall invalidate or preclude action, in relation to any state which during the Second World War has been an enemy of any signatory to the present Charter, taken or authorized as a result of that war by the Governments having responsibility for such action.

Chapter XVIII: Amendments

Article 108

Amendments to the present Charter shall come into force for all Members of the United Nations when they have been adopted by a vote of two thirds of the members of the General Assembly and ratified in accordance with their respective constitutional processes by two thirds of the Members of the United Nations, including all the permanent members of the Security Council.

Article 109

1. A General Conference of the Members of the United Nations for the purpose of reviewing the present Charter may be held at a date and place to be fixed by a two-thirds vote of the members of the General Assembly and by a vote of any nine members of the Security Council. Each Member of the United Nations shall have one vote in the conference.

2. Any alteration of the present Charter recommended by a two-thirds vote of the conference shall take effect when ratified in accordance with their respective constitutional processes by two thirds of the Members of the United Nations including all the permanent members of the Security Council.

3. If such a conference has not been held before the tenth annual session of the General Assembly following the coming into force of the present Charter, the proposal to call such a conference shall be placed on the agenda of that session of the General Assembly, and the conference shall be held if so decided by a majority vote of the members of the General Assembly and by a vote of any seven members of the Security Council.

Chapter XIX: Ratification and Signature

Article 110

1. The present Charter shall be ratified by the signatory states in accordance with their respective constitutional processes.

2. The ratifications shall be deposited with the Government of the United States of America, which shall notify all the signatory states of each deposit as well as the Secretary-General of the Organization when he has been appointed.

3. The present Charter shall come into force upon the deposit of ratifications by the Republic of China, France, the Union of Soviet Socialist Republics, the United Kingdom of Great Britain and Northern Ireland, and the United States of America, and by a majority of the other signatory states. A protocol of the ratifications deposited shall thereupon be drawn up by the Government of the United States of America which shall communicate copies thereof to all the signatory states.

4. The states signatory to the present Charter which ratify it after it has come into force will become original Members of the United Nations on the date of the deposit of their respective ratifications.

Article 111

The present Charter, of which the Chinese, French, Russian, English, and Spanish texts are equally authentic, shall remain deposited in the archives of the Government of the United States of America. Duly certified copies thereof shall be transmitted by that Government to the Governments of the other signatory states.

IN FAITH WHEREOF the representatives of the Governments of the United Nations have signed the present Charter.

DONE at the city of San Francisco the twenty-sixth day of June, one thousand nine hundred and forty-five.

Source: "Charter of the United Nations." © United Nations. Reproduced with permission.

APPENDIX C

The Universal Declaration of Human Rights

Preamble

Whereas recognition of the inherent dignity and of the equal and inalienable rights of all members of the human family is the foundation of freedom, justice and peace in the world,

Whereas disregard and contempt for human rights have resulted in barbarous acts which have outraged the conscience of mankind, and the advent of a world in which human beings shall enjoy freedom of speech and belief and freedom from fear and want has been proclaimed as the highest aspiration of the common people,

Whereas it is essential, if man is not to be compelled to have recourse, as a last resort, to rebellion against tyranny and oppression, that human rights should be protected by the rule of law,

Whereas it is essential to promote the development of friendly relations between nations,

Whereas the peoples of the United Nations have in the Charter reaffirmed their faith in fundamental human rights, in the dignity and worth of the human person and in the equal rights of men and women and have determined to promote social progress and better standards of life in larger freedom,

Whereas Member States have pledged themselves to achieve, in co-operation with the United Nations, the promotion of universal respect for and observance of human rights and fundamental freedoms,

Whereas a common understanding of these rights and freedoms is of the greatest importance for the full realization of this pledge,

Now, Therefore THE GENERAL ASSEMBLY proclaims THIS UNIVERSAL DECLARATION OF HUMAN RIGHTS as a common standard of achievement for all peoples and all nations, to the end that every individual and every organ of society, keeping this Declaration constantly in mind, shall strive by teaching and education to promote respect for these rights and freedoms and by progressive measures, national and international, to secure their universal and effective recognition and observance, both among the peoples of Member States themselves and among the peoples of territories under their jurisdiction.

Article 1

All human beings are born free and equal in dignity and rights. They are endowed with reason and conscience and should act towards one another in a spirit of brotherhood.

Article 2

Everyone is entitled to all the rights and freedoms set forth in this Declaration, without distinction of any kind, such as race, colour, sex, language, religion, political or other opinion, national or social origin, property, birth or other status. Furthermore, no distinction shall be made on the basis of the political, jurisdictional or international status of the country or territory to which a person belongs, whether it be independent, trust, non-self-governing or under any other limitation of sovereignty.

Article 3

Everyone has the right to life, liberty and security of person.

Article 4

No one shall be held in slavery or servitude; slavery and the slave trade shall be prohibited in all their forms.

Article 5

No one shall be subjected to torture or to cruel, inhuman or degrading treatment or punishment.

Article 6

Everyone has the right to recognition everywhere as a person before the law.

Article 7

All are equal before the law and are entitled without any discrimination to equal protection of the law. All are entitled to equal protection against any discrimination in violation of this Declaration and against any incitement to such discrimination.

Article 8

Everyone has the right to an effective remedy by the competent national tribunals for acts violating the fundamental rights granted him by the constitution or by law.

Article 9

No one shall be subjected to arbitrary arrest, detention or exile.

Article 10

Everyone is entitled in full equality to a fair and public hearing by an independent and impartial tribunal, in the determination of his rights and obligations and of any criminal charge against him.

Article 11

1. Everyone charged with a penal offence has the right to be presumed innocent until proved guilty according to law in a public trial at which he has had all the guarantees necessary for his defence.

2. No one shall be held guilty of any penal offence on account of any act or omission which did not constitute a penal offence, under national or international law, at the time when it was committed. Nor shall a heavier penalty be imposed than the one that was applicable at the time the penal offence was committed.

Article 12

No one shall be subjected to arbitrary interference with his privacy, family, home or correspondence, nor to attacks upon his honour and reputation. Everyone has the right to the protection of the law against such interference or attacks.

Article 13

1. Everyone has the right to freedom of movement and residence within the borders of each state.

2. Everyone has the right to leave any country, including his own, and to return to his country.

Article 14

1. Everyone has the right to seek and to enjoy in other countries asylum from persecution.

2. This right may not be invoked in the case of prosecutions genuinely arising from non-political crimes or from acts contrary to the purposes and principles of the United Nations.

Article 15

1. Everyone has the right to a nationality.

2. No one shall be arbitrarily deprived of his nationality nor denied the right to change his nationality.

Article 16

1. Men and women of full age, without any limitation due to race, nationality or religion, have the right to marry and to found a family. They are entitled to equal rights as to marriage, during marriage and at its dissolution.

2. Marriage shall be entered into only with the free and full consent of the intending spouses.

3. The family is the natural and fundamental group unit of society and is entitled to protection by society and the State.

Article 17

1. Everyone has the right to own property alone as well as in association with others.

2. No one shall be arbitrarily deprived of his property.

Article 18

Everyone has the right to freedom of thought, conscience and religion; this right includes freedom to change his religion or belief, and freedom, either alone or in community with others and in public or private, to manifest his religion or belief in teaching, practice, worship and observance.

Article 19

Everyone has the right to freedom of opinion and expression; this right includes freedom to hold opinions without interference and to seek, receive and impart information and ideas through any media and regardless of frontiers.

Article 20

1. Everyone has the right to freedom of peaceful assembly and association.

2. No one may be compelled to belong to an association.

Article 21

1. Everyone has the right to take part in the government of his country, directly or through freely chosen representatives.

2. Everyone has the right of equal access to public service in his country.

3. The will of the people shall be the basis of the authority of government; this will shall be expressed in periodic and genuine elections which shall be by universal and equal suffrage and shall be held by secret vote or by equivalent free voting procedures.

Article 22

Everyone, as a member of society, has the right to social security and is entitled to realization, through national effort and international co-operation and in accordance with the organization and resources of each State, of the economic, social and cultural rights indispensable for his dignity and the free development of his personality.

Article 23

1. Everyone has the right to work, to free choice of employment, to just and favourable conditions of work and to protection against unemployment.

2. Everyone, without any discrimination, has the right to equal pay for equal work.

3. Everyone who works has the right to just and favourable remuneration ensuring for himself and his family an existence worthy of human dignity, and supplemented, if necessary, by other means of social protection.

4. Everyone has the right to form and to join trade unions for the protection of his interests.

Article 24

Everyone has the right to rest and leisure, including reasonable limitation of working hours and periodic holidays with pay.

Article 25

1. Everyone has the right to a standard of living adequate for the health and well-being of himself and of his family, including food, clothing, housing and medical care and necessary social services, and the right to security in the event of unemployment, sickness, disability, widowhood, old age or other lack of livelihood in circumstances beyond his control.

2. Motherhood and childhood are entitled to special care and assistance. All children, whether born in or out of wedlock, shall enjoy the same social protection.

Article 26

1. Everyone has the right to education. Education shall be free, at least in the elementary and fundamental stages. Elementary education shall be compulsory. Technical and professional education shall be made generally available and higher education shall be equally accessible to all on the basis of merit.

2. Education shall be directed to the full development of the human personality and to the strengthening of respect for human rights and fundamental freedoms. It shall promote understanding, tolerance and friendship among all nations, racial or religious groups, and shall further the activities of the United Nations for the maintenance of peace.

3. Parents have a prior right to choose the kind of education that shall be given to their children.

Article 27

1. Everyone has the right freely to participate in the cultural life of the community, to enjoy the arts and to share in scientific advancement and its benefits.

2. Everyone has the right to the protection of the moral and material interests resulting from any scientific, literary or artistic production of which he is the author.

Article 28

Everyone is entitled to a social and international order in which the rights and freedoms set forth in this Declaration can be fully realized.

Article 29

1. Everyone has duties to the community in which alone the free and full development of his personality is possible.

2. In the exercise of his rights and freedoms, everyone shall be subject only to such limitations as are determined by law solely for the purpose of securing due recognition and respect for the rights and freedoms of others and of meeting the just requirements of morality, public order and the general welfare in a democratic society.

3. These rights and freedoms may in no case be exercised contrary to the purposes and principles of the United Nations.

Article 30

Nothing in this Declaration may be interpreted as implying for any State, group or person any right to engage in any activity or to perform any act aimed at the destruction of any of the rights and freedoms set forth herein.

Source: "Universal Declaration of Human Rights." © United Nations. Reproduced with permission.

References and Suggested Reading

The literature on international organizations is vast, and the list that follows here comprises those works used in the writing of this book and a selection of other important works. The readings are listed under the chapter for which they were used.

Almost every international organization mentioned in this book has a website, which I have used for the wealth of information they contain. Many post significant collections of their documents on their websites. Many research institutions and groups publish books, articles, reviews, and documents dealing with international organizations, and all have their own websites as well. Some of these are the Academic Council on the United Nations System; the UN Library Geneva; The United Nations Intellectual History Project; the International Coalition for the Responsibility to Protect; The Internet Modern History Sourcebook; the Cold War International History Project; the Institute for the Study of Conflict, Ideology, and Policy; the Society for the Study of American Foreign Relations; the National Security Archive; the Avalon Project: Documents in Law, History, and Diplomacy; US Diplomatic History Resources Index; and H-Diplo, the Diplomatic History Discussion List.

Many governments also publish foreign policy documents collections, and there are other published sources including the *Annual Review of United Nations Affairs*, the *Public Papers of the Secretary-General of the United Nations*, and the *Yearbook of International Organizations*. Finally, there are several journals that specialize in international organizations if not in the *history* of international organizations, including *International Organization, International Affairs, Global Governance, International Journal, Review of International Studies,* and *International Studies Quarterly.*

Chapter 1

An Introduction to International Organizations

Archer, Clive. *International Organizations.* 2nd ed. London: Routledge, 1992.

Barnett, Michael, and Martha Finnemore. *Rules for the World: International Organizations in Global Politics.* Ithaca: Cornell University Press, 2004.

Berkovitch, Nitza. *From Motherhood to Citizenship: Women's Rights and International Organizations.* Baltimore: Johns Hopkins University Press, 1999.

Claude, Inis. *Swords into Plowshares: The Problems and Progress of International Organizations.* New York: Random House, 1971.

Cmiel, Kenneth. "The Recent History of Human Rights." *American Historical Review* 109, 1 February 2004: 117–35.

Cox, Robert W., and Harold K. Jacobson. *The Anatomy of Influence: Decision Making in International Organizations.* New Haven: Yale University Press, 1973.

Forsythe, David P. *The Humanitarians: The International Committee of the Red Cross.* Cambridge: Cambridge University Press, 2005.

Haas, Ernst B. *Beyond the Nation-State: Functionalism and International Organization.* Stanford: Stanford University Press, 1964.

Hull, William I. *The Two Hague Conferences and Their Contributions to International Law.* 1908; New York: Kraus Reprint Company, 1970.

Iriye, Akira. *Global Community: The Role of International Organizations in the Making of the Contemporary World.* Berkeley: University of California Press, 2002.

Jacobson, Harold K. "Studying Global Governance: A Behavioral Approach." In Charlotte Ku and Thomas G. Weiss, eds., *Toward Understanding Global Governance.* ACUNS, Reports and Papers 2 1998: 13–25.

Karns, Margaret P., and Karen A. Mingst. *International Organization: The Politics and Processes of Global Governance.* Boulder: Lynne Reinner Publishers, 2004.

Luck, Edward C. *Mixed Messages: American Politics and International Organization, 1919–1999.* Washington: Brookings Institution Press, 1999.

Mitrany, David. *A Working Peace System.* Chicago: Quadrangle Books, 1966.

Morgenthau, Hans J. *Politics Among Nations: The Struggle for Power and Peace.* 4th ed. New York: Knopf, 1967.

Murphy, Craig N. "Global Governance: Poorly Done and Poorly Understood." *International Affairs* 76, 4 2000: 789–803.

———. *International Organization and Industrial Change: Global Governance since 1850.* New York: Oxford University Press, 1994

Reinalda, Bob, and Bertjan Verbeek, eds. *Autonomous Policy Making by International Organizations.* London: Routledge, 1998.

Taylor, Paul. *International Organization in the Modern World.* London: Pinter, 1993.

Vreeland, James Raymond. *The International Monetary Fund: Politics of Conditional Lending.* London: Routledge, 2007.

Yoder, Amos. *The Evolution of the United Nations System.* 2nd ed. Washington: Taylor and Francis, 1993.

Weiss, Thomas, David Forsythe, and Roger Coate. *The United Nations and Changing World Politics.* 2nd ed. Boulder: Westview Press, 1997.

Zweifel, Thomas D. *International Organizations and Democracy: Accountability, Politics, and Power.* Boulder: Lynne Rienner Publishers, 2006.

Chapter 2

The League of Nations

Barros, James. *Betrayal from Within: Joseph Avenol, Secretary-General of the League of Nations, 1933–1940.* New Haven: Yale University Press, 1969.

————. *The Corfu Incident of 1923: Mussolini and the League of Nations.* Princeton: Princeton University Press, 1965.

————. *The League of Nations and the Great Powers: the Greek-Bulgarian Incident, 1925.* Oxford: Oxford University Press, 1970.

————. *Office Without Power: Secretary-General Sir Eric Drummond, 1919–1933.* Oxford: Oxford University Press, 1979.

Bendiner, Elmer. *A Time for Angels: The Tragicomic History of the League of Nations.* New York: Knopf, 1975.

Burkman, Thomas W. *Japan and the League of Nations: Empire and World Order, 1914–1939.* Honolulu: University of Hawaii Press, 2008.

Callahan, Michael D. *Mandates and Empire: The League of Nations and Africa, 1914–1931.* Brighton, UK: Sussex Academic Press, 1999.

————. *A Sacred Trust: The League of Nations and Africa, 1929–1946.* Brighton, UK: Sussex Academic Press, 2004.

Clavin, Patricia, and Jens-Wilhelm Wessels. "Transnationalism and the League of Nations: Understanding the Work of Its Economic and Financial Organisation." *Contemporary European History* 14, 4 2005: 465–92.

Cooper, John Milton. *Breaking the Heart of the World: Woodrow Wilson and the Fight for the League of Nations.* Cambridge, UK: Cambridge University Press, 2001.

Crozier, Andrew J. "The Establishment of the Mandates System, 1919–25: Some Problems Created by the Paris Peace Conference." *Journal of Contemporary History,* 14 1979: 483–513.

Dexter, Byron. *The Years of Opportunity: The League of Nations, 1920–1926.* New York: Viking Press, 1967.

Egerton, George W. *Great Britain and the Creation of the League of Nations: Strategy, Politics, and International Organization, 1914–1919.* London: Scolar Press, 1979.

Fink, Carole. "Minority Rights as an International Question." *Contemporary European History* 9, 3 2000: 385–400.

Gorman, Daniel. "Liberal Internationalism, the League of Nations Union, and the Mandates System." *Canadian Journal of History* 40 December 2005: 449–77.

Henig, Ruth B., ed. *The League of Nations.* Edinburgh: Oliver and Boyd, 1973.

Kimmich, Christoph M. *Germany and the League of Nations.* Chicago: University of Chicago Press, 1976.

MacMillan, Margaret. *Paris 1919: Six Months That Changed the World.* New York: Random House, 2002.

Northedge, F.S. *The League of Nations: Its Life and Times, 1920–1946.* Leicester: Leicester University Press, 1986.

Ostrower, Gary B. *The League of Nations from 1919 to 1929.* Garden City: Avery, 1996.

Scott, George. *The Rise and Fall of the League of Nations.* London: Hutchinson, 1973.

Steiner, Zara. *The Lights That Failed: European International History, 1919–1933.* Oxford: Oxford University Press, 2005.

Stone, David R. "Imperialism and Sovereignty: The League of Nations' Drive to Control the Global Arms Trade." *Journal of Contemporary History* 35, 2 2000: 213–30.

Thorne, Christopher. *The Limits of Foreign Policy: The West, the League, and the Far Eastern Crisis of 1931–1933.* New York: Putnam, 1973.

Veatch, Richard. *Canada and the League of Nations.* Toronto: University of Toronto Press, 1975.

Walters, F.P. *A History of the League of Nations.* Oxford: Oxford University Press, 1952.

Webster, Andrew. "Making Disarmament Work: The Implementation of the International Disarmament Provisions in the League of Nations Covenant, 1919–1925." *Diplomacy and Statecraft* 16 2005: 551–69.

————. "The Transnational Dream: Politicians, Diplomats and Soldiers in the League of Nations' Pursuit of International Disarmament, 1920–1939." *Contemporary European History* 14, 4 2005: 493–518.

Yoder, Amos. *The Evolution of the United Nations System.* 2nd ed. Washington: Taylor and Francis, 1993.

Chapter 3

Wartime Internationalism and International Organizations

Alcock, Antony. *History of the International Labour Organization.* London: Macmillan, 1971.

Black, Maggie. *Children First: The Story of UNICEF, Past and Present.* Oxford: Oxford University Press, 1996.

Chapnick, Adam. *The Middle Power Project: Canada and the Founding of the United Nations.* Vancouver: University of British Columbia Press, 2005.

Chesterman, Simon, ed. *Secretary or General? The UN Secretary-General in World Politics.* Cambridge: Cambridge University Press, 2007.

Food and Agriculture Organization. *FAO: The First 40 Years.* Rome: FAO, 1985.

Grigorescu, Alexandru. "Mapping the UN–League of Nations Analogy: Are There Still Lessons to Be Learned from the League?" *Global Governance* 11 2005: 25–42.

Hanhimäki, Jussi M. *The United Nations: A Very Short Introduction*. Oxford: Oxford University Press, 2008.

Hilderbrand, Robert C. *Dumbarton Oaks: The Origins of the United Nations and the Search for Postwar Security*. Chapel Hill: University of North Carolina Press, 1990.

Hoopes, Townsend. *FDR and the Creation of the UN*. New Haven: Yale University Press, 1997.

Iriye, Akira. *Global Community: The Role of International Organizations in the Making of the Contemporary World*. Berkeley: University of California Press, 2002.

Johnstone, Andrew. *Dilemmas of Internationalism: The American Association for the United Nations and US Foreign Policy, 1941–1948*. London: Ashgate, 2009.

Krasno, Jean E. "Founding the United Nations: An Evolutionary Process." In Jean Krasno, ed., *The United Nations: Confronting the Challenges of a Global Society*, 19–45. Boulder: Lynne Rienner, 2004.

Lee, Kelley. *The World Health Organization*. London: Routledge, 2009.

Luck, Edward C. *UN Security Council: Practice and Promise*. London: Routledge, 2006.

MacKenzie, David. *ICAO: A History of the International Civil Aviation Organization*. Toronto: University of Toronto Press, 2010.

Mazower, Mark. "The Strange Triumph of Human Rights, 1933–1950." *The Historical Journal* 47, 2 2004: 379–98.

Normand, Roger, and Sarah Zaidi. *Human Rights at the UN: The Political History of Universal Justice*. Bloomington: Indiana University Press, 2008.

Russell, Ruth B. *A History of the United Nations Charter: The Role of the United States, 1940–1945*. Washington: Brookings Institution, 1958.

Ryan, Stephen. *The United Nations and International Politics*. New York: St. Martin's Press, 2000.

Schlesinger, Stephen C. *Act of Creation: The Founding of the United Nations*. Cambridge, MA: Westview Press, 2003.

Sherwood, Marika. "'There Is No New Deal for the Blackman in San Francisco': African Attempts to Influence the Founding Conference of the United Nations, April-July, 1945." *The International Journal of African Historical Studies* 29, 1 (1996): 71–94.

Sills, Joe. *The Role of the United Nations in Forming Global Norms*. International Relations Studies and the United Nations, Occasional Papers 2 (2002). www.acuns.org.

Valderrama, Fernando. *A History of UNESCO*. Paris: UNESCO Publishing, 1995.

Vreeland, James Raymond. *The International Monetary Fund: Politics of Conditional Lending*. London: Routledge, 2007.

Williams, Douglas. *The Specialized Agencies and the United Nations: The System in Crisis*. London: C. Hurst and Company, 1987.

Chapter 4

The UN in the Cold War Years

Anderson, Carol. *Eyes Off the Prize: The United Nations and the African American Struggle for Human Rights, 1944–1955.* Cambridge: Cambridge University Press, 2003.

Barros, James. *Trygve Lie and the Cold War: The UN Secretary-General Pursues Peace, 1946–1953.* DeKalb, IL: Northern Illinois University Press, 1989.

Bellamy, Alex J., Paul Williams, and Stuart Griffin. *Understanding Peacekeeping.* Cambridge, UK: Polity Press, 2004.

Boothby, Derek. *The United Nations and Disarmament.* International Relations Studies and the United Nations, Occasional Papers (2002). www.acuns.org.

Carozza, Paolo G. "From Conquest to Constitutions: Retrieving a Latin American Tradition of the Idea of Human Rights." *Human Rights Quarterly* 25, 2 (2003): 281–313.

Clapham, Andrew. *Human Rights: A Very Short Introduction.* Oxford: Oxford University Press, 2007.

Firestone, Bernard J. *The United Nations Under U Thant, 1961–1971.* Lanham, MD: Scarecrow Press, 2001.

Gaglione, Anthony. *The United Nations Under Trygve Lie, 1945–1953.* Lanham, MD: Scarecrow Press, 2001.

Glendon, Mary Ann. "The Forgotten Crucible: The Latin American Influence on the Universal Human Rights Idea." *Harvard Human Rights Journal* 16 (Spring 2003): 27–39.

———. *A World Made New: Eleanor Roosevelt and the Universal Declaration of Human Rights.* New York: Random House, 2001.

Heller, Peter B. *The United Nations Under Dag Hammarskjöld, 1953–1961.* Lanham, MD: Scarecrow Press, 2001.

Humphrey, John P. *Human Rights & the United Nations: A Great Adventure.* New York: Transnational Publishers, 1984.

Imber, Mark F. *The USA, ILO, UNESCO and IAEA: Politicization and Withdrawal in the Specialized Agencies.* London: Palgrave Macmillan, 1989.

James, Alan. *Peacekeeping in International Politics.* London: Macmillan, 1990.

Kennedy, Paul. *The Parliament of Man: The Past, Present, and Future of the United Nations.* New York: Harper Collins, 2006.

Kilgore, Arthur. "Cut Down in the Crossfire?" *International Relations* 8, 6 (November 1986): 592–610.

Lankevich, George J. *The United Nations Under Javier Pérez de Cuéllar, 1982–1991.* Lanham, MD: Scarecrow Press, 2001.

Lie, Trygve. *In the Cause of Peace: Seven Years with the United Nations.* New York: Macmillan, 1954.

Meisler, Stanley. *United Nations: The First Fifty Years.* New York: Grove/ Atlantic, 1995.

Melvern, Linda. *The Ultimate Crime: Who Betrayed the UN and Why.* London: Allison and Busby, 1995.

Morsink, Johannes. *The Universal Declaration of Human Rights: Origins, Drafting, and Intent*. Philadelphia: University of Pennsylvania Press, 1999.

Murphy, Craig N. *The United Nations Development Programme: A Better Way?* Cambridge, UK: Cambridge University Press, 2006.

Normand, Roger, and Sarah Zaidi. *Human Rights at the UN: The Political History of Universal Justice*. Bloomington: Indiana University Press, 2008.

Oberleitner, Gerd. *Global Human Rights Institutions: Between Remedy and Ritual*. Cambridge, UK: Polity Press, 2007.

Ostrower, Gary B. *The United Nations and the United States*. New York: Twayne Publishers, 1998.

Price, Richard M., and Mark W. Zacher, eds. *The United Nations and Global Security*. New York: Palgrave Macmillan, 2004.

Rajan, M.S., V.S. Mani, and C.S.R. Murthy, eds. *The Nonaligned and the United Nations*. New Delhi: South Asian Publishers, 1987.

Ramcharan, Bertrand G. *Preventive Diplomacy at the UN*. Bloomington: Indiana University Press, 2008.

Roberts, Adam, and Benedict Kingsbury, eds. *United Nations, Divided World: The UN's Roles in International Relations*. Oxford: Oxford University Press, 2000.

Rothstein, Robert. *Global Bargaining: UNCTAD and the Quest for a New International Economic Order*. Princeton: Princeton University Press, 1979.

Ruggie, John Gerard. "The United States and the United Nations: Toward a New Realism." *International Organization* 39, 2 (Spring 1985): 343–56.

Ryan, James Daniel. *The United Nations Under Kurt Waldheim, 1972–1981*. Lanham, MD: Scarecrow Press, 2001.

Ryan, Stephen. *The United Nations and International Politics*. New York: St. Martin's Press, 2000.

Souaré, Issaka K. *Africa in the United Nations System, 1945–2005*. London: Adonis and Abbey, 2006.

Urquhart, Brian. *Hammarskjöld*. New York: Knopf, 1972.

Ziring, Lawrence, Robert E. Riggs, and Jack C. Plano. *The United Nations: International Organization and World Politics*. Fort Worth: Harcourt College Publishers, 2000.

Chapter 5

Regional and Other International Organizations

Acharya, Amitav. *Constructing a Security Community in Southeast Asia: ASEAN and the Problem of Regional Order*. London: Routledge, 2001.

Andemicael, Berhanykun. *The OAU and the UN: Relations Between the Organization of African Unity and the United Nations*. New York: Africana Publishing, 1976.

Armstrong, David, Lorna Lloyd, and John Redmond. *From Versailles to Maastricht: International Organizations in the Twentieth Century*. London: Palgrave, 1996.

Ball, M. Margaret. *The OAS in Transition*. Durham: Duke University Press, 1969.

Beeson, Mark. *Institutions of the Asia-Pacific: ASEAN, APEC, and Beyond.* London: Routledge, 2009.

Boniface, Dexter S. "Is There a Democratic Norm in the Americas? An Analysis of the Organization of American States." *Global Governance* 8 (2002): 365–81.

Brown, Judith M., and Wm. Roger Louis, eds. *The Oxford History of the British Empire, Volume IV: The Twentieth Century.* Oxford: Oxford University Press, 1999.

Clawson, Robert W., and Lawrence S. Kaplan, eds. *The Warsaw Pact: Political Purpose and Military Means.* Wilmington: Scholarly Resources, 1982.

Foot, Rosemary, S. Neil MacFarlane, and Michael Mastanduno, eds. *US Hegemony and International Organizations.* Oxford: Oxford University Press, 2003.

Galbreath, David J. *The Organization for Security and Co-operation in Europe.* London: Routledge, 2007.

Hajnal, Peter I. *The G8 System and the G20: Evolution, Role and Documentation.* Aldershot: Ashgate, 2007.

Hemmer, Christopher, and Peter J. Katzenstein. "Why Is There No NATO in Asia? Collective Identity, Regionalism, and the Origins of Multilateralism." *International Organization* 56, 3 (Summer 2002): 575–607.

Henig, Stanley. *The Uniting of Europe: From Discord to Concord.* New York: Routledge, 1997.

Hettne, Björn, and Fredrik Söderbaum. "The UN and Regional Organizations in Global Security: Competing or Complementary Logics?" *Global Governance* 12 (2006): 227–32.

Hoffman, Andrea Ribeiro, and Anna Van Der Vleuten, eds. *Closing or Widening the Gap? Legitimacy and Democracy in Regional Integration Organizations.* London: Ashgate, 2007.

Huysmans, Jef. "Shape-shifting NATO: Humanitarian Action and the Kosovo Refugee Crisis." *Review of International Studies* 28, 3 (July 2002): 599–618.

Kaplan, Lawrence S. *NATO 1948: The Birth of the Transatlantic Alliance.* Lanham, MD: Rowman and Littlefield, 2007.

Le Scouarnec, Françoise-Pierre. *La Francophonie.* Montréal: Editions du Boréal, 1997.

Makinda, Samuel M., and F. Wafula Okumu. *The African Union: Challenges of Globalization, Security, and Governance.* London: Routledge, 2008.

Mayall, James. "Democratizing the Commonwealth." *International Affairs* 72, 2 (April 1998): 379–92.

McAllister, Richard. *From EC to EU: An Historical and Political Survey.* London: Routledge, 1997.

McIntyre, W. David. *Colonies into Commonwealth.* Rev. ed. London: Blandford Press, 1974.

Naldi, Gino J. *The Organization of African Unity: An Analysis of Its Role.* 2nd ed. London: Mansell, 1999.

Narine, Shaun. "From Conflict to Collaboration: Institution-Building in East Asia." *Behind the Headlines* 65, 5 (October 2008): 1–22.

Nye, J.S. *Peace in Parts: Integration and Conflict in Regional Organization.* Boston: Little, Brown, 1971.

Pentland, Charles. "The Regionalization of World Politics: Concepts and Evidence." *International Journal* 30, 4 (Autumn 1975): 599–630.

Powell, Kristiana, and Thomas Kwasi Tieku. "The African Union's New Security Agenda: Is Africa Closer to a Pax Pan-Africana?" *International Journal* 60, 4 (Autumn 2005): 937–52.

Ramcharan, Bertrand G. *Preventive Diplomacy at the UN*. Bloomington: Indiana University Press, 2008.

Rupp, Richard E. *NATO after 9/11: An Alliance in Continuing Decline*. New York: Palgrave Macmillan, 2006.

Schmidt, Gustav, ed. *A History of NATO—The First Fifty Years*. 3 vol. London: Palgrave Macmillan, 2001.

Srinivasan, Krishnan. *The Rise, Decline, and Future of the British Commonwealth*. Houndmills, Basingstoke: Palgrave Macmillan, 2005.

Stoetzer, O. Carlos. *The Organization of American States: An Introduction*. New York: Praeger, 1965.

Thody, Philip. *An Historical Introduction to the European Union*. New York: Routledge, 1997.

Chapter 6
The World of International NGOs

Bebbington, Anthony, Samuel Hickey, and Diana C. Mitlin, eds. *Can NGOs Make a Difference? The Challenge of Development Alternatives*. London: Zed Books, 2008.

Boli, John, and George M. Thomas, eds. *Constructing World Culture: International Nongovernmental Organizations Since 1875*. Stanford: Stanford University Press, 1999.

Boothby, Derek. *The United Nations and Disarmament*. International Relations Studies and the United Nations, Occasional Papers 1, 2002.

Carpenter, Ted Galen, ed. *Delusions of Grandeur: The United Nations and Global Intervention*. Washington: Cato Institute, 1997.

Charnovitz, Steve. "Two Centuries of Participation: NGOs and International Governance." *Michigan Journal of International Law* 18, 2 (Winter 1997): 183–286.

Clark, Ann Marie. *Diplomacy of Conscience: Amnesty International and Changing Human Rights Norms*. Princeton: Princeton University Press, 2001.

Collingwood, Vivien. "Non-governmental Organisations, Power and Legitimacy in International Society." *Review of International Studies* 32, 3 (July 2006): 439–54.

Cooley, Alexander, and James Ron. "The NGO Scramble: Organizational Insecurity and the Political Economy of Transnational Action." *International Security* 27, 1 (Summer 2002). 5–39.

Gaer, Felice D. "Reality Check: Human Rights Nongovernmental Organizations Confront Governments at the United Nations." *Third World Quarterly* 16, 3 (1995): 389–404.

Heins, Volker. *Nongovernmental Organizations in International Society: Struggles over Recognition*. New York: Palgrave Macmillan, 2008.

Iriye, Akira. *Global Community: The Role of International Organizations in the Making of the Contemporary World.* Berkeley: University of California Press, 2002.

Jordan, Lisa, and Peter van Tuijl, eds. *NGO Accountability: Politics, Principles, and Innovations.* London: Earthscan, 2006.

Kaufmann, Chaim D., and Robert A. Pape. "Explaining Costly International Moral Action: Britain's Sixty-Year Campaign Against the Atlantic Slave Trade." *International Organization* 53, 4 (Autumn 1999): 631–68.

Kennedy, Paul. *The Parliament of Man: The Past, Present, and Future of the United Nations.* New York: Harper Collins, 2006.

Mathews, Jessica T. "Power Shift." *Foreign Affairs* 76, 1 (January/February 1997): 50–66.

Orbinski, James. *An Imperfect Offering: Humanitarian Action in the Twenty-First Century.* Toronto: Random House, 2008.

Power, Jonathan. *Like Water on Stone: The Story of Amnesty International.* London: Penguin, 2001.

Price, Richard. "Reversing the Gun Sights: Transnational Civil Society Targets Land Mines." *International Organization* 52, 3 (Summer 1998): 613–44.

Reimann, Kim D. "A View from the Top: International Politics, Norms, and the Worldwide Growth of NGOs." *International Studies Quarterly* 50 (2006): 45–67.

Ripinsky, Sergey, and Peter Van Den Bossche. *NGO Involvement in International Organizations: A Legal Analysis.* London: British Institute of International and Comparative Law, 2007.

Ryan, Stephen. *The United Nations and International Politics.* New York: St. Martin's Press, 2000.

Simmons, P.J. "Learning to Live with NGOs." *Foreign Policy* 112 (Fall 1998): 82–96.

Strong, Maurice. *Where on Earth Are We Going?* Toronto: Knopf, 2000.

Weiss, Thomas G., and Leon Gordenker, eds. *NGOs, the UN, and Global Governance.* Boulder: Lynne Rienner, 1996.

Weyler, Rex. *Greenpeace: How a Group of Ecologists, Journalists, and Visionaries Changed the World.* Vancouver: Raincoast Books, 2004.

Willetts, Peter, ed. *"The Conscience of the World:" The Influence of Non-Governmental Organisations in the UN System.* Washington: Brookings Institution, 1996.

———. "From 'Consultative Arrangements' to 'Partnership': The Changing Status of NGOs in Diplomacy at the UN." *Global Governance* 6 (2000): 191–212.

Chapter 7

The UN in the Modern Era

Adebajo, Adekeye, and Helen Scanlon, eds. *A Dialogue of the Deaf: Essays on Africa and the United Nations.* Johannesburg: Jacana, 2006.

Bellamy, Alex J., Paul Williams, and Stuart Griffin. *Understanding Peacekeeping.* Cambridge, UK: Polity Press, 2004.

Black, David R., and Paul D. Williams. "Darfur's Challenge to International Society." *Behind the Headlines* 65, 6 (December 2008): 1–23.

Bolton, John. *Surrender Is not an Option: Defending America at the United Nations and Abroad.* New York: Simon and Schuster, 2007.

Boulden, Jane, and Thomas G. Weiss, eds. *Terrorism and the UN: Before and After September 11.* Bloomington: Indiana University Press, 2004.

Boutros-Ghali, Boutros. *Unvanquished: A US-UN Saga.* New York: Random House, 1999.

Burgess, Stephen F. *The United Nations Under Boutros Boutros-Ghali, 1992–1997.* Lanham, MD: Scarecrow Press, 2001.

Caballero-Anthony, Mely, and Amitav Acharya, eds. *UN Peace Operations and Asian Security.* London: Routledge, 2005.

Carpenter, Ted Galen, ed. *Delusions of Grandeur: The United Nations and Global Intervention.* Washington: Cato Institute, 1997.

Cooper, Andrew F., John English, and Ramesh Thakur, eds. *Enhancing Global Governance: Toward a New Diplomacy?* New York: United Nations University Press, 2002.

Coulon, Jocelyn. *Soldiers of Diplomacy: The United Nations, Peacekeeping, and the New World Order.* Toronto: University of Toronto Press, 1998.

Dallaire, Roméo, with Major Brent Beardsley. *Shake Hands with the Devil: The Failure of Humanity in Rwanda.* Toronto: Random House, 2003.

Egeland, Jan. *A Billion Lives: An Eyewitness Report from the Frontlines of Humanity.* New York: Simon and Schuster, 2008.

Evans, Gareth. *The Responsibility to Protect: Ending Mass Atrocity Crimes Once and For All.* Washington: Brookings Institution, 2008.

Gallagher, Peter. *The First Ten Years of the WTO, 1995–2005.* Cambridge: Cambridge University Press, 2005.

Guerrina, Roberta, and Marysia Zalewski. "Negotiating Difference/Negotiating Rights: The Challenges and Opportunities of Women's Human Rights." *Review of International Studies* 33, 1 (January 2007): 5–10.

Hanhimäki, Jussi M. *The United Nations: A Very Short Introduction.* Oxford: Oxford University Press, 2008.

Hannay, David. *New World Disorder: The UN after the Cold War: An Insider's View.* London: I.B. Tauris, 2008.

Heinbecker, Paul, and Patricia Goff, eds. *Irrelevant or Indispensable? The United Nations in the 21st Century.* Waterloo: Wilfrid Laurier University Press, 2005.

Hochstetler, Kathryn, Ann Marie Clark, and Elizabeth J. Friedman. "Sovereignty in the Balance: Claims and Bargains at the UN Conferences on the Environment, Human Rights, and Women." *International Studies Quarterly* 44 (2000): 591–614.

Howard, Lise Morjé. *UN Peacekeeping in Civil Wars.* New York: Cambridge University Press, 2008.

International Development Research Centre. *The Responsibility to Protect: Report of the International Commission on Intervention and State Sovereignty.* Ottawa: International Development Research Centre, 2001.

Iriye, Akira. *Global Community: The Role of International Organizations in the Making of the Contemporary World.* Berkeley: University of California Press, 2002.

Lebor, Adam. *"Complicity with Evil": The United Nations in the Age of Modern Genocide.* New Haven: Yale University Press, 2006.

Ludwig, Robin. *UN Electoral Assistance.* www.acuns.org.

Malone, David, M. *The International Struggle over Iraq: Politics in the UN Security Council 1980–2005.* Oxford: Oxford University Press, 2006.

Meisler, Stanley. *Kofi Annan: A Man of Peace in a World of War.* Hoboken: John Wiley and Sons, 2007.

Mingst, Karen A., and Margaret P. Karns. *The United Nations in the Post-Cold War Era,* 2nd ed. Boulder: Westview Press, 2000.

Normand, Roger, and Sarah Zaidi. *Human Rights at the UN: The Political History of Universal Justice.* Bloomington: Indiana University Press, 2008

Ogata, Sadako. *The Turbulent Decade: Confronting the Refugee Crises of the 1990s.* New York: Norton, 2005.

Paris, Erna. *The Sun Climbs Slow: Justice in the Age of Imperial America.* Toronto: Knopf, 2008.

Power, Samantha. *Chasing the Flame: Sergio Vieira de Mello and the Fight to Save the World.* New York: Penguin, 2008.

Puchala, Donald J., Katie Verlin Laatikainen, and Roger A. Coate. *United Nations Politics: International Organization in a Divided World.* New York: Prentice Hall, 2007.

Ryan, Stephen. *The United Nations and International Politics.* New York: St. Martin's Press, 2000.

Thakur, Ramesh. *The United Nations, Peace, and Security: From Collective Security to the Responsibility to Protect.* Cambridge: Cambridge University Press, 2006.

Traub, James. *The Best Intentions: Kofi Annan and the UN in the Era of American World Power.* New York: Farrar, Straus, and Giroux, 2006.

United Nations. *An Agenda for Peace: Preventive Diplomacy, Peacemaking, and Peace-keeping.* A/47/277—S/24111 (17 June 1992).

Urquhart, Brian. *Hammarskjöld.* New York: Knopf, 1972.

Weiss, Thomas G., and Sam Daws, eds. *The Oxford Handbook on the United Nations.* Oxford: Oxford University Press, 2007.

Weiss, Thomas G. *What's Wrong with the United Nations and How to Fix It.* Cambridge: Polity Press, 2008.

Welsh, Jennifer, Carolin Thielking, and S. Neil MacFarlane. "The Responsibility to Protect: Assessing the Report of the International Commission on Intervention and State Sovereignty." *International Journal* 57, 4 (Autumn 2002): 489–512.

Williams, David. "Aid and Sovereignty: Quasi-states and the International Financial Institutions." *Review of International Studies* 26, 4 (October 2000): 557–73.

Index